Reclaiming Composition for Chicano/as
and Other Ethnic Minorities

Iris D. Ruiz

Reclaiming Composition for Chicano/as and Other Ethnic Minorities

A Critical History and Pedagogy

palgrave
macmillan

Iris D. Ruiz
Merritt Writing Program
University of California, Merced
Clovis, California, USA

ISBN 978-1-137-53672-3   ISBN 978-1-137-53673-0   (eBook)
DOI 10.1057/978-1-137-53673-0

Library of Congress Control Number: 2016940207

Cover Image © Trish Gant / Alamy Stock Photo

Printed on acid-free paper

This Palgrave Macmillan imprint is published by Springer Nature
The registered company is Nature America Inc. New York

ACKNOWLEDGMENTS

First, I want to express my many thanks to all the people who are responsible for the technological processes that made this project possible and allowed it to come to fruition over time. I'm very much an advocate for the use of technology as a vehicle to spread social justice, social awareness, specialized research, and unique life experiences. I feel that this book is my first attempt at spreading all of the above with a sincere concern for the direction of literacy education in the USA. Second, I would like to thank the Creator for giving me the abilities, spiritually, mentally, and physically, to do this work. It has always been a childhood dream of mine to help others in any profession that I chose, and, with my abilities, I have been able to see this dream come true through working with others on a day-to-day basis in my job, where I am committed to critical literacy education.

This brings me to thanking the people who are most responsible for planting the seed of this dream in my mind at a young age so that I could strive for and achieve it. The first of these people is my dear grandmother, Zulema G. Trevino. Her motto was to always "Remember the Dream," and she was a strong advocate for education as a means to elevate from poverty of both the mind and the body. I have written her story and I hope to be able to share it with you one day, as she was one of the most special *abuelas* I've ever known (no, really, she was!). She was my inspiration, my touchstone, my best friend, and my greatest ally. With her, age was just a number and knowledge equaled power. These things I learned from her are priceless. Thank you, Grandma. On a day-to-day, tedious writing schedule, I want to acknowledge my mother, Ida T. Ruiz, who raised my sister and me by herself while being an educator herself and later became a school administrator. She taught me the love of language and teaching. I spent many summers with my mom doing everything related to becoming the passionate educator that I am today. I owe that to her. Thank you to my family, in general, for believing in me, never giving up on me, and being by my side every step of the way.

Next, I would like to thank the many mentors I've had along the way. At the University of California, San Diego, I had the privilege of being one of Linda Brodkey's last graduate students, and she served on my committee for the first two years of dissertation study. She became ill in my last year of writing and was not able to follow-through with our mentor–scholar relationship. I thank her for encouraging me to follow my intuition with the theory of Critical Historiography and for allowing me to teach the course in her writing program, which served as the lab school in which the research for this book took place. She was an excellent mentor, brilliant scholar, and talented educator. It was because of Linda that this book was written. To my fortune, I had Rosaura Sánchez, who was willing to take on my project at its final stages when I decided that I had to look beyond the Midwest to both the South and the Southwest in this study. She was more than instrumental in helping to guide me through the thickets of Latinx history, sociolinguistics, demographics, and current national issues which helped this study tremendously. She also insisted by calling me by my Spanish pronounced name, which I will never forget. Her scholarship is equally amazing and provides a rich locale for further development of Critical Historiography that seeks to add to the field of Composition and Rhetoric and the "Latinx Renaissance."

Other mentors who have had their hands in this work are Victor Villanueva, whose writing advice is insurmountable. He has been there since the first day of my grad school trials. Thank you. Jaime Mejía is a very genuine, smart, and careful reader. I am indebted to him for his comments on drafts of this manuscript. His editing skills are as close to perfection as I have witnessed. Others that I must mention are: Jorge Mariscal, Jody Blanco, Cristina Kirklighter, and Damían Baca for their mentorship and support along the way. Last, I want to thank my children, Ali, Eliana,

Jordan, and Lucas for being so patient with me while I sought to bring this project to publication. It is my hope that they will one day benefit from the critical work that we do as Compositionists to make education more relevant and connected to the changing demographics and cultural and epistemic shifts taking place today.

A note on terminology: While the title of this book is reflective of traditional Spanish markers of gender identity, apparent in the words "Chicano/as", decolonial theory has influenced my use of identity terms within the pages of this book. I've chosen to use both Latinx and Chicanx as syntactic forms of both delinking and agency. I was once asked, for example, what the relationship between Latinx and Malcolm X is. I thought, there is none, but then I continued to think about why Malcolm chose the X as his last name, and that aspect of delinking and agency still applied. He rejected his master's imposition of a last name on him in a similar manner to how decolonized peoples, whether physically or psychologically, reject the language of the colonizer, even when that is what Latinxs speak...we speak Spanish. I use the x at the end of both Latinx and Chicanx to indicate that I acknowledge the need to be inclusive of various gender and indigenous identies that are limited by the use of the "o", "a" , or even the symbol "@", as gender markers before European colonization.

CONTENTS

LIST OF TABLE

CHAPTER 1

Introduction

Reading Composition histories and scholarship is like reading Shakespeare. I can't see myself, and, oftentimes, I can't see my friends or those who look like me. We don't look like the authors who wrote them. We are not white men. I can't see my history. It's buried in there somewhere, they tell me, but where? I try to imagine myself in it, but it's hard. I'm not a princess or a queen. I'm not white. I'm not a fairy; I'm not a witch. I do get a glimpse at what I might look like in Shakespeare's "The Tempest." I see a hint of myself alluded to in the presence of Caliban, but I'm not a cannibal, and my relation to Caliban's Puerto Rican reference is very dim. Plus, unlike Shakespeare, I don't talk or write in Early Modern English nor in sonnets and couplets (though they are beautiful and articulate). The same tension happens when I'm reading Composition histories. The language of this history does not represent me, and I can't imagine myself there in the Harvard halls walking to my next writing class (first-year composition [FYC]), in Harvard classrooms looking studiously at the distinguished white-male professor, or even in the Harvard bathrooms getting refreshed for my next class (and, no, not even cleaning them). So I suppose it is a bit worse when reading Composition histories in comparison with Shakespeare's plays because I don't see myself even implicitly referred to in any of the "characters" of these histories. The more I can't imagine myself there, the more I wonder why I'm not there. Is there something wrong with me? Why can't I hear how my voice would sound if I asked the professor, "What do you mean that rhetoric started in Greece?" Wait a minute, I can't ask that, because I'm not there. No, I can't imagine

© The Editor(s) (if applicable) and The Author(s) 2016
I.D. Ruiz, *Reclaiming Composition for Chicano/as and Other Ethnic Minorities*, DOI 10.1057/978-1-137-53673-0_1

it. I can't imagine any of this because I'm not even implicitly there. I'm not alluded to in the words, the phrases, the dates and the events, or in the critical discussions of "changing demographics" and the changing political landscapes. I continue, however, to read the histories of the field I'm engaged in because I want to be there. I want to be worthy of Harvard; I want to show that I understand this history, that I know it. I know that slaves helped build Harvard and that they were often the backdrop of the University as freedmen, once emancipation was offered,[1] but where were the Latinxs: those who look like me with similar backgrounds and last names? Surely they were around; I mean, we were here before Harvard. So I know we were around. Maybe it's just an oversight. It's not really a blind spot, is it?

So, I keep reading. In grad school they gave us James Berlin, David Bartholomae, Patricica Bizzell, and Kenneth Burke to read. Graduate Seminars in Composition and Rhetoric, however, often saved the marginal scholarship (those written by People of Color [PoC]) for the last week (if there was time to get to them). In 1999, there were three scholars of color whose work I read toward the end of the course, no, four that I can think of: Victor Villanueva, Juan Guerra, Norma González, and Ralph Cintron. Finally, a hint of myself and my experience had surfaced, but were there more? I was the only Latina in many of my grad seminars, so I always felt awkward asking. I needed a mentor, but no Latina Comp/Rhet people were around. No, not at the Master's or PhD level. What was going on here?

I held on to the books authored by Latinxs in Comp for dear life. They were my salvation. They were my oxygen when I needed to come up for air, when reading theoretical taxonomies or reading about how students like me must invent the University (like magic) if we were to be counted and seen in the University. We had to imitate—imitate that which we read at the undergraduate level and the discourse of Composition theory at the graduate level (at the beginning of the seminars, not the end—the colored scholarship). Graduate students do have to imitate forms, even if assumed to have mastered the discourse of the field. They have to follow conventions—the "They say/I say" rules of academic discourse in order to gain entry into the profession of Composition Studies, even when they don't see themselves in the history of the field; this is a common phenomenon but not regarded as any kind of real literacy violence, nor as Gloria Anzaldúa would say, "linguistic terrorism."

---

[1] "Ebony & Ivy: Race, Slavery, and the Troubled History of America's Universities," Massachusetts Institute of Technology American history professor Craig Steven Wilder reveals how the slave economy and higher education grew up together.

Victor Villanueva was the only one brave enough to challenge these rules; he played with genre and format, even tone in Bootstraps. But we read him at the end. Why? Was he marginal? Could I write like him and not be marginalized? Imitation of academic discourse is one thing I "mastered" as a graduate student, but I wondered, who was I imitating and were there more Latinx Compositionists? So the impetus for this book is the obvious discord between my personal experience and the requirements of initiation into academia, specifically into the field of Composition Studies and Rhetoric. Today, I continue to look through tables of contents of various publications associated with the field, specifically for names that look Latinx, like mine.

Sadly, a present survey of the field shows little change over the past decade. People of Color (PoC), including Latinx, Composition scholarship are limited in quantity and often deal with a narrow set of topics: linguistic diversity issues such as English as a Second Language (ESL), translingualism, Generation 1.5, and, now, historical recovery work has begun (Ramírez (2015), Baca (2008), Pimentel (2015)) and they are still read at the end of the semester, if there is time. Where are PoC in the theoretical realm, the realm of the unmarginalized, the realm of the serious, structural conversations, such as research methodology and Composition Studies history that ultimately influences the way Composition gets taught and talked about? We've shown that we can master the discourse, and everyone knows that these conversations are important in an increasingly diverse society where the Latinx population is growing rapidly. PoC influence the ways the field changes, evolves, grows, and gets reconceived. Where are PoC in Composition's History? Are they there implicitly? No. They are invisible. Composition histories, even "critical" Composition histories, do not account for PoC, and it is not until we look at other geographical locations and educational institutions not found in traditional histories of Comp Studies that we find hints of what literacy meant for PoC when these histories seem to originate in the late nineteenth century.

* * *

With the above inquiries as the motivation for entering PoC's or other "ethnic minorities" into traditional histories of Composition, this book argues that nineteenth-century-based histories of Composition Studies do not account for PoC, especially Latinx, and that post-civil rights Composition Studies still shows signs of excluding PoC in its main scholarly journals (*Journal of Advanced Composition, College Composition and Communication*, and *Composition Studies*) with the exception of "special issues." Looking at these two historical moments, as this book does, it is apparent that PoC are almost unaccounted for in over a century in the field. These two moments reveal rhetorical blind spots (Ramírez 28). These blind spots call for rhetorical recovery that reveals the growing presence of Latinxs in Composition and Rhetoric programs. We are not only growing in numbers in society at large; now, we are also in the field as scholars, researchers, professors, administrators, adjuncts, and leaders. We are here to stay. Latinxs are now in the halls of Harvard as students. This is a fact, while there are also Latinxs (very young ones) sitting on the bus awaiting shelter in a warehouse and court decisions regarding their welfare and possible deportation. While at least one of us sits at the Supreme Court, others of us are crossing the border, fleeing that which threatens those human rights we are fighting for in our courts every day. While many of us have crossed borders to be here, many of us were already here before Harvard was built. Our experiences are multifaceted, some more tumultuous and violent than others. We seek justice, but to achieve that, we must first be recognized for our historical contributions, our present contributions, and our continued, growing presence here in the USA.

Missing from traditional histories of the field from a Compositionist of Color perspective, I wanted to know where these PoC were. Indeed, they were reading, writing, printing, and distributing their own newspapers while holding town meetings, country-club and civic-club meetings during this time. Where are their literacy histories? How do they figure into the history of our field? When they were not present in postsecondary education, what were they doing to develop their composing skills? How can their experiences effectively inform Composition theory and pedagogy?

While the first part of this book looks at Composition's history tied to late-nineteenth-century renditions of the Harvard history to account for the absence of PoC, the second part considers the state of our field after the Civil Rights Movement and the growing presence of students of color. It seeks to examine how the field responded to those changes in terms of its scholarship and pedagogical attention to civil rights gains of both African Americans and Mexican Americans. For example, different theories of writing were formed after the Civil Rights Movement as a way to meet the challenges new students brought with them to the writing classroom challenging traditional writing models, such as what we have come to know as "current-traditional rhetoric."

With the passing of civil rights and the era of open admissions came the cognitive model (Flower and Hayes), the process model (Peter Elbow), the epistemic model (James Berlin), and the post-structuralist/postmodern model (Sharon Crowley and Gloria Anzaldúa, as introduced into Composition Studies by Andrea Lunsford in a "special issue" of *JAC: A Journal of Composition Theory* called "Exploring Borderlands: Postcolonial and Composition Studies"). These were defined and disseminated through Composition publications and classrooms; however, one still sees a vast absence of scholars of color within the field in the midst of these changes, and Composition scholarship paid little attention to understanding students' cultural backgrounds. Most Composition scholarship that deals with PoC concentrates on how current teachers should not accommodate ethnic minority students' literacy practices and focuses on how students should accommodate universities' literacy standards and teachers should teach process writing models that will educate students on how to imitate standard academic English as a means of initiation into the University (Bartholomae, Elbow, Shaughnessy, Flower and Hayes, Vgotsky, Delpit, and Heath). There were a variety of approaches available to "initiate" new students of color into universities during the era of Open Admissions, but their individual and group cultural identities, histories, rhetorical practices, and learning styles were not widely considered, at least not in the field's scholarship.

Victor Villanueva would agree with my assessment of the field's inattention to PoC. He insightfully argues in "Rhetoric, Racism, and the Remaking of Knowledge Making in Composition" that PoC were only implicitly included in some of the major scholarship of the field in the mid-1980s. More explicitly, he indicts Stephen North's *The Making of Knowledge in Composition: Portrait of an Emerging Field* (1987) for not accounting for PoC in his taxonomy of research methodological communities in the field of Composition. While North identifies eight key methodological communities—practitioners, historians, philosophers, critics, experimentalists, clinicians, formalists, and ethnographers—each one written about in a chapter noting their entry in the field, he also reveals and critiques their underlying assumptions and common procedures, and lists the kinds of knowledge the community has contributed to the field. In North's book, Villanueva sees that there is not one scholar of color who contributes to this foundational disciplinary text. He wonders why this huge blind spot has not been accounted for, even while North included Shaughnessy, Perl, Sommers, and Graves, who were obviously working with students of color. Specifically, Villanueva states,

North was seeking to explain research methods, with the people intended as illustrations of methods. And folks of color were implicit in those examples: the students that Shaughnessy, Perl, Sommers, Graves looked at, worried about, studied, tried to help. But that they were in fact students of color seems only implicit, never fully developed. (2)

Villanueva starts to uncover this blind spot in the field and its foundational works. This book is discussing *the making of knowledge* in a field to legitimize its disciplinary strong hold and reputation with its own distinct field of inquiries and methods but at the cost of doing what many disciplines have done in the past, ignoring the subjects taught by those fields during this time period.

Blind spots, thus, are not uncommon. If they were, then there would be no need for historical recoveries or for critical race theorists who look beyond that which is written to locate the missing voices. In this case, those voices would be Composition scholars of color or those that wrote about students of color and their linguistic particularities as they related to the evolution of Composition at this moment, such as William Labov, Roseann Dueñas González, and Geneva Smitherman. Villanueva critically argues why it might have made some kind of sense to have left these important scholars out, but had they been included, this blind spot would not be so vast:

And conscribed by a field, he would not discuss Smitherman (1977) or Roseann Dueñas González (1983), as active as they were in composition studies during the same decade that North observes. Smitherman and González are linguists. And maybe, in his choosing to stay focused on compositionists, he can't discuss William Labov (though Heath and Scribner and Cole do turn up in The Making of Knowledge, the linguistic anthropologist and the two psychologists, more white folks studying those of color; one tires of being a subject and a specimen)...Labov's great (even if obvious in retrospect) contribution to language research methodology was his pointing out that the cultural and racialized make-up of the researcher affects the research outcome. (4)

Wow, had that last insight about Labov been considered in the North's book, how might it have been accepted and read? How might pedagogy have been altered if Labov's insights were given credibility in North's book? Villanueva notes that North was conscribed by a field and that this is why he could not account for these inclusions; however, what could he have accounted for within the field if he wanted to account for PoC? This is a subject for another book and some of it will be covered herein; however, North is still guilty of the negation of PoC, nicely put, and he is not the only one.

This negation is not only one of people but of writing pedagogy and practices. Notably, the personal essay has seen its criticism (see Bartholomae (1995), Holdstein and Bleich (2001), and Villanueva (2004)) and has been accused of being nonacademic, while there is constant preference for academic discourse associated with a disciplinary respect for "current-traditional" rhetoric. A field's preference for scientific and academic discourse supports the need for North's book to demonstrate that the research of Composition Studies can be seen alongside other disciplines that adhere to respected scientific research methodologies that claim objectivity and reliability. However, the personal narrative is seeing its way back into writing across the disciplines as a way of communicating the fact that research is positional; that is, research is performed by a researcher, and there are no predetermined structures which make science fall outside of the realm of the personal observer—the scientist. Science cannot be carried out or explained by a detached observer; the observer is always attached to the observation with his or her personal experience as a part of the observation. Because of this attachment, "Personal Academic Discourse" provides a way of discovering the lives and experiences of students of color and can inform Composition Studies, but it did not count as a serious methodology in North's book. How is that? Villanueva argues that scholars and students of color can't just do "science" that ignores the personal because the personal is their science:

> The men and women of color who pulled this profession into the world of Personal Academic Discourse, of storytelling mixed with evidence of various other sorts have been pointing to what so many others see, that understanding humanity's humanity can best be attained with how we articulate our understanding. This is our "science," not to be relegated to the Scholars resisting composition's ties to literature in English departments, not to be relegated to the Historians who are tied to a rhetoric that rises Adam-like out of Athens and then Rome, inevitably tied to the story of European expansion, when we would all of us have had our own rhetorics. (16)

Villanueva gives North the benefit of the doubt, however, and acknowledges that the limits of North's available scholars had to stay narrow because in legitimizing a field's modes of inquiry, North could not simply make claims to all types of research methodologies that fell outside of the realm of how an "emerging field" made claims to making knowledge for a specific part of the University curriculum: Composition Studies and FYC. Personal academic discourse was not part of this trend. North could have, however, accounted for how the field had been impacted by the ethnic varieties that were also contributing to the legitimacy of our field, for without students of color and those that challenge the middle-class meritocratic University makeup, our field would not have evolved as it has today. For example, we can now consider the complicated genesis of what we can critically consider as falling under the realm "rhetoric" and histories of rhetoric. We can now legitimately look to the Americas, to the indigenous, to the African American, to the Chicanx, or to the Puerto Riqueña to inform new understandings of rhetorical functions and histories. Maybe if North were to rewrite his notorious book today as Villanueva has imagined,

> he would no doubt [have] acknowledge[d] not just ethnography but the symbolist ethnography of a Clifford Geertz and, likely, the rhetorical ethnography of a Ralph Cintron. And he would likely acknowledge the artistically-rendered research of Personal Academic Discourse. And I would hope, he would recognize the current work on the rhetorics historically tied to people of color. (16)

Like Villanueva, I seek to contribute to the tradition of recovering that which has been lost through the exclusion of PoC in histories of the field and subsequently in the scholarship of the field. While I turn to the inclusion of African American voices to highlight ways African American Composition scholars have approached their absence in traditional histories of Composition, my emphasis ultimately falls on how to better account for the absence of Latinxs in these histories and in the field in toto. Furthermore, I am Latina, and I have resided in the Southwest and West my entire life, including the duration of this research study, which took place in the state of California, a state with one of the largest Latinx populations.

To gain an idea of the vastness of Latinxs in the present USA, the 2010 U.S. Census Bureau reports that 37.6 % of the State of California's total population is composed of Hispanics, or Latinxs, of any race, and in the span of 10 years from 2000, this population grew almost 28 %. In San Diego, where I carried out my research, 32 % of the population is composed of Latinxs, 28 % of whom are designated as "Mexicans," with 55.7 percent of the city's population speaking Spanish and English. As the 2012 U.S. Census Bureau reports, the language spoken more often by Americans other than English is Spanish. Yet, despite this large Spanish-speaking population, many of our educational institutions still practice English-only curricula, except for "magnet" schools where educational experiments are carried out without looking closely at what is needed to enable the Spanish-speaking or bilingual populations of California and, more specifically, San Diego, to be successful in higher education. While these statistics are county-specific, California is a border state and these demographics are roughly representative of most California counties.

Today, Latinxs are the majority population of the entire state. I go into some of these demographic details about Latinxs in the USA periodically throughout the book because race and identity politics are going to serve as lenses of analytics throughout; I acknowledge that even though race is a biological fiction, it is a socially induced category which creates a burden for many PoC and has specific economic opportunities and material rewards and losses associated with each racial category. Many people, however, disagree with this position and instead argue that we live in an era of post-racism and color blindness and that racism is a phenomenon of the past. Yet, PoC still deal with white racism because it is still part of our history; it is embedded in our collective and individual consciousness. Americans react to PoC based upon their expectations of how PoC are supposed to act, talk, and dress, and they make guesses about our level of intelligence or points of view, what kind of family we come from, and PoC are judged according to how ethnic we are because of how we meet or challenge socially ingrained ethnic expectations. These expectations are responsible for assumptions such as if a young black teenager is walking in a middle-class neighborhood with a hoodie, he must be a hoodlum. We expect that Blacks listen to Hip Hop music. We expect Mexicans to be short and brown, speak Spanish, and have many children. We expect Black men to be angry and Black women to be outspoken. We expect Asians to be good at math. We also expect them to talk about all things Asian, including literacy practices (as felt by Min-Zhan Lu).

Due to these expectations and assumptions, PoC should not be "okay" with very little self-representation in the scholarship of the field. However,

PoC have been expected to remain silent when they are being overlooked, and it is time to break this silence. Tradition says, however, that PoC should remain invisible and that their issues are "special"—reserved for "special editions." All of these ideas abound, even while mass cultural appropriation is on the rise (as felt by the Rachel Dolezal incident, an American civil rights activist who presented herself as an African American NAACP officer although she is racially a white Anglo). Furthermore, we all continue to experience and witness hate crimes directed toward PoC and the reality of unfair sentencing practices for PoC comes to mind (the case of Marissa Alexander in Florida), as do conservative backlashes to the teachings of ethnic-related pedagogies (HB 2281, Arizona House Bill). With such disparities and silences surfacing out into the open corridors of educational institutions and printing presses, cultural wars come to mind within the context of the decline of support for the humanities and the fight for ethnic studies alongside conservative immigration policies (SB 1070, Arizona Senate Bill). Due to the reality of histories of prejudice and exclusion, PoC often experience an identity crisis; thus, this book is also intended to serve as a vehicle for positive cultural recovery and healing and as a source of pride while in the midst of the corporatization of the University and Composition Studies, where most attention has been paid to the role of adjuncts and the increasing technological takeover of education in general. It's important to keep these twenty-first-century issues that plague our higher education institutions in mind because it is within this context that PoC are attempting to make and remake what they lost and what others have hidden.

Within this context, this book was written with the goal of PoC cultural recovery in mind as scholars and as writing practitioners. This book's most important aim, for me, is to offer a Critical Historical Writing pedagogy for students and Compositionists committed to teaching in an era of continued racism and to helping students recover their histories. In the process of this historical recovery, the battle might become even more muddled, but should we look for a pedagogy of simplicity or one of complexity, where students learn the intricacies of weaving textual experiences together with an intent to represent a unified experience and understanding of a past historical event?

Complex social relations, as those noted above, seem to be the norm of twenty-first-century social realities and are the backdrop within which to consider implementing a Critical Historical Writing pedagogy, as this book encourages. Pedagogy is important when thinking about social inclusion and exclusion. Educational institutions, once thought to be immune to outside social realities and somewhat of a sanctuary away from what was happening in surrounding communities, are instead a direct reflection of those social realities. They respond to them, they reflect them, and they alter their practices according to them in reactionary ways. Instead of being duped by the idea that we are in an era of post-racism and societal harmony, we would be better off acknowledging that we are in the era of twenty-first-century cultural wars, still trying to deal with our racist past and the effects of it on race relations today. The past informs the present, and if we turn to the present, we might see something familiar.

Today, the University is again faced with serious questions about what should be taught in writing classrooms and who should be teaching, even reaching the question of whether human beings should teach writing. The humanities are again under attack, as they are often the first division to experience cutbacks when budgets get low. Ethnic Studies programs are glorified in some states and not even a factor in others. In the climate of today's U.S. universities, one is reminded of the Texas Culture Wars of the 1990s. There are still disagreements about what the meaning of "academic freedom" is, and whether or not the left or right (politically speaking) runs the University. Given this contextual background with which to consider this study, a Critical Historical Writing pedagogy might be reminiscent of some of those same concerns that were vividly evident in the 1990s culture wars. This connection, then calls for a need to pay attention to the 20 or so years that have passed since then and ask: is what we are doing in our writing curricula, programs, and departments working to create a more egalitarian and successfully diverse society? If we desire to live in a post-racist state, which seems like the direction we are headed in, with the apology for slavery issued by Congress only recently, then we need to answer this question.

If I were to go back to my Shakespeare seminars, I would undoubtedly be more prepared to deal with the absence of PoC given my acquired education about the histories of conquest, the expansion of the New World, and the enchantments Europe developed with the magical allure of the Americas. There is comfort in knowing that I am in those plays, even if implicitly so, because my history is inextricably tied to what Shakespeare envisioned for some of his characters and settings for a select few plays. I feel comfort in knowing I'm not invisible but that my history contributed to the richness and beauty of this literature. I feel redeemed in some sense.

So I want to go back to the histories of Composition; I want to account for what is not there. That is what this book seeks to do for Latinxs and allies in our field: recover our dignity and pride in the process of teaching college students to be better writers and thinkers.

LATINXS IN AND OUT OF THE FIELD:
THE PROBLEM UNFOLDS

It is evident that in states along the US–Mexico border, the majority of public school students are ethnic minorities; in fact, today, people of Mesoamerican descent constitute the majority of Texas public school students.[2] As the Latinx population continues to grow, so does the need for the Composition profession to change how we teach writing. Chicano Compositionist Jaime Mejía believes that current cross-cultural and multicultural textbooks and readers Composition publishers are currently producing have yet to provide reasons for being endorsed by the Latinx Caucus associated with the Conference on College Composition and Communication. These publishers, according to Mejía, are committing gross oversights of current domestic realities associated with the growing, heterogenous Latinx population. If this trend continues, not only the publishers but also the scholarship associated with the field of Composition that overlooks the pedagogical needs of Latinxs will result in the low scholastic attainment of these students. These texts will also continue to contribute to the creation of cultural misunderstandings that have plagued people of Mexican descent and Anglos in the USA for over a century and a half, since the Treaty of Guadalupe Hidalgo.

The tertiary aim of this book, as mentioned above, is to elaborate the theory, history, and practice of critical historiography as a pedagogical approach for teaching Composition in an increasingly multicultural and multilingual society. Critical historiography is founded on the premise that college Composition classes have much to gain from the incorporation of lost or neglected histories in writing curricula. The field of Composition itself needs to be aware of the lost histories of Composition. Some of this work has begun; for example, the history of Composition in Midwestern and Black normal schools and African American rhetorical contributions has been written about (see Fitzgerald, Gold, Skinnel, Royster, Salvatori, and Gilyard). In addition to these identified rhetorical blind spots in Composition's history, Composition histories are also incomplete in their attention to Chicanxs/Latinxs. Once this blind spot becomes visible, the next step is to logically develop alternative Composition

[2](see: http://www.huffingtonpost.com/2013/06/12/hispanics-majority-texas-schools_n_3427239.html).

pedagogical approaches as part of this recovery process in the spirit of cultural loss prevention.

To give a more specific idea of the journey I took to uncover this historical blind spot, in the first part of this book, I examine the histories of Composition written by John Brereton, James Berlin, Albert Kitzhaber, and Richard Ohmann. I do so to argue, in part, that these histories do not adequately address minority populations such as Chicanxs/Latinxs or African Americans. While Sharon Crowley, Lynn Z. Bloom, and Susan Miller provide a critical analysis of histories of Composition, these histories also overlook these populations. This book's purpose is to call into question the very historiographies of Composition, even those by scholars who would identify as revisionist historians. In order to effectively complicate these traditional and "revisionist" histories, I turn to critical race theorists, Richard Delgado and Kimberlé Crenshaw, to inform my racial analysis and critique of Composition histories, to critical historians, Michel Foucault and Eric Foner, to inform my historical analysis, and a critical education theorist, Paula Moya, to challenge notions of traditional multicultural curricula. Like our field's attention to and respect for multidisciplinarity, my study relies on a multidisciplinary pyramid of theories to inform my analyses.

After considering both traditional and critical Composition histories, I look at what has been the response to civil rights in the field's attention to race-based civil rights and inclusion in our field's scholarship and its attention to changing student demographics. After a look at the 1960s, I turn to the culture wars that stemmed out of changes that resulted from paradigm shifts in our field's attention to texts and formalist approaches to invention and arrangement. I then turn to my own case study performed in 2007 to argue that an inclusive multicultural writing pedagogy can be one that makes use of alternative accounts of history for the purpose of looking at subordinated experiences so as to benefit all students, not just minority students. This approach goes beyond the use of culturally relevant material by focusing on developing students' argument skills through a critical reading of histories of particular periods or groups.

Book Summary

In order to complicate traditional histories of Composition Studies, I take a comparative historical approach to the field. I compare the first and second civil rights eras. Composition Studies is a field dating back to the nineteenth century when education in the USA was seen as playing a significant role in establishing a national community after the divisive Civil War. This war, largely about race, had to do with the abolition of slavery and the state of the Union divided on what to do with the "Negro" problem. After the Civil War, a reconstructive period sought to create and promote equal rights and the inclusion of various cultural minority populations in society. Inclusion and equality were definitely major educational and political objectives during this time, but were more about class than race. In the 1870s, during the Reconstruction era, for example, attempts were made to incorporate lower- to middle-class Anglos and African Americans into the national body through a more inclusive educational system that sought to educate, in a segregated manner, the common man and prepare those to teach these common folk, whether white or black.

This reconstructive period is then compared with social, cultural, educational, and political shifts of the second "reconstructive period," which was the Civil Rights Movement that occurred a century later. Interestingly, 100 years later, in view of the failure of earlier attempts, it was clear that various communities, including African Americans and Chicanxs/Latinxs, had still not been granted equal access to education. Eric Foner, Civil War historian, affirms that these are two decisive reconstructive moments in American history: "the parallels between the period after the Civil War and the 1950s and 1960s are very dramatic, as are the retreats from the Reconstruction ideal of racial justice and social equality in the latter decades of the nineteenth century and again in our own time" (18).

Despite major subsequent retreats and backlashes to reconstructive measures, the inclusion of minority populations reached levels previously unheard of during these two historical moments. Both periods were marked by the inclusion of previously disenfranchised populations into civil society at large by providing a wider opening to the doors of higher education. The formation of new course offerings, departments, and disciplines in institutions of higher education in the aftermath of struggles during these two historical moments was meant to attract marginalized groups of students (see Kathryn Fitzgerald, Jacqueline Jones Royster, and Richard Griswold del Castillo and Arnoldo de León). However, neither attempt was successful in reaching a satisfactory level of inclusion of minority populations.

According to Foner, "[j]ust as the failure of the first Reconstruction left to future generations an unfinished agenda of racial and social justice, the waning of the second has shown how far America still has to go in living up to the ideal of equality" (18). For example, one inclusionary practice of the 1870s led to educational practices that sought to include a larger segment of lower- to middle-class white students, the sons and daughters of farmers in the Midwest, to facilitate quality education for all: the creation of the normal school. However, there were still large populations of Americans not included in the educational reform mission headed by Horace Mann and the spread of the common school. These excluded populations were located in the South (African Americans) and the Southwest (Mexican Americans). The formation of Black normal schools and colleges in the South was recognition of this exclusion (see Jones Royster); however, there is no parallel institutional formation for Mexican Americans, who were largely concentrated in the Southwest USA at this time.

A partial explanation for this institutional neglect is likely based on the absence of a large Latinx middle-class population interested in pressing for educational reforms. Thus, while aims at educational inclusion are apparent in the 1870s, the presence of a large number of U.S. citizens still disenfranchised from American educational institutions clearly points to the fact that this historical moment did not live up to its promise of education for all, nor was it inclusive (see Rosaura Sánchez' "Mapping the Spanish Language").

Almost a century passes between the 1870s and the civil rights era; nevertheless, these moments have been characterized as having parallel historical effects by Composition historian Albert Kitzhaber as well as Eric Foner. The parallel is found in calls for reform and social change during both periods. The first reconstructive moment was a result of the Civil War, and the second reconstructive moment was a liberal response to American conservatism heightened by the Cold War, the assassinations of John F. Kennedy and Martin Luther King, Jr. (MLK), and protests against the Vietnam War. The civil rights era was in large measure, although not exclusively, about equal educational and employment opportunities for African Americans and other minority populations such as Chicanxs. In discussing the aftermath of inclusive traditions brought about by the civil rights era, Foner specifically discusses his experience with the City University of New York (CUNY), which "was in the throes of adjusting to open admissions, with a faculty bitterly divided against itself" (13). Creating a policy of open admissions at CUNY was another attempt to provide equal educational opportunities to those who might not have had them otherwise.

Furthermore, the civil rights decade of the twentieth century, widely known as a moment of the struggle for freedom, equality of opportunity, and equal rights, in both the popular and the political arena, is also known for the enfranchisement of various "alternative" knowledges within institutions of higher education that brought about the creation of Ethnic Studies programs and a move toward considering "social histories," also known as "new histories" (Foner, *The New American*).

After considering this comparative historical analysis of both Civil Rights Movements, I then consider the present moment, almost 40 years later, and ask: what do we see when we look back and evaluate the inclusive attempts of the civil rights eras? Today, we continue to witness attempts at inclusion of cultural minorities in the public and private sphere in the face of exclusionary measures like Proposition 209, Arizona's new anti-immigration law, SB 1070, and Arizona's ban on Ethnic Studies in public schools, and, lastly, the attempt by the Texas Board of Education to erase certain Latinx historical figures from public school history textbooks. Furthermore, in an age of increasing conservatism and backlash against liberal notions of "academic freedom," there is still a significant gap in the number of African Americans and Chicanxs/Latinxs present in universities and the number of those living in the surrounding communities. How, then, can educators in the sphere of English Studies continue to foster the inclusive tradition evident in the Reconstruction period of the 1870s and the civil rights era while teaching in an era of conservative admissions policies?

Some of the answers to this question have already surfaced but are largely relegated to the margins of Composition pedagogy. For example, critical educational practices can play a role in helping retain minority students in school, as evidenced by the use of multicultural pedagogies within Hispanic-Serving Institutions (HSIs) (see Kirklighter and a discussion of HSIs in Chap. 6) and the success of their students, but are these suggestions practiced? If so, where? I will argue that literacy educators can play a major role in addressing this issue of inclusiveness by providing culturally relevant curricula, also known as critical educational practices that often contrast with traditional curricula in place to maintain the status quo (such as Common Core in K-12 or current-traditional rhetoric in higher education). However, because of the sometimes controversial nature of culturally relevant curricula and critical educational practices, Composition Studies has struggled with creating and implementing a variety of pedagogical approaches in Composition classrooms that serve cultural and linguistic minorities, such as African Americans and Chicanxs/Latinxs. The difficulty with coming up with an appropriate curriculum can be traced to the ultimate aim of the Composition classroom: that is, to impart Standard English literacy skills in order to function in the category of the "literate," according to U.S. higher educational standards.

So, multicultural pedagogy is not a new concept to Composition Studies. Critical and culturally relevant Composition scholarship does, in fact, exist and has been put into practice in some schools and colleges. Likewise, there are Composition theories that are inclusive of cultural and linguistic minorities who may be in need of a writing pedagogical practice which concentrates on demystifying the Academy, as David Bartholomae claims in his famous Composition article titled "Inventing the University." However, even attempts to demystify the Academy by exposing the particulars of academic writing have not succeeded in enfranchising both linguistic and cultural minorities in institutions of higher education. For example, a group called The Concilio (a community of Chicanx/Latinx faculty, staff, and students at the University of California, San Diego [UCSD], where my study took place) attributes the lack of underrepresented students at the UCSD to certain factors. These include a hostile campus environment, a lack of critical mass of Raza (Chicanx/Latinx faculty, staff, and students), low numbers of Chicano/a faculty, and the limited visibility of Chicano/a issues in the curriculum. The group argues that this lack of representation is particularly unacceptable because some areas of the San Diego County are over 30% Chicanx/Latinx.

Even worse, the African American student body is virtually invisible at the UCSD (see "Report Card on the University of California, San Diego: A Legacy of Institutional Neglect"). Disparities between the number of minority populations present at institutions of higher learning and in the community at large point to major social and educational problems that need to be addressed. At the level of education, Composition is clearly in need of finding innovative ways to enfranchise minority populations through critical literacy. Since Composition is an entry-level college course, it is a site where writing skills as well as social activism can be promoted. I would argue that Composition courses can be fruitful sites for trying to deal with problems of unequal access to a university education when a Composition instructor implements a critical writing pedagogy that meets the needs of both minority and mainstream student populations. These theories, however, need to be closely associated with the process and production of written texts (see Raúl Sánchez, *The Function of Theory in Composition Studies*).

Implementing a critical writing pedagogy in Composition classes, however, has not always been easy. At times, there have been detrimental conservative backlashes to what is being taught in university classes and attempts to dictate what should be taught in the Composition classroom. One extreme example of the public's control over what happens at universities is the case of Linda Brodkey, known as a critical Compositionist and a Foucauldian. Brodkey attempted to utilize legal texts in Composition classes in order to provide students with critical tools with which to read and analyze Supreme Court cases surrounding racial discrimination issues (Faigley 74–75). This attempt at providing students with critical literacy was met with a blatant conservative backlash and criticism. Such conservative attacks are akin to present attacks on academic freedom, attacks which make it very difficult for educators to implement critical versions of writing pedagogy in the classroom.

Such considerations serve broader social interests. For example, the obvious current discrepancy between what is said to be equal access to education and what is actually practiced, especially if we consider who is allowed into college and who is put in jail or prison, calls for a reexamination of current admission policies and sentencing practices (Sánchez 542–43). If as much time as is devoted to policing were expended on finding creative avenues to teach cultural minorities, more minorities would be in school and out of jail. I argue that culturally relevant curricula can lead to higher levels of minority representation at all institutions of higher education, not just at HSIs (which I will discuss in more detail in Chap. 6).

In my pedagogical implications section of this book, I argue that a historiographic method can provide students with the critical analytical tools needed to analyze current social problems of inequality as well as to combat feelings of inadequacy or alienation from mainstream academic culture (See L. Esthela Banuelos' "Here They Go Again with the Race Stuff"). By providing students with these critical tools, education can continue in the tradition of the 1870s and the 1960s by providing students with critical perspectives on history and current social inequalities. The inclusion of these critical practices also necessarily implies making previously excluded histories of minorities or subordinated experiences available to students. Thus, publications in Ethnic Studies, Ethnic Literatures, and Cultural Studies programs have become important sources of textual material that can be incorporated in the writing curriculum.

These publications include "new histories" which concentrate on history written from the bottom up—moving away from historical accounts which only concentrate on the role of institutions in shaping historical change while ignoring the popular effect on historical change. Foner describes them as contributing to a "far more complex and nuanced portrait of the American past, in all its diversity and contentiousness" (11). These "alternative knowledges" are now available to those wishing to be critical literacy educators within English Studies. Through a continual commitment to critical pedagogy, one that relies on a critical historiographic method, educators, I suggest, will be able to continue the tradition of reform that has characterized periods marked by attempts at inclusion of cultural minorities in institutions of higher education. Thus, in the very last chapter of my book, I suggest the writing of a "new history" of Guatemalan immigrants in the USA to give another example of a critical historical case study.

The above explanation gives an overall picture of what I envision for this book, and what follows here is a more detailed explanation of the contents of each chapter.

CHAPTER-BY-CHAPTER OUTLINE

In Chap. 2, I present the theoretical pyramid for both my study and a historiographic writing methodology. I used this pyramid to provide a comparative analysis of traditional Composition histories and alternative histories. At the top of the pyramid are the voices of Foucault and Moya. First, I consider the way Foucault questions the idea that history serves as the consciousness of man (Foucault, *Archaeology of Knowledge*, 12). I also consider the way he presents a post-structural understanding of history as always being incomplete and contingent. While this post-structural understanding of both history and experience has been largely accepted within the field, there are reservations about the post-structural school of thought as expressed by Paula Moya, a critical post-positivist realist theorist, that are not completely unlike Maxine Hairston's criticism of post-structural theory's entrance in Composition Studies in the late 1980s. Post-structuralism was also harshly criticized in the culture wars of the 1990s as being too progressive: read "nontraditional." Nevertheless, post-structuralism and post-positivist realist theory are at point one at the top of the pyramid.

While Foucault allows me to question the legitimacy of historical narratives as uncomplicated texts, I also consider the voices and guidance of "revisionist" historians as point two of the pyramid to inform my critical historical analysis. Here, I turn to two critical historians: Eric Foner and Michel-Rolph Trouillot. Both critical historians allow me to problematize seemingly coherent and complete historical narratives; in this case, the traditional histories of Composition that ignore subaltern experiences.

Since my focus is on contributing subordinated experiences to contested traditional histories of Composition, in the third point of the pyramid, I also consider critical race theory (CRT). Given its focus on race and ethnicity, CRT allows me to concentrate on the experiences of racial groups not addressed in texts representative of a discipline or field of knowledge, like Composition. The way these theories come together for me influences how I understand textual representations and textual artifacts. A critical historical approach, which relies on the focus found in CRT—race as its motivation for textualizing the experiences of minorities, is also consistent with Moya's post-positivist realist theory, which validates experience, and post-structural theory, which questions the ability of texts to represent total experience. I think of this pyramid as fluid in that each of its points informs and is connected to the other.

After presenting these theories and how they work together to inform this study, in Chap. 3, I take a look at late-nineteenth-century histories of Composition Studies. I call upon Foner to give a contextual background which concentrates on the nation's status right after Reconstruction. Foner, as previously noted, describes this time period as a foundational moment in U.S. history, marking the beginning of an evolving nation that was trying to unite itself after a major war and after the prohibition of slavery. This time period forced the nation to confront new social relations as well as new means of production as industrialization increased, especially in the Northern part of the country. Thus, this chapter serves as a traditional historical review of Composition's history beginning in the 1870s. The historical context of the nation also established herein serves to contextualize the changing nature of the University during this era. Here, I argue that the role of politics in Composition becomes evident through comparing and contrasting the traditional history of Composition with critical histories of Composition written by Composition historians, such as Sharon Crowley, Richard Ohmann, Wallace Douglas, Susan Miller, and Lynn Bloom, who see Composition as being involved in the cultural endeavor of middle-class creation.

Chapter 4 focuses on the first Reconstruction era of the mid-to-late nineteenth century and begins the comparison between the Reconstruction era and the civil rights era. This chapter focuses upon time periods right before, during, and after the Civil War. Here, I begin to concentrate upon nineteenth-century alternative institutions and geographical locations after considering the common taxonomy of pedagogical theories offered by James Berlin to provide an analytical tool to visualize what was taking place beyond the traditional, "Harvard history" of Composition Studies. I start out with the Midwest normal school institutions. I discuss pedagogical varieties and the creation of the common school as attached with the spread of normal schools, which also contributed to pedagogical history and innovation. This location is interesting when compared with traditional Composition histories because it provides insight into uncharted territory for our field's current conversations about alternative writing pedagogies.

It becomes evident when I look at these historical junctures and geographical locations that the field of Composition has changed along with changing educational institutions. I find that American educational institutions, such as normal schools, faced with many types of U.S. citizens and residents seeking an education, have called for alternative Composition pedagogies while attempting to form an English-literate middle class in the late nineteenth century.

In Chap. 5, I look beyond the East and away from the Midwest normal school history and pedagogical practices in order to consider Southern states so as to consider large African American populations; I then look toward the Southwestern United States because doing so allows me to look at large Spanish-speaking populations. Considering these alternative geographical areas in conjunction with the Eastern United States creates a more accurate and informative analysis of the history of Composition and also enables me to mark the omissions in the field's traditional histories.

In Chap. 6, I look at the impact of the decade of the 1960s on the field. I present Lester Faigley's discussion of the influence that MLK's death had on Composition Studies. During this era, Compositionists began to encourage students to think critically about their current positions in society and to question the power structures that were largely responsible for their situation. From the 1960s onward, Composition begins anew to reconsider many of the concerns previously raised in its history, albeit under new theoretical and political lenses. These resurfacing considerations, however, were given a name and have been referred to as "critical pedagogy," and are oftentimes accompanied by the likes of Henry Giroux and Paulo Friere.

Furthermore, I emphasize the connection between the inclusive and changing 1870s, as evident in Eastern and Midwestern educational institutions, and the accomodationist and revolutionary 1960s and their effects upon the field of Composition Studies and consider the Chicano Movement as a possible missing historical contribution to the field and to "critical pedagogy." While my account does not focus on the participation of Chicanxs in the field of Composition Studies in the 1960s, it does deal with the impact of the Chicano Movement on educational institutions and especially on curriculum and suggests that Composition was indeed influenced by this educationally focused struggle.

In Chap. 6, I examine the conservative backlash of the 1990s because it stemmed from the gains made in the revolutionary 1960s. Also known as the "culture wars," this backlash was successful in reversing gains made in the 1960s. After the 1960s and 1970s, American citizens witnessed the decline of civil rights, and in the 1980s, there was a backlash to the gains associated with equality rhetoric common in the prior two decades; this backlash manifested itself as the heated response to "reverse-discrimination" as no one, many Americans argued, should receive special treatment or preferential treatment in the professional or academic arena.

In Chap. 7, I concentrate upon the political climate of the 1990s and its effects upon multicultural curricula despite the culture wars. I provide some important statistics relating to the heterogeneous and growing Chicanx/Latinx population within the USA to establish the importance of providing appropriate pedagogical strategies with which to meet the needs of this growing population. Because of the population increase of Chicanxs/Latinxs in the USA, I also argue that it is imperative for mainstream students to learn more about these populations. I then examine "brands" of multiculturalism defined by Paula Moya and consider the ways these "brands" of multiculturalism are practiced at HSIs.

I chose to look at HSIs because I want to take a closer look at these institutions by defining what they are and what their educational mission is and examining how the populations present at these institutions have influenced the way Composition pedagogy is practiced there. Such considerations challenge traditional conceptions of Composition pedagogy such as current-traditional rhetoric and the Harvard model.

I rely on Cristina Kirklighter et al.'s path-breaking book, *Teaching Writing with Latino/a Students: Lessons Learned at Hispanic Serving Institutions* (2007), to provide a snapshot of the type of pedagogical innovations taking place at these nontraditional institutions that are another part of excluded experiences in the history of Composition. One of my initial findings reveals that there is a conflict between traditional multicultural pedagogies and more universal multicultural pedagogies among and in between HSIs.

In Chap. 8, I briefly explain Moya's taxonomy of various types of multicultural curricula (145–46); moreover, in this chapter, I concentrate on illustrating an example of the fifth item of her taxonomy titled "Education that is multicultural and social reconstructionist." It asks students to look at the social structures that create inequalities, such as racial, gender, and class disparities, in an effort to better understand the dynamics of social relationships and possibly alter them. Thus, it seems to be representative of a critical universal multicultural pedagogy or curriculum.

Because no instructional model is provided in Moya's work, I provide a pedagogical moment in a Composition class as one example of an instructional model that can be labeled "Education that is multicultural and social reconstructionist." It allows one to critically analyze the social structures that have historically been put in place in order to ensure certain social relations that are inextricably linked to positions of power and prestige in U.S. society.

Thus, another purpose of this chapter is to provide a detailed case study of a Composition class which took place at the UCSD in 2007. This case study also serves as a basic model for how I currently conceive of and teach FYC at an HSI, UC Merced. The Composition class concentrated on in this chapter was based upon teaching a critical historical approach through the use of textual representations of the Spanish Conquest. Through the description and analysis of this course, I make the case that critical historiography in the Composition classroom allows one to teach a multicultural curriculum that is universal and not exclusive, following Paula Moya's universal multicultural educational theory called post-positivist realist theory (see Chap. 2). Because of constant criticism of multicultural curricula, it is very important that any curriculum that appears inclusive of the minority experience and affirms minority identities also make clear its "sound intellectual and universalist justifications" (Moya 144). This chapter provides those justifications by demonstrating that a critical historical approach to a minority experience provides universal critical thinking skills while paying particular attention to a minority experience; in this case, the experience that is salient to Mexican American students is the Spanish Conquest of Mexico. The study of the history of one's ancestors is a way to cement identity. I agree with Moya's claim that experiences are real, and that because these experiences form identity, identity is also real. I am also a proponent of multicultural education and ethnic studies because I think the progressive movements that took place in the 1960s and 1970s were a step in the right direction for educational institutions that claimed to be inclusive of a wide variety of students.

I end this chapter with this particular classroom example in order to ground my pedagogical implications, which have largely been implicit until this chapter. The pedagogical tasks proved to be social reconstructionist in that the students were encouraged to consider a variety of critical historical texts. In this class, all students, regardless of their race or cultural affiliation, considered the history of a U.S. cultural minority group. This group's history, relayed through both primary and secondary historical sources, became important content to analyze when thinking about their current social standing and status. The material discussed in this class allowed students to problematize a colonial and imperialist history from the eyes of the conquered. It allowed students to critically consider this group's current status as a U.S. cultural minority with a conquered past that is different from the usual black versus white dichotomous histories often discussed in more common and traditional U.S. historical accounts. It also allowed us to see that categories such as Mexican, Chicano/a/x, and Latino/a/x all have particular definitions that can be historically traced and problematized in order to challenge stereotypical notions of these groups.

I end this book with Chap. 9, which serves as a reminder of why it is important to consider the various histories of Latinx populations in the USA. I argue that as this population continues to grow, it is important for educators and Composition scholars to become aware of the heterogeneity of this population and its histories. In doing so, I present statistical data on immigration trends of various Latinx populations to the USA and remind the reader that within the fairly narrow conception of writing instruction and the rhetorics of Composition Studies, there needs to be an expanded knowledge of these various populations as they continue to enter our writing classrooms. I do this by looking at what both James Berlin and Jaime Armin Mejía say about the traditional goals of Composition Studies (Berlin) and the lack of Latinx scholarship within the field (Mejía). Furthermore, I include Rosaura Sánchez and Beatrice Pita's concept of the "Latino Bloc" to demonstrate the many complexities Latinx populations bring to educational and civic institutions that are often overlooked or misunderstood. Their concept enables me to problematize common misconceptions of the Latinx population as only being one monolithic group such as immigrants, Spanish-speaking, uneducated, and uninterested in politics.

I then move on to discuss a specific Latinx population, namely Guatemalans. I introduce this group to problematize common notions of Latinxs as homogeneous and as, perhaps, coming from Mexico and in search of jobs. I argue that immigration is a complicated matter. Through a more in-depth understanding of the turbulent history of Guatemala, we discover that this group came here seeking political asylum. These immigrants were often escaping violent political circumstances, even genocide. Thus, I argue that looking at some historical documents that study the tumultuous history of immigration for Guatemalans allows students in Composition classrooms to problematize notions of immigrants as possessing monolithic and homogenous characteristics and rationales for their growing presence in the USA. I end here because the possibilities for the inclusion of Critical Historical Writing pedagogy become hopeful and endless at this point.

CHAPTER 2

Post-Structuralism, Historical Theory, and Critical Race Theory: A Pyramid for Critical Historical Analysis

I begin this chapter by discussing my own theoretical leanings as well as my writing methodology for two reasons. The first obvious reason is that I am a Composition scholar and it is my duty to do so. I'm not blind to the fact of biased research. I feel my perspective and my experience, though, are my strength and my edge, if you will. Also, I find it necessary to share my methodology, even though by doing so, I run the risk of being marginalized as a Composition scholar of color. I am a Latina interested in the field's attention to Latinxs in the field and in the Composition classroom. However, I am also a Latina who is familiar with "mainstream" scholarship in Composition Studies that serves as its disciplinary "foundation." As a Latina Compositionist, I have noticed that this foundational scholarship is not necessarily concerned with the education of minority students. Like I noted earlier, I don't see myself in Composition's mainstream scholarship, but I have taught Composition in a variety of settings composed of various populations of students ranging from lower- to upper-middle-class students and ranging from classes dominated by minority students (90–95 %) to classes dominated by majority students (white and Asian) (85–90 %). My experience has allowed me to test the theories underlying these foundational texts, and I have found the need to be more inclusive in my theoretical and pedagogical approaches. Thus, while I realize that both the subject matter of this book and my last name may lead to my being marginalized as a "colored" Composition scholar (much like Richard Delgado's professed "colored" legal scholar in "The Imperial Scholar"), I still write

© The Editor(s) (if applicable) and The Author(s) 2016   27
I.D. Ruiz, *Reclaiming Composition for Chicano/as and Other Ethnic Minorities*, DOI 10.1057/978-1-137-53673-0_2

with the intent to be considered by mainstream scholars in Composition, Cultural Studies, and History. My familiarity and understanding of main-stream Composition scholarship and writing theories allow me to place the needs of Latinxs in Composition classrooms in a larger context, and doing so is one of the main goals of this book.

My theoretical leanings are plural, and this is not meant to portray a the-oretically irresponsible position. Indeed, it is my intention to bring together the main tenets of several critical theories in my study that will allow me to problematize and question concepts such as current-traditional rhetoric, objectivity, and positivism. In positing the importance of pursuing alter-native histories, I recognize that historical narratives are never neutral or objective. Post-structural theory, as delineated by Michel Foucault, exposes the interested positionality of discourse as it is intricately involved in power relations. More pointedly, Foucault's notion of history as the consciousness of man and of society is of particular interest to me (Foucault, *Archaeology of Knowledge*, 12). Traditional historians postulate that history is capable of weaving an obscure synthesis that leads one endlessly toward the future. This type of approach to history would provide a privileged shelter for the sovereignty of consciousness and directly affects how one views and acts in the world and participates in civil society. However, for Foucault, history is not continuous; it bears the feeling of continuity and provides a stable narrative structure that appears total and complete. Foucault was aware, however, that many historians question as they also legitimize the value of history. Historians present history as continuous and it is their very presen-tation that Foucault questions. Foucault's notion of history is also found within post-structuralist literary studies, especially in relation to question-ing stable subject positions in literature. Post-structural theory has also made its way into the field of Composition Studies.

While the above notions have been largely accepted and written about within the field (Susan Miller, Raúl Sánchez, Linda Brodkey), there are reservations about Foucauldian notions of post-structuralism as expressed by some critical educational scholars like Paula Moya, a critical post-positivist realist theorist, who argues that post-structural theory severely limits the role of discursive structures to be able to meaningfully com-municate stable states that describe human experience, such as identity, culture, gender, and even humanity. She states that

> postmodernist scholars in the United States...have been influenced by post-structuralist theory [which has] undermined conventional understandings of identity by discounting the possibility of objective knowledge. Instead of asking

how we know who we are, poststructuralist-inspired critics are inclined to suggest that we cannot know...The self, the argument goes, can have no nature because subjectivity does not exist outside the grammatical structures that govern our thought; rather, it is produced by those structures. (7–8)

Moya, however, critiques post-structuralism's reduction of individuals to discursive constructs which allows scholars who do not value identity politics to dismiss notions of a stable identity altogether. The dismissal of experience as serious empirical evidence, Moya argues, is dangerous if one is seeking to understand the experiences of marginalized students and scholars of color as alluded to in the introduction by Villanueva. The personal essay is our sanctuary and our lab. However, while Foucault says that it is okay to dismiss notions of stability when thinking about narratives, Moya counters that when thinking about subjectivities which result in groups of similar identities, dismissing notions of stable structures begins to break down critical dialogue about the value of lived experience, especially for minority groups.

Moya agrees that discourses do construct lived experience and that understanding experience as the material results of those constructions is crucial in any discussion of minority subjectivities. This connection between discourse and experience is a dynamic that this book seeks to problematize as I argue that bringing both elements of post-structuralist theory and post-positivist realist theory in the classroom is crucial for understanding how constructs function to assist in maintaining current power structures. (See Chap. 7 for an in-depth discussion of Critical Historical pedagogy theory as a multicultural strategy that asks students to look at the discursively maintained social structures that create inequalities such as racial, gender, and class disparities.) Looking at experience and history as discursively structured allows us to gain a better understanding of the dynamics of social relationships and possibly alter and disrupt them.

Like Moya, I highlight the importance of experience and subjectivity. Just as subjectivity is created through linguistic structures, experience is also constructed in relation to particular contexts and practices that enable one to situate what is observable and capable of making meaning for groups of people. This position would be similar to the importance of identity politics and multiculturalism in the 1980s, which was based on the notion that what can be known about a people can only be known through a textualized experience. A previously unknown group's customs, beliefs, values, and achievements can only be known through its use of discursive practices that convey them even while not in a totalized uncomplicated manner. The personal essay brings us into visibility.

Multicultural narratives, at once, benefit from and challenge post-structural theory. This double-edged sword occurs because while post-structualism disrupts the continuity of constructed experience, it cannot deny that there is continuity amid discontinuity. Even as one rejects essentializing, one also has to bear in mind, as noted by post-positivist realists, that the consideration of experience is fundamental to any study of minority populations. Experience is more than discourse. It is material and produces real consequences for groups of people who share common experiences. This book postulates that excluded historical accounts can inform misrepresentations of and misunderstandings of both African Americans and Chicanxs/Latinxs in the USA. For example, the experiences of an undocumented student challenge the dominant narrative of citizenship and security within the USA. The very act of being discursively labeled as "undocumented" produces very real and material consequences that all lead back to papers and letters.

It is no secret that the field of Composition Studies has also benefited and built upon Foucauldian notions of subjectivity as it relates to writing pedagogy. One critical perspective that considers discourse or discursive structures as being concerned with the notion of contingent individual experience, both empirical and situational, is James Berlin's "social-epistemic rhetoric," where he argues that discourses are ideological and entangled in power relations. Academic discourses only provide one version of reality or history from a particular social position as proposed in Berlin's third rhetorical writing theory in "Rhetoric and Ideology in the Writing Class." It should be easy to see, then, that the way in which historical continuity is communicated is always in the interest of those who share the same social position (such as the same class, race, gender, geographical location, and historical time period). My yearning to problematize historical narratives is situated in these critical discussions and theories from the standpoint of a Latina Compositionist.

It is important, then, to look at dominant historical narratives in Composition Studies and classrooms as they serve to form the U.S. subject's consciousness. It is not surprising that these narratives are found in U.S. classrooms. Interestingly, these narratives and the discursive fields to which they belong, in effect, determine who will identify with them, who will be encompassed in them, and who will be marginalized from them (similar to what Eric Foner and Michel-Rolph Trouillot argue below). Interrogating dominant historical narratives while keeping Foucault's questioning of the process of historical continuity in mind is crucial to understanding the constructed nature of one's reality. So too, Moya's call to legitimize experience as a form of "objective" truth is crucial to recovering experience otherwise unknown, underresearched, or ignored altogether. Moya argues that texts and experiences of marginalized people are important to understand because of the subjects these texts concentrate upon and the subjects these texts also contribute to and create:

> In the course of making an extended theoretical argument for the epistemic significance of identity, I demonstrate that studying the texts and lived experiences of Chicanas/os (and other marginalized people) is necessary to construct a more objective understanding of the (social and economic) world we live in. (2–3)

I agree that it is important to understand a number of subjectivities texts create so as to have a better view of our social networks and the social networks of others. Again, I would like to stress that these subject experiences, once understood, should not be essentializing but should provide opportunities to engage otherwise understudied populations.

While the ultimate goal of this book is to postulate and endorse a Critical Historical pedagogy in the writing classroom, I lean on but do not completely surrender to post-structuralist understandings of historicity and historiography. I don't believe that the purpose of writing history should be to promote the idea that history is a *transparent* reflection of the "real" and, as always, progressive. While Foucault is not a self-proclaimed critical historian, he is often appropriated as one; so, I turn to two self-proclaimed critical historians to support my theory of historiography and the production of history as processes that produce contingent but seemingly closed texts. The connection between these theories, I argue, is one of a parallel nature. History is composed of narratives, and these narratives are important, as they are all that we have at our disposal to experience the past. Yet, these narratives should also not be thought of as totalizing and essentializing. Thus, I turn to critical historians, Eric Foner and Michel-Rolph Trouillot. Foner claims that as a result of the social movements of the 1960s and the 1970s, American history has been remade. He further claims that

> American historians redefined the very nature of historical study...[They were] inspired initially by these social movements, which shattered the "consensus" vision that had dominated historical writing—and influenced by new methods borrowed from other disciplines. The rise of the "new histories," the emphasis of the experience of ordinary Americans, the impact

of quantification and cultural analysis, the eclipse of conventional political and intellectual history—these trends are now so widely known (and the subject of much controversy) that they need little reiteration. The study of American history today looks far different than it did a generation ago. (vii)

Similar to Foner, Rolph Trouillot, author of *Silencing the Past: Power and the Production of History*, claims that the production of history, which consists of narratives, involves the uneven contribution of competing groups and individuals who have unequal access to the means of such production. He considers both the material means needed for such production as well as the academic qualifications needed. Rolph-Troulliot calls for a better rounded approach to history. This approach can be initiated by asking such questions as, why is the word "history" itself accepted as meaning an unambiguous account of events as if the words that make up the history are transparent conveyers of historical facts? What happens when historical events are told in isolation? Who benefits from such unified historical accounts, and who is unduly marginalized in the process? What does power have to do with the way historical "facts" are revealed? According to Rolph Trouillot, asking such questions begins to problematize a "one-sided" history based on positivist views. Rolph Trouillot positions Western scholarship as misguided by positivism which sees the role of the historian as that of a researcher who reveals the past and the truth with only one side in mind (5).

The alternative to this positivist response is to regard history as merely another form of fiction. However, Trouillot claims that deciding that history is only fiction does not problematize historicity in a productive manner. Of course, there is some truth to every historical story; at least, this is what Rolph Trouillot would posit. Instead of a positivist point of view or a capitulation to history as mere fiction, Rolph Trouillot offers a third perspective on the complication of a "one-sided" history: the constructivist view of history. He defines it as "a particular version of these two propositions [;] it contends that the historical narrative bypasses the issue of truth by virtue of its form [;] they necessarily distort life whether or not the evidence upon which they are based could be proved correct" (6). This view contends that historical narratives are not just fiction; they are a production of an attempted conglomeration of the social historical processes of events (he calls them referents that combine to produce events). Rolph Trouillot's understanding of historical theory is stated as follows, "I have noted that while most theorists acknowledge at the outset that history involves both the social process and narratives about that process, theories of history actually privilege one side as if the other did not matter" (22).

Both critical historians, Foner and Rolph Trouillot, problematize seemingly coherent and complete historical narratives, such as those making up the traditional history of the field of Composition Studies that either obviously or covertly ignore subaltern experiences. I consider this particular history in the next two chapters. For now, I simply want to emphasize that critical historical practice is consistent with the positions found in post-structural, Foucauldian theory and post-positivist realist theory as outlined by Moya above. To put Foucault's contribution and usefulness to this book in the words of another critical Foucauldian and Composition scholar, it is helpful to consider Brodkey's discussion of the violence of literacy in "Poststructural Theories, Methods, and Practices." At the end of this essay, Brodkey states her theoretical position:

> In much the same way that theorists argue that the unity of discourse is a necessary illusion, I view resistance or interruption as a necessary illusion, if only because I need to believe that social change is possible and, further, that the possibility of shifting discursive positions and articulating positive representations of oneself is a more effective, a more inclusive and lasting, form of political resistance than either silence or violence. (23)

This quotation, for me, represents the possibility that discursive structures provide for agency in the same way they provide for limitations to experience since subject positions change. *The possibility for agency and change lies in the demystification of the oppressive effects of discursive practices as well as the liberating effects of discursive practices.* A pedagogical writing theory, such as Critical Historiography, allows silenced voices to express experience in a critical, credible, and scholarly manner suitable for an analysis of the experiences Moya validates as representative of identities, also known as discursive subjectivities.

This type of discursive possibility is one that can be found in critical race theory (CRT). Given its focus on race and ethnicity, CRT concentrates on the experiences of racial groups not addressed in texts representative of a discipline or field of knowledge, like Composition Studies. An analysis of texts representative of a field or discipline is crucial toward establishing the credibility of the field, but so is an analysis of what and who is left out of these texts. A scholarly field is also composed of discursive practices, albeit exclusive discursive practices; and when particular populations are left out of texts thought to represent a foundational understanding of a field, then the needs of those populations will also be marginalized—such is the case with the field of Composition Studies. The exclusion of minority pedagogical considerations will have drastic effects upon minority students. These absences need to be especially considered when addressing the largest minority population within the USA—Latinxs.

Now that it has been established that historical narratives are always incomplete but equally important when searching for exclusivity and inclusion, I briefly turn to CRT as a method that allows students and scholars to identify and recover exclusions in any given narrative. CRT, as outlined by Kimberlé Crenshaw, allows for the examination of covert racist practices which depart from the outright racist practices that are associated with the Jim Crow South—the outright exclusion of people from public facilities and places such a schools, buses, restaurants, universities, and even restrooms. Because the language and practice of jurisprudence determine race relations and minority rights, the practice and language of law are the critical focus of CRT. Legal practices, decisions, and laws are discursive just as narratives are discursive, so the practice of CRT can easily carry over into any practices that seek to critically question objective narratives that convey experience and truth unproblematically. History is one such discursive construct as the debate to whether the discipline of History is a social science or a human science is never-ending.

While CRT explicitly embraces a critical race consciousness of law and public policy-making, it aims to reexamine the terms by which race and racism have been negotiated in the American consciousness. It also aims to recover and revitalize the radical tradition of race consciousness among African Americans and other cultural minorities, such as those addressed by Richard Delgado as being in the realm considered "colored scholarship." Further elaborating CRT, Crenshaw states that those who claim a critical race theorist approach do not necessarily commit to a

> canonical set of doctrines or methodologies...But CRT is unified by two common interests. The first is to understand how a regime of white supremacy and its subordination of people of color have been created and maintained in America, and, in particular, to examine the relationship between that social structure and professed ideals such as "the rule of law" and "equal protection." The second is a desire not merely to understand the vexed bond between law and racial power but to change it. (xvi)

Like critical historians not easily swayed by dominant historical narratives, critical race theorists are deeply dissatisfied with traditional civil rights discourse first popularized in the *Brown v. The Board of Education* case and often referred to as the color-blind rhetoric utilized by civil rights leader Martin Luther King, Jr. This "color-blind" rhetoric rests upon the ideal of equality of opportunity for all Americans regardless of color or creed.

One progressive discursive practice found to be common among critical race theorists is counter-storytelling, described by Edward Said as a type of "antithetical knowledge" which is characterized by the development of counter-accounts of social reality by subversive and subaltern elements of the reigning order. This position is also consistent with a post-positivist realist theoretical stance discussed earlier by Moya.

Since dominant narratives, often found in traditional canonical texts and in traditional histories, are utilized to create one's consciousness and keep dominant populations in positions of dominance, minority populations will not be accounted for or represented in these texts. The effects of this exclusion are detrimental to these populations because they will not have access to the same representation, consideration, and, thus, equal opportunities in society at large. Brodkey calls these types of textual practices violent. She argues that language has real consequences on the ways society operates and the ways people interact with one another; minorities will notice their absence or subordinate status within society in the ways language is utilized in dominant narratives that exclude their experiences and thus negate their consciousness (22–23). More specifically, she argues that there exists a covert relationship between discursive practices and authoritative institutions:

> The conjunction of violence and the word in a legal interpretation is grounded in the powerful discursive hegemony of the state, which confers on judges the authority to reconstruct the lives of plaintiffs and defendants with words. Legal discursive practice may be a powerful interpretive practice, but it is the authority of the state in the person of the judge that makes legal discursive practices (both legislative and juridical) consequential. And it is the authority of the state in the person of the teacher that makes educational discursive practices, such as the teaching of writing and the teaching of History consequential. (23)

The power of discursive practices can be understood in various ways, but one obvious concept that allows one to identify and analyze absence and violence in discursive practices is textual racism. Thus, CRT allows me and others (such as Aja Martinez) to focus on the absence of different U.S.

minority populations in various historical narratives and practices found in mainstream educational institutions and in mainstream U.S. scholarship and academia.

In his book, *White Supremacy and Racism in the Post-Civil Rights Era*, Eduardo Bonilla-Silva gives a useful understanding of racism as practiced in contemporary society. While his analysis parts ways with the "cynicism" of CRT (see Derrick Bell's "Racial Realism"), he also embraces many of its tenets. He specifically acknowledges the subtle racist practices that have taken place since the civil rights era, often alluded to as "color-blind" racism, or that choose to ignore that color has anything to do with the differences in experience for various racial groups in U.S. society. He also gives suggestions for scholars who wish to focus on the concept of race in their scholarship. He states:

> Racism should be conceptualized in structural terms. Whereas the collective interests of the dominant race (Whites in contemporary United States) lie in preserving the racial status quo, the interests of the subordinate race or races (blacks and other minorities) lie in attempting to change their position in the system; one group tends to fight to maintain the social, political, economic, and even psychological arrangements that provide them privileges and the other tends to struggle to alter them...[Thus,] analysts of racial orders must study the practices, institutions, and ideologies that help sustain white privilege. (11–12)

In trying to analyze the practices, institutions, and ideologies that help to sustain dominant privilege, post-structural methods of finding silences, ruptures, challenging continuity, coherence, order, and objectivity enable one to always question the obvious and lead me to also embrace a brand of CRT that questions subtle racial exclusions and distortions within texts while validating both the identities and the experiences of these same excluded peoples.

These theories allow me to focus on what is not obvious on the surface of experiences, whether textual, personal, or political. If educational scholarship can be said to be imperialist (see Delgado's "The Imperial Scholar") because most humanities disciplines are dominated by white, Anglo males, then it is important to question the implications of this scholarship for other racial populations that are also part of those bodies of knowledge. Delgado, for example, writes of civil rights scholarship as being imperialist in the sense that it marginalizes legal scholars of color. In the process of marginalizing scholars of color, a monopoly of mainstream legal scholarship is created at the expense of marginalizing "colored" scholarship. Even after ten years, when Delgado decided to revisit critical legal scholarship, he argued that "colored" scholarship, although cited more often now than a decade ago, is still connected to a marginal status by mainstream legal scholars (see "The Imperial Scholar: Reflections on a Review of Civil Rights Literature," 1984). Delgado states that this 1984 article "showed that an inner circle of twenty-six scholars, all male and white, occupied the central arenas of civil rights scholarship to the exclusion of contributions of minority scholars" ("10 Years Later," 1349) He argued that this exclusion of minority scholars' writings about key issues of race law caused the "literature dealing with race, racism, and American law to be blunted, skewed, and riddled with omissions." He also states that in 1994, ten years later, marginalization of minority voices is still occurring but in a different light: "With a few notable exceptions both the original group and the newcomers rely on a panoply of devices, ranging from the dismissive Afterthought to the wishful Translation, to muffle and tame new voices" (1372). These devices are responsible for the covert textual racism that occurs in many humanities disciplines. Marginalization of voices that do not contribute a melodious addition to existing hegemonic scholarship is the result of the use of such textual devices (listed above) seen in traditional venues for scholarship such as the most well-known journals of a discipline as well as the canonical version of a discipline such as those that constitute the mainstream historical narratives of Composition Studies written by Berlin, Connors, Kitzhaber, and Brereton.

Because of the tendency, then, for much scholarship in the U.S. academic institution to ignore minority perspectives and suggestions for curricular change at every level of the education tier, there is a need to engage in a different type of scholarship. This different kind of scholarship distinguishes itself from the objectified, heavily cited kind of prose found in much academic, postsecondary scholarship representing the "elite culture of knowledge" responsible for creating and maintaining dominant perspectives. This type of textual engagement has been termed "critical counter-storytelling" by many critical race theorists, a textual engagement consistent with Moya's post-positivist realist theory discussed earlier. Racism is not as blatant as it was in the Jim Crow era and happens at more structural levels (in the ways institutions, laws, politics, and powerful, wealthy people interact). So, it is not enough merely to engage in the scholarly conventions manifested in the main textual productions dominated by these institutions. In addition to engaging in these scholarly conventions to show credibility, critical counter-storytelling needs to be engaged in by scholars of color and needs to be considered as a scholarly convention within traditional scholarly venues of a discipline. Critical counter-storytelling departs from traditional academic prose and argumentation to show a realist side of one's experience or of a group's experiences. This type of textual realism which relies on the telling of events from a personal perspective is a crucial textual maneuver that should be utilized by minorities in the academy. Engaging in such a practice allows the focus of such texts to show how race plays an important role in the ways they navigate the "higher academic track."

Tara J. Yosso, author of *Critical Race Counterstories along the Chicana/Chicano Educational Pipeline*, argues that scholars who identify as racial minorities should challenge the dominant ideology. Specifically, she states:

> Critical Race Scholars argue that traditional claims of race neutrality and objectivity act as a camouflage for the self-interest, power, and privilege of dominant groups in U.S. society. A CRT [Critical Race Theory] in education challenges claims that the educational system offers objectivity, meritocracy, color-blindness, race neutrality, and equal opportunity. A critical race praxis (practice informed by critical race theory) questions approaches to schooling that pretend to be neutral or standardized while implicitly privileging White, us-born, monolingual, English-speaking students. (7)

Thus, the act of relying upon critical counter-storytelling for challenging dominant ideology seems appropriate in its reliance on personal storytelling that is often deemed subjective and nonacademic. However, these labels are another attempt to marginalize and thus object to the experiences of those who are most likely not to be considered worthy of academic initiation. But if one looks at the basic tenets of positivist realist theory, experience is a credible source of scholarship research. Critical race counter-storytelling is also part of a Critical Historiographic pedagogy.

Relying on this complementary set of theoretical schools, the next chapters will seek to rely on these precepts referred to here on an "as needed" basis. What this means is that when I run the risk of being politically neutral or seemingly objective, I will stop and ask myself and the reader what is missing. What race is missing? What geographical area is missing? What historical story is being ignored? What are the implications of these silences? I will then attempt to add to these missing portions and then analyze these gaps and see what contributions these additions might produce for both the theory and the practice of contemporary Compositionists of the twenty-first century.

The pedagogical implications discussed in this book for first-year Composition classrooms are also based on these premises. Aja Martinez, Damían Baca, Victor Villanueva, Raúl Sánchez, Cruz Medina, Cristina Kirklighter, Christina Ramírez, and Jaime Armin Mejía are Latinx Compositionists who are all contributing to this tradition today.

CHAPTER 3

Introduction to the Field of Composition: Politics from the Start

This chapter critically considers the current field of Composition Studies (Composition) from a traditional historical perspective while acknowledging its role in the creation and maintenance of culture. Since my intention is to expose omissions in this traditional history in the next chapter, the history of Composition presented in this chapter is most commonly known as the traditional "Harvard" history because Harvard is the location where initial Composition courses are said to have been taught. Harvard, as the locus of Composition, is largely accepted as the dominant history of Composition. It is important to critically understand the scope and contours of the "Harvard" history so that current Compositionists can understand what has already been tried, critiqued, and/or dismissed, pedagogically and theoretically. This familiarity would enable them to answer the following questions: Have previous practices been concerned with inclusiveness? Does one's current pedagogy consider the peculiarities of students in its precepts and ultimate goals? Finally, Compositionists can also add to and complicate this history as I have done here.

Interestingly, Composition Studies, on the surface, looks like a simple field which has as its only goal to teach first-year college Composition (writing). When looking at its traditional history, writing practices are largely seen as positivist, scientific, academic, and objective. On the other hand, when one exposes the silenced history of Composition Studies, one sees that the teaching of college writing addresses much more than just the production of academic, objective essays. Familiarity with Composition's

© The Editor(s) (if applicable) and The Author(s) 2016   41
I.D. Ruiz, *Reclaiming Composition for Chicano/as and Other Ethnic Minorities*, DOI 10.1057/978-1-137-53673-0_3

silenced past enables the discernment of the purposes behind various forms of writing, writing courses, and the theories that might support these different writing practices. What is evident and somewhat constant across histories of Composition, including its traditional history, is that the practice of teaching Composition, since its first appearance on university campuses in the late nineteenth century, has been and is still a political practice in that it teaches a certain view of academic writing and enforces, then, a certain cultural conception of what the definition of good writing is even if that definition changes across contexts. The political function of Composition becomes evident through comparing and contrasting the traditional history of Composition with a more critical, contested history of Composition.

Prior scholarship written by Composition historians, such as Wallace Douglas, has argued that Composition has been involved in constructing culture, specifically middle-class, white male culture, since its inception at Harvard. As a direct result of such scholarship, Compositionists understand the practice of teaching Composition as being involved in creating culture as well as being affected by larger national, cultural goals. The practice of teaching Composition, like any educational practice which creates and maintains culture, is inherently political; it ensures that certain nationalistic goals and cultural climates of a historical period will find their way into the writing classroom to affect and alter the culture of individual students even in a manner that supports cultural assimilation for many students from various social classes as well as for students of color. Composition scholar Sharon Crowley argues that "[i]nstitutional practices in composition typically represent the general history of the course as well as the history of influential teachers and administrators on a given campus" (220). One does not need to perform a lengthy research study to show what those histories reveal about the cultural associations of administrators and their institutions.

Along with Sharon Crowley's book, *Composition in the University*, other Composition scholarship has been devoted to examining the historical politics of the field, the political nature of Composition Studies, as well as the politics involved in Composition pedagogy. For example, Composition historians such as Richard Ohmann, Wallace Douglas, Susan Miller, and Lynn Bloom see Composition as involved in the cultural endeavor of middle-class creation. Before looking at traditional, elite versions of Composition's history written by majority Composition scholars, the following is a look at these critical Composition historians' scholarship.

I want to look briefly at these critiques in order to provide the reader a critical eye with which to view the traditional history of Composition.

The critical focus on middle-class values present within Composition pedagogy touched upon in more traditional Composition histories is elucidated by popular Composition historians Susan Miller, Sharon Crowley, and Lynn Bloom. For example, Miller states that the history of Composition is political because it stresses certain middle-class values. However, according to Miller, the field's history has been largely depoliticized by using abstract terms to describe curricula for writing. She states that the predominant images associated with Composition are associated with developing traditional, middle-class values that

> encompass popular images of what it means to write well. It [Composition] stresses upward mobility, imitation of a largely hidden American upper class, and stringent mores, as against improprieties imagined to be shunned by that upper class. The history of English in America has been depoliticized by imagining this particular scholastic brand of writing. Abstractions like "the curriculum," "regressive education," and "rhetoric" hide many considerations for nationalistic, colonizing, and pointedly political programs. (34–35)

Similar to Miller's argument, Sharon Crowley and Lynn Bloom would agree that Composition's continuity of purpose is and always has been to create and maintain a hegemonic middle class.

Bloom claims in her essay, "Freshman Composition as a Middle-Class Enterprise," that freshman Composition encourages students to think and write in ways that will make them good citizens of the academic (and larger) community and viable candidates for good jobs upon graduation. She further identifies a number of major notions pertaining to social class that freshman Composition often emphasizes, such as self-reliance, responsibility, respectability ("middle-class morality"), decorum, propriety, moderation, temperance, thrift, efficiency, order, cleanliness, punctuality, delayed gratification, and critical thinking. These characteristics all pertain to the creation and maintenance of the U.S. middle-class population. Many may disagree with Bloom, who believes Composition has always had this normalizing function. However, she makes clear that although many Composition models are possible, "the middle-class pedagogical model, replete with Franklinesque virtues, has remained normative and dominant from the emergence of composition as a college course in the late nineteenth century to the present (see Brereton)" (658).

Regarding Composition's role in the creation of the citizen/subject or the bourgeois subject, Crowley similarly argues that Composition, since its inception, has metamorphosed with society's expectation of what skills an ideal national subject should possess:

> Over the years...first year composition has been remarkably vulnerable to ideologies and practices that originate elsewhere than its classrooms. An amazing number of rationales have been advanced to justify the universal requirement in composition. [These are] in rough historical order:...to develop taste, to improve their grasp of formal and mechanical correctness, to become liberally educated, to prepare for jobs or professions, to develop their personalities, to become able citizens of a democracy, to become skilled communicators, to develop skill in textual analysis, to become critical thinkers, to establish their personal voices, to master the composition process, to master the composition of discourses used within academic disciplines, and to become oppositional critics of their culture. (6)

These rationales, which Crowley discusses above, are undoubtedly tied to the greater cultural and historical goals of the university in creating and maintaining the middle-class subject/citizen. The variability seems to stem from what the educational institution regarded as appropriate literate behavior for its students in the interest of larger political and cultural goals. Only recently has the last goal (to become oppositional critics of culture) become part of the critical pedagogical practices of Composition. By recently, I mean since the late 1960s, when other cultural groups started to become more visible in the field of Composition (i.e., the increased presence of African Americans in colleges associated with desegregation and the Civil Rights Movement).[1]

Continuing this critical discussion of the creation of the middle class in which Composition participates, Miller argues in *Textual Carnivals* that the Composition course has both indoctrinating and normalizing functions:

> Acting from its own traditions, composition can repress and commonly assimilate the majority of American writers who obtain credentials in higher education, indoctrinating them into openly middle-class values of propriety, politeness, and cooperation. By taking as one of its goals the "conventional,"

---

[1] This time period will be discussed in further detail in Chap. 5.

composition assures that these values will maintain their continuing, if disguised or displaced, status. (7)

Considering these critical Composition comments before reading a traditional history of Composition may provide the reader with a critical historical perspective with which to view Composition's commonly accepted history.

Before considering a traditional post–Civil War history of Composition, a brief contextually aligning historical backdrop to this history can be summoned by the reader if he or she consults works devoted to the U.S. historical period of the Reconstruction Era. Eric Foner, a critical historian, addresses this period exclusively and makes connections between the Reconstruction Era and the civil rights era. He characterizes this era as follows:

> The era of Civil War, Slavery and Reconstruction raised the decisive questions of America's national existence; the relations between local and national authority, the definition of citizenship, the meaning of equality and freedom. As long as these issues remain central to American life, scholars are certain to return to the Civil War period, bringing to bear the constantly evolving methods and concerns of the study of history. (89)

As Foner describes, this time period was a foundational moment in U.S. history, marking the beginning of the solidification of a nation that was trying to unite itself after a major war and after the dismantling of a very oppressive institution—slavery. With the destruction of this institution also came the need to confront new social relations as well as new means of production as industrialization increased at this time, although more pronounced in the northern part of the country. This period can be compared with the civil rights era of the 1960s, which also looked at ideas such as the meaning of equality and the definition of citizenship. For this reason, Foner's work makes interesting connections between these two time periods for the field of Composition Studies.[2]

The Reconstruction period can be characterized as one of extreme national transformation and upheaval. Every institution was affected by the union of the North and the South as well as by industrialization, including the University. It was undoubtedly affected by the changing demographics

---

[2] See Foner's "Slavery, the Civil War, and Reconstruction" in *The New American History*.

and economic interests of an increasingly capitalistic nation. Since slavery was no longer legally sanctioned and education was a goal sought not only by previously disenfranchised African American slaves (referred to as "Negroes" at this time) but also by the sons and daughters of previous plantation owners, the training of teachers to teach these growing student populations became a priority. However, in the North and specifically in the Northeast, the elite Ivy League university was more interested in maintaining and continuing to contribute to an elite class of white male managers and a culturally and technically trained capitalist class. While the training of teachers was also a goal of these universities, much of the teacher training took place at teacher's colleges, also known as normal schools.[3]

The history of Composition Studies shows us how the practice of rhetoric and teaching writing underwent transformations in an effort to serve the needs of this newly conceived society: a society that was interested not only in becoming a stronger capitalist nation-state, but also in disseminating a unified nationalist ideal through curricula that were suitable to the various populations entering universities and normal schools. Furthermore, when analyzing these two sites of education varying in geographical concentration, it becomes apparent that whites were considered for certain social roles, while blacks were delegated to different social roles. Moreover, white men were trained for public sector jobs, while women were trained for private sphere jobs, with the exception of teaching. Thus, women, in general, were meant to be domestic queens with the ability to teach children, while white men would ensure the economic management (not necessarily manpower) of our increasingly bourgeois nation. With this short historical background, I now move on to the traditional history of Composition, and I will then give a more contested history which includes both African American and Mexican American contributions to this history as well as the normal school mission which sought to train teachers.

COMPOSITION'S TRADITIONAL HISTORY

Albert R. Kitzhaber wrote a book titled *Rhetoric in American Colleges, 1850–1900*. It was completed in 1953; however, it was not published as a book until 1990. Kitzhaber was, thus, the author of the first book-length historical study of rhetoric in Composition. His study helped make the paradigm shift in Composition during the 1970s possible. John T. Gage, author of the introduction to Kitzhaber's book, claims that this book was long called for,

---

[3] The parallel history of the normal school will be discussed in depth in the next chapter.

since, previously, students of Composition had access only to Kitzhaber's dissertation. The importance of Kitzhaber's study lies in his initiation of the reevaluation of rhetoric in American education. He made a very important claim for Compositionists who wish to understand the current history of Composition in relation to the past. In his book, he describes the second half of the nineteenth century as a "transitional" period for the field of composition and rhetoric. John Gage states that, according to Kitzhaber's book, the current shifts that the field has experienced in the past 20 years (this book was published in 1990) are not unlike those of the mid-nineteenth century:

> If the watershed year were changed from 1870 to 1970 and "eighteenth" changed to "nineteenth," few, I think, would quarrel with the accuracy of such a description [of the dissatisfaction with college curriculums] applied to our own more recent history. The words raise the salient possibility that the discipline of composition, which seems to have changed so much in the past twenty years, has in fact changed relatively little, or has changed along familiar lines. (ix)

Gage makes this controversial historical claim by recognizing the move from rhetorical training to the teaching of practical skills in Composition classrooms of the late nineteenth century as noted by Kitzhaber. One cannot make historical connections between these two time periods without considering, however, both traditional and nontraditional histories of Composition. What follows is a review of Composition's history beginning in the 1870s. It is my hope that the historical context of the nation established above will serve to contextualize the changing nature of the University during this era.

THE BEGINNING

> By 1900, every college had an array of Composition and English literature courses. The creation of the modern university transformed writing instruction. Of all the complex factors that influenced the university's formation, four stand out: the influence of the German university model, the changing nature of knowledge, the dramatic expansion of higher education, and the efforts of a few visionaries to update the university's purview. (Brereton 4–5[4])

[4]As a result of the influence of the German university, of the impact of science, of the Morrill Act, and of a weakening faith in the credibility of the old faculty psychology, the 1870s saw the beginnings of extensive revisions in the traditional curriculum (Kitzhaber 17).

Composition is a field of knowledge that grew out of classical rhetorical training common at universities such as Harvard and Yale. Rhetorical training was common for most nineteenth-century colleges, which were reserved for the prosperous elite who were predestined, because of their socioeconomic status and gender, to become the nation's clergymen, doctors, and lawyers. Most of these college students were white Anglo-Saxon males. However, because of the move from a *laissez-faire* market economy to a managed economy which was intimately tied to governmental alliances, colleges changed their educational mission. This mission was to "train certified experts in the new sciences, experts who could turn their knowledge to the management of the production, distribution, exchange, and consumption activities of society for profit" (Berlin *Writing Instruction* 185). Thus, the elitist institution was transformed by both economic and social changes taking place within our nation as a result of Reconstruction and industrialization. The mid-and late-nineteenth-century U.S. called for and required a managerial class to maintain its progress. This managerial class could be created by specialization and training in the sciences. These specialists were to become well-equipped by education and specialization to contribute to the economic development of our burgeoning nation.

Wallace Douglas also understands the elite university responding to a growing college population and the scientific needs of late-nineteenth-century society. He confirms that Harvard was one of these colleges where men from all walks of life could be refined and "was to be a selection mechanism, a recruiting ground for new men for the apparatuses of state and industry, some few of whom might even come to walk the corridors of power themselves" (132).

This new educational mission was also largely influenced by the German model of education and the passing of the Morrill Federal Land Grant of 1862.[5] Under such educational legislation, populations granted

[5] Within five years after the act became law, 23 states had availed themselves of its provisions. These new state institutions, founded squarely on the notion that it was the responsibility of American colleges to offer a wider selection of courses than had been commonly available before, were very influential in breaking up the older pattern and in supplying a new one for the next century (Kitzhaber 12). This act funded educational institutions by granting federally controlled lands to the states. The mission of these institutions, as set forth in the 1862 Act, is to teach agriculture, military tactics, the mechanic arts, and home economics, not to the exclusion of classical studies, so that members of the working classes might obtain a practical college education. In 1890, this act was again enforced on the Confederate states, which began the creation of some of the well-known historically black colleges.

admissions into higher education were no longer solely white upper-class males. Brereton states that "the American college moved from a unified small, elite school to a diverse, large fragmented university organized by academic disciplines" (4).[6] Thus, as more populations were gaining access to higher education, elite colleges were also faced with a more eclectic, nonelite student population with differing abilities and talents. Law, medicine, and the ministry were no longer the only options for higher education; instead, the new goal was to create a managerial class to oversee businesses or to fulfill governmental bureaucratic roles. Thus, more white Anglo-Saxon males, who represented a wider range of social castes, began to attend college along with the elite upper class. As such, the old curriculum of classical language training and rhetorical recitation common in Harvard's previous rhetorical program became impractical.

In addition to a growing population of students, the formation of the modern university also included an increasing interest in specialization. This interest developed in elite institutions along with the American exposure to the German model of education. Brereton comments on the influence of the German model in the early nineteenth century:

> Americans in search of advanced degrees went to Germany and returned imbued with the university ideal. The German universities they studied at stressed research, the creation rather than the transmission of knowledge. In 1876, Johns Hopkins University was founded on the German model and overnight became the single most potent force for upgrading the educational standards of American scholarship. (5)

However, the German university did not include rhetoric, and Americans interested in English studies came home with a German doctorate in philology (study of classical language and literature), not rhetoric (the art of persuasion, oratory, and recitation). Brereton further informs us that the German model influenced an increasing interest in science in American universities, and the move from a required curriculum to an elective system which allowed students to specialize:[7]

---

[6] W.E.B. Dubois was a graduate student at Harvard in the early 1890s.

[7] "While German universities were approaching their peak in prestige and enrollment, there were in 1868–1869 only eight graduate students in residence at Yale, five at Harvard, and none at all at Brown, Columbia, Princeton, or the University of Pennsylvania" (Kitzhaber 13).

The German model stressed innovation, electives, and specialization. Following this German ideal, professors immersed themselves in their studies or laboratories to produce research, the disciplines organized themselves on scholarly rather than pedagogical lines, and universities slowly abandoned much low-level teaching to an underclass of instructors and graduate student assistants. (6)

Brereton hints at the future of Composition professionals and their lowly status; however, what interests me here is the turn to scientific research and specialization in the American university, which influenced rhetoric departments to focus more on the study of English language and literature.

Thus, by 1869, when Charles W. Eliot was inaugurated as Harvard's president, the conditions were ripe for a transformation of the American college into a modern university and of what we now know as English Composition. In 1872, Eliot appointed Adams Sherman Hill to develop Harvard's Composition program: "Harvard went about composition, like everything else, in a big way. At its height in 1880–1910, the Harvard system included three elements: a particular kind of writing; a wide array of course work; and an eminent, highly visible staff" (Brereton 11). Under Hill, the Harvard Entrance Exam (1873–1874) was implemented to test the incoming students' familiarity with both English language and literature by writing about "great cultural works" in grammatically correct Standard English. In fact, the first-year required Composition course was created partly because of the results of this exam and the university's increasing specialization. The results of the Harvard Entrance Exam showed a less-than-literate entering class.

Thus, the first-year Composition course was created to accommodate and cultivate the increasingly diverse populations Harvard was admitting. It strived to remedy students' English language and literary knowledge so as to prepare them for arguably more "advanced" and cultured subjects such as English Literature. Brereton confirms that "[b]y the time the literature-based composition course became popular a hierarchy began to develop: the better the student, the more literature in the composition course" (16). These new populations were to be cultivated into cultured men through the act of reading and writing about English Literature in current-traditional rhetoric (see definition in the next section). They would later serve the larger economic need for a managerial class. And, as a result of a very pointed curricular aim, the push toward scientific research caused the University's English department to be dominated by a positivist view of knowledge.

This focus on positivism influenced Harvard's focus on scientism and specialization, also influenced by the German model as well as the results of the Harvard Entrance Exam. Harvard thus became under Charles William Eliot "the most extreme in its elective system, reducing required courses to freshmen in 1894, and decreasing even these to a year of freshman rhetoric in 1897" (Berlin *Writing Instruction* 59).[8] Freshman Composition became solidified as a required freshman class in the late nineteenth century, with its conception at Harvard and its proliferation at other well-known colleges and universities.

Contributing to this traditional history of Composition, Richard Ohmann provides a "radical" view of the English profession. This critique of the profession of English logically includes critiquing the purpose of Composition. He concludes that Composition was responding to the needs of powerful groups in the larger society at this time. Ohmann also explains how Composition assumed the place it currently holds in the university curriculum. He states that "there are complex causal relationships among the university teaching of composition, social class, and the management of our society" (173). Douglas, who wrote a chapter in Ohmann's book,[9] argues that the first-year required Composition class was created in response to the growing needs of society for a managerial class while also trying to accommodate a broader range of students attending Harvard before, during, and especially after World War I.

In his chapter, Douglas states that in the nineteenth century, "[c]omplex industrial firms needed a corps of managers who could size up needs, organize material, marshal evidence, solve problems, make and communicate decisions" (93). In other words, writing became a tool of production and management and veered away from being mainly a private art to being a public art. Douglas takes special care to make the transformation from rhetorical training to modern composition very explicit. According to him, this conversion led toward the creation of a required freshman Composition course that focused upon problem-solving and

[8] "The entering student, [Eliot] said, 'ought to know what he likes best and is most fit for. If his previous training has been sufficiently wide, he will know by that time whether he is most apt for language or philosophy or natural science or mathematics. If he feels no loves, he will at least have his hates (p. 14)'" (Eliot quoted in Kitzhaber 18).

[9] Titled "Rhetoric for the Meritocracy."

discipline (and perhaps taste), catering to the needs of an economically changing society which needed individuals who could manage capital, both human and monetary (131–32). In addition to supporting a society which increasingly relied upon an individual's ability to perform managerial tasks, another partial explanation for the creation and continuance of Composition is its focus on the scientific rhetoric that it espoused at this time, namely current-traditional rhetoric.

While the next section of this chapter provides a detailed definition of current-traditional rhetoric, I would like to briefly mention that the traditional history of Composition and the dominant writing theory, namely current-traditional rhetoric, are historically interdependent. The type of writing theory espoused during this historical era undoubtedly reflected the needs of a larger nation. However, it is my intention to show how this type of writing theory marginalizes minority populations when taking a critical look at its definition and asking who benefits from this type of rhetoric and, at the same time, who is excluded.

The Rise of Composition/Rhetoric Outdated: Scientism, Managerialism, and Current Traditional Rhetoric

Current-traditional rhetoric (CTR from this point on) grew out of the impracticality of classical rhetoric. Classical rhetoric was configured into a more practical use of language which aided in creating a managerial class because of the changing nature of the modern university. This configuration was related to the scientific concentration of the elite university. Thus, CTR does not consider pedagogy so much as the product to be evaluated. The practice of teaching CTR, as a result, contrasts with other practices within pedagogically centered educational institutions such as normal schools. Identifying this contrast allows underrepresented populations to problematize the legitimacy of CTR by looking at the value placed upon CTR in elite universities in contrast to normal schools (discussed in depth in the next chapter). The difference can be summarized as follows: Unlike the psychological theories which underlie the pedagogical practices of Composition in Midwestern and other normal schools, CTR does not consider critical pedagogical questions such as: Who is writing? Why might he/she have difficulty producing CTR? Is CTR in close proximity to her home culture or usual manners of speaking/writing? Furthermore, populations that have not been considered in elite universities or that were located in normal schools come to light when questioning the history, use, and value of CTR. The following section thus seeks to expose how the redefinitions of classical rhetoric within the new scientifically oriented university led to the creation of CTR.

Rhetoric Outdated

Rhetorics arise, fall, or alter in accordance with the conditions that make for a change in society as a whole. They are engaging in themselves, but, because they are sensitive indicators of the extent of change in society, they are also a useful index of larger social developments. Thus, studying a rhetoric in its relationship to society reveals a great deal about both a rhetoric and the society producing it. (Berlin *Writing Instruction* 3)

Producing a managerial, working middle class was the aim of the modern university, and this aim was not unlike training individuals in a language that would promote mental discipline such as classical rhetorical exercises claimed to do. Brereton states that proponents of classical rhetoric "claimed that the ancient languages provided mental discipline and trained the powers of the mind, pointing to the extremely close attention to the details of language…that characterized college Greek and Latin classes" (4). However, as Ohmann claims in "Writing and Reading, Work and Leisure," "the emergence of the new university would make a traditional, unified subject like rhetoric obsolete and replace it with a new, utilitarian writing course, more attuned to the times" (quoted in Brereton 7).

The influence of an Aristotelian view of language was especially noticeable in classical rhetoric. According to Berlin and other contemporary rhetoricians, the influence of Aristotelian rhetoric can be explained as follows: "[C]lassical rhetoric defines the real as rational. The universe is governed by the rules of reason, and the human mind is so constructed that, at its best, it is governed by the same rules. Knowledge is, therefore, found through the formalization of these rules of reason—in Aristotelian logic" (*Writing Instruction* 4). Because the focus on logic was already found in Aristotelian rhetoric, it was easy to forge connections between classical rhetoric and CTR. Objective logic was needed for the managerial class to function according to the new focus of the university. Thus, a scientific purpose of language was easy to connect to classical rhetoric. For example, Berlin states that "[l]anguage for Aristotle is little more than a simple sign system, with thought and word enjoying a separate existence, to be brought together only for purposes of communication" (7). Language was capable of conveying truth, scientific truth, in uncomplicated ways. Thus, rhetoric's connection to Composition is very much in line with the new scientific mission of the university. Language was regarded as a sign system which conveyed something without ever considering who is conveying what.

Because elite universities were focusing more upon scientific theories which represented truth in an objectified manner, English departments followed suit. Therefore, the view in English departments became dominated by the belief that language (Standard English) could transparently relate the derivation of truth or experience, but only in standardized forms or modes—narration, description, exposition, and argument without any attention to the individual student and his/her background. Fortunately, for the field of Composition Studies, CTR has increasingly come under critique even while it remains the dominant writing theory and practice in most U.S. universities. Critics of CTR, such as Donald Stewart, share this sentiment. He stated the following in his Conference on College Composition and Communication (CCCC) Chair's address:

> I have become convinced that a writing teacher's development can be measured by the degree to which that person has become liberated from current-traditional rhetoric. And the progress of that liberation, I further believe, is closely linked to that person's accumulating knowledge of the history of composition as a discipline. (105)

Thus, familiarizing oneself with Composition Studies' history allows for the possibility of becoming liberated from CTR, which seems necessary because learning any language (whether to speak, read, or write) should involve much more than merely the relaying of facts. There is, without a doubt, always a situated author behind every text who has a perspective and a purpose to his/her writing, even if that author is a socially constructed individual as Foucault would claim.

After considering a traditional account of Composition's history and becoming more aware of the dominant writing theory connected with this theory, I believe it is logical to return to the critical perspective introduced before the recounting of this history and of CTR. This critique is based largely on the connection between Composition's historical roots in Eastern elite universities and the types of composition taught and produced at this time for the creation of the late-nineteenth-century, middle-class, white, male subject.

However, the creation of the middle-class subject through the act of writing has been established in the field's scholarship by Ohmann, Douglas, Crowley, Bloom, and, Miller, yet certain aspects of these histories are not questioned and thus are largely accepted as complete and official accounts of the genesis and practice of Composition in the late nineteenth century. Some immediate noticeable omissions are: (1) Due to the focus on a North American view of teaching writing as a set of skills to be mastered under CTR, a European view of teaching writing which emphasizes pedagogical and psychological aspects of learning is omitted. This is a striking omission in itself as European-centered teaching concepts and skills are, rather, based upon the psychology of learning[10] or psychologically based pedagogical practices, which were present in many normal schools in the late nineteenth century (to be discussed shortly). (2) Largely, in these critical histories of Composition, a racial and culturally blind version of Composition pedagogy is prevalent. Thus, critiques that address nonelitist views of Composition's history that arose from (1) European pedagogical influences on Midwestern normal schools and (2) a consideration of race are omitted.

Both of these considerations bring up pertinent absences in traditional and even critical histories of Composition. For example, when considering a critical race theoretical perspective, where an otherwise race-neutral approach seems the norm as in traditional histories, the concept of race becomes central, and from such a perspective, the absence of African Americans and Mexican Americans in higher education and in histories of Composition Studies comes to light. Still, Miller's, Crowley's, and Bloom's critiques of Composition as multidisciplinary, yet still regulatory, are noteworthy in their contribution to the current understanding of the field; their focus, however, is not on race but on class. When focusing on race, one can look to other U.S. geographical locations to inform how other races might have been involved in the untold history of Composition Studies. The same would be the case when looking at other races that were being educated in U.S. institutions while this history was taking place. These considerations guide the next two chapters.

---

[10] This distinction will be further explained in the next chapter. Heinrich Pestalozzi, the most influential European theorist, argued that "education's aim was to 'fit' or adjust, all children to society and that all learning begins with the child's perceptions" (Fitzgerald 231).

CHAPTER 4

A History Untold: Composition's Connected Past to the Educational Reforms of the Reconstructive Era

Various historical moments—the Civil War (1861–1865), the Morrill Federal Land Grant (1862), World War I (1914–1918), World War II (1939–1945), and the Vietnam War (1959–1975)—affected the status and practice of Composition across the U.S.A. Due to the scope of this book, however, I will focus on the periods right before, during, and after the Civil War in this chapter, and the next chapter will focus primarily upon the civil rights era, which also closely correlated with the time period of the Vietnam War. Along with the two time frames of this and the next chapter's focus, I concentrate upon alternative geographical locations; that is, I look beyond the East, the area on which common histories of Composition focus. Looking toward the Southwestern and the Southern U.S. states allows me to consider Spanish-speaking populations and large African American populations. Considering these alternative geographical areas in conjunction with the Eastern U.S.A. allows for a more accurate and informative analysis of the history of Composition and of the blind spots that mark the field.

It becomes evident when looking at these historical junctures and geographical locations that the history of Composition is commensurate with a changing educational institution inhabited by Americans who derived from various cultures and social classes. However, regardless of color, culture, or social class, the educational institution's mission has always been, since the reform era (1830s), to train able individuals to fulfill various socioeconomic roles in the larger society, ranging from handmaids to presidents of the U.S.A.

© The Editor(s) (if applicable) and The Author(s) 2016   57
I.D. Ruiz, *Reclaiming Composition for Chicano/as and Other Ethnic Minorities*, DOI 10.1057/978-1-137-53673-0_4

The American educational mission, faced with many types of U.S. citizens and residents who sought an education, called for a challenge to traditional Composition pedagogy as its practitioners attempted to maintain a literate middle class in the late nineteenth century. For example, in the Southwest, the predominantly Spanish-speaking population posed new challenges to English-only legislation, and when looking at the South, teachers often discounted literate practices because of the color of the person's skin (see Royster). Thus, some key considerations have emerged in view of these historical changes within the field of Composition, including: (1) What should be taught? (2) What is the desired result from what is being taught? (3) Whom are we teaching? These changes are described by Berlin, who argues that larger political and social developments led to transformations in society's rhetorics[1] (*Rhetoric and Reality* 4).

For example, he discusses the control of rhetoric in a democratic society which seeks to regulate who can and cannot speak and write:

> In a democracy, those whose power is based on a particular notion of rhetoric (for example, a rhetoric maintaining that only certified experts may speak or write, or only those who have attained a certain level of financial success) will...restrict challenges to their conception of rhetoric because such challenges constitute a threat to their continued claim to eminence. [While a] free play of possibilities [exists] in the rhetorics that appear...these possibilities are obviously never unlimited. (5)

Thus, there are always rhetorical limits to who can speak and what one can say in a democratic society, even with First Amendment rights. However, because language and rhetoric are interdependent, and change and adapt to populations and political purposes, the regulating function of rhetoric and Composition can actually shape and form competing rhetorics, also known as alternative rhetorics.[2] The racial and cultural realities of the many populations that make up the U.S.A. affect these changes,

---

[1] Or better yet, the sanctioned communicative methods of persuasion and identification. For further discussion of the relationship between rhetoric and identification, see "Hybridity: A Lens for Understanding Mestizo/a Writers" by Louise Rodríguez Connal from *Crossing Borderlands: Composition and Postcolonial Studies*, edited by Andrea A. Lunsford and Lahoucine Ouzgane.

[2] See Louise Rodríguez Connal's "Hybridity A Lens for Understanding Mestizo/a Writers" from *Crossing Borderlands: Composition and Postcolonial Studies*, edited by Andrea A. Lunsford and Lahoucine Ouzgane.

even within rhetorical limits and language exclusions (such as Spanish). Each cultural group present in the U.S.A. has its own rhetorics (manners of communication and persuasion). Berlin notes that changes in dominant rhetorics are largely influenced by notions of what it means to be literate in a democratic society such as ours. More specifically, he states that "the kinds of graduates colleges prepare have a great deal to do with the conditions in the society for which they are preparing them" (5). Thus, writing curricula are almost always responsive to changes within the economic, social (including racial), and political conditions in a given society. If colleges desire to create a middle class, then the way in which Composition responds to this goal has largely to do with what the requirements for middle-class initiation are at any given historical moment and who is being initiated. These requirements are chosen and created by the dominant class. Today, the knowledge of correct Standard English and U.S. American rhetorics is part of what is required for middle-class initiation. Composition, again, is involved in creating culture, but it has to start from where the subject/citizen is or these requirements will not be met easily.

As previously mentioned, racial diversity is absent from the histories I referred to in Chap. 3 by Crowley, Miller, Ohmann, Douglas, and Bloom. Although very important for the field when analyzing the role of class creation in Composition, these histories are limited by a focus that dwells primarily on issues of class. This focus leaves the consideration of race and geographical locations out of their histories, and understandably so. Considering the racial dynamics and politics behind the history of Composition is not an easy task, and it is not conducive to a seamless, nice, and tidy historical account of the field. I have only begun to uncover some of these considerations. However, since the examination of various geographical, gender, and racial characteristics of Composition's history is left wanting, new grounds need to start being forged in order to begin to grapple with the many complexities of Composition's past and present.

It becomes important, then, to look at earlier alternative Composition pedagogies other than current-traditional rhetoric associated with the education of white males. For example, what were some alternative pedagogical views associated with the normal school? Was current-traditional rhetoric the dominant pedagogy in the normal school as it was for the Composition Program practiced at Harvard? What contemporary theories are associated with the rise and fall of the normal schools of the late nineteenth century? As far as the minority populations are concerned (African Americans and Mexican Americans), one needs to consider additional factors, like alternative schools. Here, however, we find that the concentration of black normal schools in the South is not telling a story much different from the Midwestern normal school. What is different, however, is the new population attending these normal schools—African Americans. While practicing a common brand of English-language teaching for the black common schools, the South also was characterized by the literary training of African Americans through alternative institutions such as the Church, community activist groups, and the public press (i.e., National Association of Colored Women [NACW] and the African American periodical press[3]).

Thus, it is apparent that African Americans were, from the start, developing alternative rhetorics—alternative ways of knowing, critical means of seeing the world from an outsider's distance, with a worldview that was colored by an alternative lens (everything seemed a different hue from an African American perspective as W.E.B. Dubois' concept of the veil describes). These alternative rhetorics are those Berlin describes as being a challenge to the dominant rhetoric but which were also able to come into dialogue with democratic rhetoric in a society where equal consideration of opinions is permitted and where freedom of speech is guaranteed even as it is limited. He alludes to alternative rhetorics in his discussion of competing rhetorics above. Modes of communication differed for groups situated in a socio-historical place, or subject position, that falls into one of three spheres: (1) white, middle-class male; (2) non-white but willing to adapt to the communicative patterns of white, middle-class males; or (3) as non-white and distinct from the cultural attributes categorized as being associated as white, middle class, and male.

Unfortunately, it was not until the civil rights era that these alternative ideas and alternative rhetorics begin to seriously shake the fabric of a seemingly unified nation, and at the same time, they began to be considered equal to the intellectual spheres of inquiry, such as that afforded to current-traditional rhetoric.[4] This chapter, however, exclusively deals

---

[3] There were literally dozens of women who, since the 1830s, found the African American periodical press to be the platform from which they could speak and be heard both as creative writers of poetry, short stories, and serialized novels, and as fiction writers of informative prose, persuasive essays, personal narratives, biographical sketches, tributes, opinion pieces, and so forth (Royster 221).

[4] These alternative rhetorics are not to be confused with contrastive rhetorics associated with William Labov. These alternative rhetorics are more in line with those that are associated with identity in mainstream society. While the dominant rhetoric is closely correlated to the

with the late-nineteenth-century Midwest, South, and Southwest, as well as with the racial dynamics of the groups associated with these regions at this moment.

The goal of this chapter is to shed light on the absence of both geographical and, as a result, gender and racial concerns in traditional histories of Composition by Douglas, Crowley, Miller, and Bloom. The chapter's intent is to provide a more complete story of Composition and to contribute to the more common story of Composition connected to Eastern elite colleges such as Harvard.[5] Looking beyond the historical references in "elitist versions" of Composition's history allows the traditional/elitist and the forgotten history of Composition to come into dialogue with one another so that the future of Composition can be better informed.

An example of an alternative historical text is Kathryn Fitzgerald's "A Rediscovered Tradition: European Pedagogy and Composition in Nineteenth-Century Midwestern Normal Schools." In this article, she documents a nineteenth-century presence of Composition in Midwestern normal schools beginning shortly after Composition's inception at Harvard in 1875. She argues that

> the unique social environment, educational aims, and intellectual traditions of the normal school gave rise to attitudes about composition theory, methods, teachers, and students that are much more compatible with composition's contemporary ethic than those associated with the elite Eastern colleges where the origins of composition have most often been studied. (224)

Interestingly, connected to the Midwestern normal schools and their attention to pedagogy are connections between Composition and a critical history of pedagogy. It becomes evident that Composition enjoyed a higher status in normal schools because of its association with German pedagogy and European psychological theories of learning.[6]

white, male, and middle-class identity, alternative rhetorics are seen as somewhat in contrast and in competition with this dominant identity and, instead, identify a minority identity (i.e., people of color, women, and LGBT [stands for lesbian, gay, bisexual, and transgender] populations).

[5] See Sharon Crowley's discussion of the hierarchy of educational institutions in *Composition in the University* (222).

[6] This theory and pedagogy were based "on natural developmental patterns of the young mind, of the child's interest in a subject as a starting point for effective learning, and of

In order to understand the complexity of varying versions of Composition pedagogy taking place at the same historical moment, one should be aware of the main competing writing theories which represent the field of Composition, not comprehensively, but broadly. These theories are the most commonly practiced, and if one is familiar with these theories, then one can better gauge what was taking place at Harvard in comparison with, let's say, Fisk University or the University of Wisconsin in the late nineteenth century. Although studies analyzing these theories were not popularized or even published until the 1980s, they provide a progressive history of Composition by tracing Composition's ancient rhetorical past, tied to the Greco-Roman tradition, to Composition's more political and practical present in very interesting ways.

Composition theory taxonomies are interesting to note here for three reasons. The first is that it becomes evident that Berlin's taxonomy of theories were practiced in the late nineteenth century, although we only find constant references to the first theory (current-traditional rhetoric) in more traditional histories of Composition. Second, these normal school pedagogical histories enable us to see that all three of the following theories are practiced today. Lastly, these alternative histories also allow Compositionists to note particular absences in the history that do not speak to today's classrooms. If the reality of our country's populations in the late nineteenth century posed new challenges to the practice of teaching Composition, today's constantly evolving diverse pool of students clearly presents new challenges to the purpose and function of Composition, if it is to create a literate middle class. As Composition has become solidified as a field since 1949 (when the College Conference on Composition and Communication was formed), many scholars are devoting much of their research, time, and publications toward defining, promoting, and categorizing various practices and theories associated with the teaching of academic writing. Such taxonomies have been written not only by James Berlin, but also by Alastair Pennycook and Lester Faigley.[7]

One of these taxonomies especially interests me: that of James Berlin, a Composition historian. He is known for the revival of rhetoric in the field of Composition in the 1980s. His taxonomy of writing theories is based on the premise that pedagogical theories in writing courses are

instruction organized to move inductively from the familiar and concrete toward the unfamiliar and abstract" (Fitzgerald 231).

[7] See Pennycook's "Incommensurable Discourses" and Faigley's "Competing Theories of Process: A Critique and a Proposal."

grounded in rhetorical theories. The ways these theories are conceived to be different are the ways each one conceives of the relationship between writer, reality, audience, and language. So, for each one of these theories, the way reality can be communicated through language differs. For example, one of the key questions is: Does language creates reality or whether reality exists prior to language?

Briefly, the first of these theories is called positivist or current-traditional rhetoric. This writing theory is affiliated with the Harvard Composition program, which began in 1875. This theory views the world as rational, and its system is to be discovered through experimental methods of scientism. It is in contradistinction to the old science of Aristotle, which rested upon syllogisms. What is considered truth is only what could be shown to conform to the realities behind it. The world readily surrenders its meaning to anyone who observes it properly, and no operation of the mind—logical or otherwise—is needed to arrive at truth (Berlin "Contemporary Composition"). Discourse is then organized according to the faculties that it appeals to. As a result, college writing courses are to focus on discourses that appeal to the understanding of individuals. One can communicate one's version of verifiable truth through writing modes such as exposition, narration, description, and argumentation. Thus, this rhetorical writing theory, while dominant in many Composition textbooks today, according to Berlin, does not account for the distance between the student and the discourse to be engaged in through various writing assignments. This writing theory is not very interested in democratizing the classroom.

The next rhetorical writing theory is claimed, by Berlin, to derive from Plato, who believed that truth is discovered through an internal apprehension, a private vision of the world that transcends the physical. It is largely referred to today as expressionist rhetoric, which allows one to express and discover his/her authentic self. There is a collaborative element in this theory in that it is dialectic in its attempt at arriving at truth and allows for interaction among individuals to help one individual arrive at his or her own truth. This theory is correlated to the personal essay. The personal, expressive essay is taught in a variety of educational settings, but is not considered academically expository. The personal essay, however, is often used as an "entryway into academic prose" (see Haefner).

This brings me to the last rhetorical writing theory given to us by Berlin, the New Rhetoric, also known as epistemic rhetoric. In this view, rhetoric is thought to be epistemic, as a means at arriving at truth. Truth is viewed as dynamic and dialectical, the result of a process involving the interaction of opposing elements. Truth is created; it is not preexisting, waiting to be discovered. Thus, communication is basic to the epistemology underlying this writing theory. Truth is always truth for someone standing in relation to others in a linguistically circumscribed situation. As such, the social context, consisting of the backgrounds, social circumstances, and linguistic variabilities, and other cultural variables, such as gender, class, and race, are considered in the discovery and communication of truth in this theory. I think this is the smartest writing theory and the most democratic, and it also allows for the consideration of critical pedagogies such as those by Paulo Friere and Henry Giroux that enable the consideration of alternative genres such as those written by Gloria Anzaldúa.

A further description of this theory holds that the world requires interpretation, which is the result of transactions between events in the external world and the mind of the individual—between the world "out there" and the individual's previous experience, knowledge, values, attitudes, and desires (Berlin "Contemporary Composition" 243). According to this theory, language embodies and generates a version of truth and reality.

The belief that language creates a version of reality is much in line with the concept of discourse communities. Meaning can only be derived contextually, through interpretation; so in the academic discourse community, meaning has to be negotiated in ways that have already been established by an already formed body of truth in the form of academic language and conventions. Thus, the academic discourse community and their ways of knowing, seeing, communicating, and revealing truth have to be taught in order to demystify the Academy and make interpretation feasible for various social groups. This is why I believe that of all these rhetorical writing theories, epistemic rhetoric is the most democratic. It does not discount the prior experience of the individual. At the same time, however, it does not allow for the *acceptance* of alternative texts such, as that of Gloria Anzaldúa, as an entry ticket into the University. Such a mixed genre would be more appropriate, not for a proposed gate-keeping course as first-year Composition, but for upper-division writing courses.

Besides current-traditional rhetoric, both writing theories, expressionist rhetoric and epistemic rhetoric, while being identified as contemporary Composition theories, are also visible in the beginnings of Composition. Composition may seem as if it is a new discipline, but an examination of its history makes it apparent that it is actually almost a century and a half old, if not older, if one considers the sphere of rhetoric as a way that members of society make meaning. This is a conclusive statement. It says that since we have been doing all of this stuff already, then we should learn from our history what works, what effects each pedagogical writing theory produces, and gauge what the purpose of writing should be. Why should one become increasingly literate? To learn more about oneself? To become an oppositional critic of his or her culture? Thus, what ultimately, should be the goal of Composition? My answer would be to teach students to write, of course, and to be able to critically analyze other written texts that help them to understand their present social position in current society. So I call for the inclusion of historically oriented texts to be included in diverse Composition classrooms as a vehicle to teach writing that is recursive and contingent even while it is attempting to take a position and convey meaning to an audience. These goals have a historical context and are again resurfacing in twenty-first-century Composition Studies. This resurgence in the field is curious as many claim that we live in a post-racial society, when it is clear that racial oversights are part of our field's history and continue today when we closely examine its recent scholarship and dominant pedagogical practices (see Villanueva "On the Rhetoric and Precedents of Racism" and Haney-Lopez "Is the Post in Post-Racial the Blind in Colorblind?"). Writing pedagogies and rhetorical education are still dominantly "color-blind" in that they often do not consider students' racial backgrounds. The continued inattention to both scholars and students of color is what makes this book so important. It challenges the notion that color blindness and post-racism are nonproductive ideologies for accommodating students of color. Composition histories show that continuing to espouse these ideologies will continue to commit great oversights of the many minority students who are populating our writing classrooms.

ALTERNATIVE LOCATIONS FOR COMPOSITION STUDIES HISTORY

This section seeks to locate contemporary Composition theories, similar to Berlin's theories, taking place in the nineteenth century when considering various geographical areas. The following three areas will be considered: the Midwest (Wisconsin), the South (specifically Atlanta), and the Southwest (specifically California and Texas). The populations tied to these regions will also be considered—working-class whites, African Americans, and Chicanxs/Latinxs. Since the Southwest was a growing region at the time, the theories will be put into dialogue with one of the main issues of Southwestern educational history, namely the politics of bilingualism in predominantly Spanish-speaking communities. To begin this critical historical analysis, I turn first to the Midwest and the creation of the normal school as associated with the common school movement and the state regulation of a unified public schooling system.

This book is a critical history of Composition Studies, and I am a Latina Compositionist. While I don't see myself in this history, I also notice that other populations are missing from this history; thus, the way I problematize this history comes from my own subjectivity; however, I don't want to be limited by my personal perspective only. Thus, in this section, I want to exemplify how a critical history might be conducive to efficient, publicly warranted, and worthy writing practices. So here, I put my own pedagogical practice to the test while considering alternative locations and populations which contribute to the growing account of Composition Studies in the nineteenth century, namely the history of writing practices at an alternative educational institution—the normal school. While others in the field have also recently written about this alternative site for the study of histories of composition and rhetoric,[8] I want to briefly consider Ryan Skinnell's critique of these historical considerations. In Skinnell's article, he claims that

> [t]he lessons composition historians have drawn from normal schools—about writing pedagogy, rhetorical curricula and extra-curricula, and historical precedence—are misguided inasmuch as they fail to appreciate the ways in which normal schools' unique institutional objectives shaped the conditions for rhetoric and writing. (12)

While it is true that normal schools did have a unique educational mission, to train the nation's teachers in this era of increased interest in education for all, it does not discount what actually was taking place pedagogically at these schools and how these pedagogical approaches influence what one knows about Composition history in the twenty-first century. It is interesting to note, as Skinnell does, that these institutions had a unique mission, and that part of this mission entailed secondary education in addition to postsecondary education (like Harvard). Is it so unique that traditional Composition histories do not account for them?

---

[8] Ryan Skinnell, Bordelon, Fitzgerald, "Platteville," "Platteville Revisited," and "Rediscovered"; Gold; Gray; Lindblom, Banks, and Quay; Ritter; Rothermel, "Our Life's Work" and "Sphere."

Why is the alternative pedagogical view, offered by looking at normal school history, not accounted for? What is the function and purpose of writing for the populations taught at the normal schools? It becomes clear when looking at this historical blind spot that the Harvard Composition Program had its own function and purpose for providing rhetorical education and imparting writing skills in its Composition courses. So, while the critique is true in that the mission of normal schools was different than Eastern elite institutions, that does not discount their contribution to a more detailed, complex, and complete history of rhetoric and writing practices in U.S. educational institutions of the late nineteenth century. Furthermore, it is true that "normals cannot be easily equated to colleges" (6), as Skinnell also notes. They were functioning in a particular point in history for a particular function as were the Eastern elite Ivy League. However, it is not unlike a historian's task to look beyond a geographical region to complicate a limited historical account of a nation; thus, looking at normal school history can contribute to our knowledge of the histories of education and Composition Studies and is, therefore, necessary and important.

The history behind the normal school is quite straightforward since it is tied to widespread educational reform in the U.S.A. during and after the 1830s. The creation of the common school propagated by Horace Mann, who sought for unified education as was found in Germany, leads to the great need for qualified teachers to teach a unified curriculum to be regulated and sponsored by the state. As a matter of fact, the first normal school was opened in Massachusetts, and more were created and opened shortly after the creation of the State Board of Education (1837), which was formed to regulate the common school system.

The creation of the common school brought about the possibility of imparting a common education and cultural knowledge to many American children in the Midwest and later in the South. Since Germany was deemed to have a successful method for imparting a common cultural education, it was a fruitful site for investigating how to implement a similar educational institution and program within the U.S.A. This common education would stress both common knowledge and common cultural values of a growing English-speaking nation. These values are described in *Preparing American's Teachers*, written by James W. Fraser. In this book, Fraser writes of the history of the common school as well as of the common values to be imparted through this school system:

the campaign led by Horace Mann and Henry Barnard to bring order to the preparation of teachers, and, indeed, to all aspects of the common schools... has [been summarized] by Jurgen Herbst [as being] essentially [comprised of] Whig values, "a middle-class morality, centering on a sense of human decency and on what has become known as the Protestant work ethic, a bourgeois conception of economic security based upon a commitment to hard work and the ownership of private property, civil order, security of property, decency and gentility in interpersonal relationships among the members of a white, middle class, and overwhelmingly Protestant citizenry..." (46)

Such a politically charged agenda is consistent with the goals of U.S. nation-building at this time. Other elements of nation-building and creating a unitary culture through the common school included teaching a common language and a common religion. According to Fraser, "Herbst also goes on to note that common institutions, like the common schools and normal schools, were part of an even larger campaign to strengthen national unity through a common language—an Americanized English—and a common religion..." (46).

These common schools needed teachers who could impart this common cultural language and curriculum in an effective and unitary manner. Thus, the need for teacher-training institutions was great as, thus far, teachers were not bound by a common curriculum or common pedagogical tools. In *The American State Normal School*, Christine A. Ogren explains the extreme need for a specialized class of trained teachers that would be the rationale behind the creation of the normal school. She states, "Whether virtuous or scoundrels, teachers before the antebellum period had no specialized training. They were usually hired by town elders or some sort of community group, who attempted to test applicants' subject matter and pedagogical knowledge, as well as character and religion" (11). Furthermore, the interview process was a bit of a farce. School reformers, thus, called for a wider pool of better-prepared applicants as a step toward the professionalization of teaching.

The normal school, where these new teachers would be taught, was created in direct response to the desire for a unified educational institution. The history of normal schools within the U.S.A. is also one that is connected to the educational history of Germany. Since U.S. states and boards of education looked to Germany for its educational models, it makes sense that normal school history is closely correlated with a German educational tradition and influence.

The Creation of the Normal School/Praise of the German Teacher Seminary in Prussia

The German influence on the creation of the normal school is apparent in the following three documents. The first of these documents is

> Henry E. Dwight's *Travels in the North of Germany in the Years 1825 and 1826*, published in New York in 1829, [which] praised the Prussian government for requiring teacher training and established institutions to instruct future teachers in 'the best methods of educating and of governing children as well as the subjects they are to teach'. (Ogren 14)

The second document, "American Annals of Education and Instruction," was published two years later by editor William Channing Woodbridge. This publication included published commentary and translated reports on Prussian teacher education.

While Woodbridge was spreading the word about Prussian teacher seminaries, French philosophy professor Victor Cousin, commissioned by the French government, spent several weeks visiting the school systems in the German states.

Cousin then published a third document, *Report on Public Instruction in Germany*. It was translated in English and spread throughout the Midwest. Ogren states that a large population read this document in Europe and that "the report appeared in translation in New York in 1835 and immediately made a splash among school reformers, who began to use the term 'normal schools,' a translation of the French *école normale*" (15). Ogren also states that Cousin's report was less an objective account of Prussian schools as it was a portrayal of an ideal combination of a nation's progress under responsible conservative guidance. This portrayal appealed to American education reformers who sought unified education for the purpose of U.S. nation-building.

James W. Fraser in *Preparing American's Teachers*, for instance, states that

> [a]lmost a century later, in 1923, G.E. Maxwell, president of Winna State Teachers College in Minnesota, captured the early history with his tongue-in-cheek description of '[t]hese institutions, the adaptation of a German idea, tagged with a French name, and developed in a new continent...' Clearly, the normal school idea was in the air, though it took Edmund Dwight's money and Horace Mann's political ability to pluck it out of the air and make it real on the ground of several Massachusetts towns at the end of the 1830s. (50)

It is clear that normal schools began in the Midwest and were directly influenced by a German educational model. It is also clear that the mission of this educational institution was to assist in achieving national unity and culture. The normal school, like elite schools such as Harvard, sought to contribute to the changing dynamics of our nation. *While the U.S.A. needed a managerial class in the late nineteenth century, the U.S.A. also needed to create a teaching class to teach in common schools, all resulting from educational reform associated with the late-nineteenth-century's reforms.*

The ways education was viewed by each of these educational institutions was very different, however. The processes behind becoming educated and behind teaching were a large focus of state normal schools, while these same processes were taken for granted at Eastern elite colleges which produced graduates who specialized in certain subjects, such as law, medicine, science, or engineering. Thus, one can begin to notice a closer association between the arts of pedagogy and the state normal school. Referred to as teacher's colleges now, the normal school was influenced by its unique educational mission: to train qualified teachers.

The pedagogical focus of the theories practiced in normal schools is telling of the value placed upon pedagogy. These pedagogical theories, as practiced within the writing classroom, become interesting to look at when put within the context of traditional histories of Composition which do not discuss alternatives to current-traditional rhetorical theory in late-nineteenth-century Composition classrooms. These pedagogical theories, while German influenced, resemble contemporary Composition theory such as that which relies upon psychology and writing (also known as the cognitive/process approach).[9]

The differences in pedagogical approaches between Harvard and the Midwest can be seen in the ways normal school students were taught to teach versus the inattention to learning processes at Harvard. The ways teaching modes were learned at Harvard were not based upon pedagogical research so as to offer the teacher the best way to teach, let's say, descriptive essays. In contrast, the normal school curriculum allowed for room to consider how a student would effectively learn to write a descriptive essay other than just modeling it after another's descriptive essay or merely a definition of what a descriptive essay is, as would be consistent with a current-traditional approach.

---

[9] See Flower and Hayes on the cognitive process–oriented pedagogies closely associated with psychological theories of human behavior. The results of these studies resulted in what most Compositionists today refer to as process writing.

Ogren explains that scientific theories of learning present in the normal school were found in a textbook based upon the educational methods of German educator, Johann Friedrich Herbart. This textbook is titled *How to Conduct a Recitation and Elements of General Method Based on Principles of Herbart.* Published in the early 1890s, by author Charles McMurry, this textbook

> spelled out the five formal steps that became the heart of scientific methods at American normal schools. In their methods classes, normalities in the 1890s and 1900s learned to plan and execute lessons through "preparation, presentation, association and comparison, generalization or abstraction, and practical application" (Ogren 131).

This attention to the processes of learning came about because, as Ogren states, in the 1870s, state normal schools incorporated more sophisticated topics and approaches in their teacher-training curricula (122).

This time period is consistent with the beginnings of Composition at Harvard, but normal schools and the pedagogical practices associated with them are not referred to in traditional histories of Composition. The "lower-tier" status and separation from a Greek rhetorical origin associated with normal schools could possibly be a reason for their absence. The normal school's association with pedagogy could also be a reason for its absence. For example, unlike Eastern elite universities, normal schools were influenced by an investigation into children's mental development. This investigation

> led to two overlapping movements at the normal schools beginning in the 1890's: Harbartianism and child study. Based on the teachings of German philosopher and educator Johann Friedrich Herbart (1776–1841), Herbartianism systematized psychological theories into concrete approaches to teaching based on engaging and fostering children's interests. (131)

The normal schools' commitment to the educational needs of the time is also evidenced by the courses offered by the normal school. According to historian Charles Harper, normal schools offered classes in the History of Education and in the Philosophy of Education. These classes were believed to help round out "students' liberal education in the field while also enhancing their practical training and emotional commitment to education" (Ogren 133).

Kathryn Fitzgerald also comments on these same differences between the Eastern elite institutions and normal schools. She argues that there is a tendency to overlook geographical regions and important conceptions of the meaning and derivation of pedagogy. She states that historians and rhetoricians like Kitzhaber, Berlin, and Connors made important contributions to the history of composition and rhetoric. According to Fitzgerald, they contributed the accommodation of classical theory to written discourse and this was an important endeavor since professors of this time struggled to make this connection. These historians discuss the pedagogical focus of Composition as being in contrast to the expanding research-based model that was supplanting the classical tradition in higher education. These same historians, however, do not consider both the alternative pedagogical practices of Composition and the large populations of students attending normal schools during this same time. Thus, according to Fitzgerald, when looking at a region of Composition's history not common in traditional historical accounts, it becomes evident that the history of Composition is not complete.

For example, the emphasis on current-traditional rhetoric and the American pedagogical theories of scientism (from which current-traditional rhetoric derives) were not present in Midwestern normal schools. More specifically, the mastery of skills was not the focus in Midwestern normal schools. Fitzgerald makes this distinction come to light when comparing the pedagogical practices of the Midwest in contradistinction with the East.

She states that the main difference between Eastern institutions and the Midwestern normal school can be understood by looking at the pedagogical ideologies which informed these institutions' Composition programs. Midwestern normal school ideology came from German systems of teacher training and European pedagogical theories. For example, Heinrich Pestaozzi was a Swiss teacher and philanthropist who was familiar with Rousseau's educational romanticism. His theories were passed on to his heirs John Frederick Herbart and Friedrich Froebel. This pedagogy began to spread vehemently after the Civil War. Edward A. Sheldon implemented European pedagogical thought at Oswego Normal School. In 1859–1860, the eminent educator Henry Barnard was hired as Chancellor of the University of Wisconsin and simultaneously as an agent of the Board of Regents of Normal Schools (Fitzgerald 232). Herbart, however, went further than Pestaozzi's faculty-based psychology and toward a more associationist view that held that students learn by comparing new ideas with old and reflecting on their similarities and dissonances. He also invented the lesson plan. Mariolina Salvatori, a historian of pedagogy, also comments on the influence of Herbart on normal schools: "Herbartians had more in common with later socio-psychological views of the educational process than with Romantic concepts of individual development" (Salvatori quoted in Fitzgerald 233). European educational models were undoubtedly a great influence on normal schools' pedagogical focus, which is in sharp contrast to an Eastern elite, American pedagogical model with its focus on specialization and current-traditional rhetoric as the discourse of scientism.

An example of a contemporary Composition pedagogical concern shows the difference of the pedagogical foci of Eastern elite institutions versus Midwestern normal schools. For example, Fitzgerald points out that "linguistic competence" has two different meanings for either historical account according to either of the populations involved in each historical moment at each geographical location. This difference is largely due to complex ideological, professional, and economic circumstances associated with these two types of institutions. Nonetheless, students' linguistic competence, according to Connors and Miller, resulted in professors at Eastern elite institutions often attributing grammatical errors to character deficits like stupidity, laziness, or moral turpitude. However, "when the teachers talk about the linguistic competence of their normal school students, we see explanations for poor performance based on prior experience and learning with none of the ad hominum descriptors like 'vulgar,' 'illegitimate,' and 'slip-shod' that we heard from Harvard men" (Briggs quoted in Fitzgerald 234–235). In short, teachers at the normal schools saw linguistic competence as a socially constructed and constantly modified process, not as a static, class-based character trait (244). Furthermore, teachers at the normal schools tended to regard students' errors as the "natural outcome of a combination of inadequate teaching and incomplete learning—an explanation worthy of Mina Shaughnessy" (235).[10] Shaughnessy comments on the derivation of basic writers' grammatical errors:

> [T]he grammatically less important errors these students frequently make in their efforts to write formal English, errors that do not seriously impair meaning, are often rooted in language habits and systems that go back to their childhoods and continue, despite years of formal instruction, to influence their performance as adult writers. (90)

---

[10] See Mina Shaughnessy's book, *Errors and Expectations*, for a more thorough discussion of the logic of error written in the era of open admissions at City University of New York, which began in 1970 (1).

The fact that Shaughnessy was writing in the seventies and Fitzgerald is referring to normal schools in the late nineteenth century is quite telling. Compositionists, however, would not be able to make connections between Shaughnessy and Fitzgerald if other alternative sites, such as normal schools, are not looked at.

Fitzgerald further explains that the practice of teaching and learning pedagogy in the late nineteenth century enjoyed a high status, but with the creation of the modern university, it came to be devalued. Pedagogy became relegated as a concern of Chairs of Education and Education departments at many such universities across the nation. Pedagogy served a specific vocational purpose—to train teachers—and, therefore, was not worthy of any disciplinary status. There were, however, clear learning theories behind many of the pedagogies of the normal schools of the late nineteenth century (i.e., psychological theories). Fitzgerald states that

> [b]y 1900 the changes in psychological thinking were no longer confined to Europeans like Pestalozzi and Herbart, for Americans like John Dewey, William James, and Stanley Hall were beginning their work on theories of learning and development that would render faculty psychology obsolete and begin to frame educational theory for the next century. (230)

However, the student, according to European pedagogical theories, is always the focus of such pedagogy. This idea contrasts with the current-traditional rhetoric, often connected with the Composition pedagogy at Harvard and other elite institutions. Composition pedagogy at Harvard focused more so on superficial correctness and the ability of students to produce immaculate texts. The student was not at the center of their pedagogical attention, the product was.

Furthermore, as Composition became relegated to the first year as a required course, textbooks became formulaic versions of Composition pedagogy at Harvard. Fitzgerald quotes Robert Connors, a Composition historian, referring to his discussion of the centrality of textbooks in modern composition. The intellectual heritage and the typical practice of Composition instruction largely convey the story of the nineteenth-century textual transitions from theorized rhetorics to reductive practical textbooks; however, the story at the normal schools is quite different (230).

In the case of the normal schools found in the Midwest, the focus was not on textbooks. As a matter of fact, the only reason texts were referred to in many normal school classrooms was to figure out who the author of the book was addressing and what particular view or time period that text represented. Fitzgerald confirms that "conclusions [of textbooks] could be questioned. What's more, the bias for challenging the conclusions could lie in the linguistic competence, experience, and reasoning capacity of the students themselves" (243). Textbooks in normal schools could be questioned; in other words, they were not always assumed to be right. The reason for this is that the students in many Midwest normal schools were exposed to European pedagogies which emphasized the student-learner. Therefore, the current connection that Composition pedagogy has to politics and access is actually an occurrence that can be witnessed in a broader, more inclusive history of Composition. Other critical scholars who contribute to this section are Mariolina Rizzi Salvatori, Merle Curti and Vernon Carstensen, Anne Ruggles Gere, Albert Salisbury, and Walker D. Wyman.

Midwestern Composition in the Context of Berlin's Rhetorics

Of the three major pedagogical theories outlined by Berlin, the German pedagogical practices of the normal school most resemble the New Rhetoric in which Berlin sees "the writer as a creator of meaning, a shaper of reality, rather than a passive receptor of the immediate" (245). Individuals are shaped by their realities as they shape reality. The above two examples of differences between the emphasis placed on students or upon textbooks when examining the role of pedagogy in Midwestern normal schools and Eastern elite institutions point to a consideration of the learner's background and the ability of students to be makers of their reality. In normal schools, linguistic competence was attributed to the student background, and students were regarded as the supreme authority over scientifically oriented textbooks. Consistent with the position of the New Rhetoric is the belief that "[i]n teaching writing, we are not simply offering training in a useful technical skill that is meant as a simple complement to the more important studies of other areas. We are teaching a way of experiencing the world, a way of ordering and making sense of it" (246). That way of experiencing the world that Berlin talks about can easily be applied to the ways normal schools viewed the linguistic deficiencies of students as "situation bound" instead of them being lazy or immoral as proclaimed at elite institutions. The distance between the educational institution and the student was a consideration of the normal school and is remarkably similar to some of the premises of Berlin's New Rhetoric, a contemporary Composition pedagogical theory.

The objective and personal essays associated with current-traditional rhetoric and expressionist rhetoric are not sufficient to accommodate the political nature of learning nor the social processes associated with how one learns and what the consequences are when one learns. A linear form of logic that is also supposed to be delivered in an objective manner, for example, is a way to view the world that may not be consistent with a student's individual background. Structuralism also does not account for a student's individual background in that it presupposes static forms of representation and experience. These theories, which view the invention of texts through nonproblematic and seamless processes, are ignored in Composition Studies' traditional history. A consideration of the student's social background is also consistent with Berlin's New Rhetoric and the normal school's attention to individual learners.

One may wonder what became of normal schools beginning in the early twentieth century. This history is not common knowledge for our field so far. Interestingly, the pedagogical focus of the normal school led to their transformation into "teachers colleges" and state universities:

> While a handful of normal schools became teachers colleges before 1920, the majority, including those in Pennsylvania, Alabama, Kansas, Wisconsin, and California, changed their names during the 1920's. Many normal schools, such as those in Massachusetts and Maryland, waited until the 1930's and the institutions in Maine, Vermont, and most of state normal schools in New York did not become teachers colleges until the 1940's or later. (Fitzgerald 200)

Normal schools also began to resemble larger universities with their attention to refinement and middle-class culture. This institution would offer educational opportunities to a wider population of students interested in becoming educators or going to research universities. Such a desire of cultural and intellectual refinement was witnessed by the creation of literary societies within the normal school. Ogren claims that literary societies [were] by far the most long-lived, popular, and far-reaching student organizations, where students worked hardest to refine themselves...By the 1870's, college societies were giving way to Greek letter fraternities (and later, sororities) as growth in the formal curriculum satisfied student interests and wealthier students looked for a means of distinguishing themselves socially. (108)

While the history of normal schools shows its ability to more fully accommodate a larger student population than Eastern private institutions, it is not complete without attention to other regions composed of racial minorities. Thus, the next chapter continues in this historical time period to give a history of the black normal school and then considers alternative forms of literacy present in both the antebellum South and the Reconstruction Era. In addition, I consider the Southwest and Mexican American literary practices absent in current Composition scholarship.

CHAPTER 5

Mexican Americans and African Americans: In/Visibility in Composition

What is different from the mission of late-nineteenth-century Eastern elite institutions and Midwestern normal schools is that the distance between a student and the language of the Academy (or what was expected to be mastered) seems to be a separate issue from pedagogy. This distance, if it existed, was regarded more as a "personal problem" or as an unfortunate personal characteristic that was almost akin to being regarded as illiterate. Students' various social upbringings were seldom pedagogically considered in private Eastern elite colleges such as Harvard, as noted above. Furthermore, the vast majority of students educated in elite institutions were middle-class and upper-class, white, Anglo males. Thus, there seems to be an obvious need to look beyond the East and toward geographical locations which consisted of different racial populations associated with the South and Southwest areas, that is, to consider African Americans and Mexican Americans who were seeking educational opportunities also in the late nineteenth century. What was happening educationally to these populations in this and other parts of the country around the same time? It seems an obvious fact that in the late nineteenth century and since then, female, African American, and Chicanx/Latinx populations were also seeking to attain economic rewards through receiving a college education previously considered exclusive to white Anglo, Protestant males. Brereton confirms that

> [s]imilar to feminist efforts in education, African American writers were forging a distinctive voice (or series of voices) in nineteenth-century America,

© The Editor(s) (if applicable) and The Author(s) 2016   79
I.D. Ruiz, *Reclaiming Composition for Chicano/as and Other Ethnic Minorities*, DOI 10.1057/978-1-137-53673-0_5

but any concerns black educators had about college writing instruction were not at all part of the general discourse. In writing, black college faculty and students were forced to assume the white world's styles and standards, as Fisk University graduate W. E. B. DuBois did when he elected Barrett Wendell's writing course at Harvard (23) [...] Black or Latino or Native American concerns seem invisible in the professional literature of writing instruction between 1875 and 1925, while most black colleges seem to have taught writing in strict accord with the standards of white America. (21)

Brereton rightfully acknowledges the absence of Black, Latinx, and Native Americans in the "professional literature of writing instruction" in the late nineteenth century, and it is quite a task to find out what happened to voices that are not part of a field's history. These voices have to be located in other places than in traditional professional/academic venues. Thus, I decided to look at some early-twentieth-century school texts such as the Harvard *Crimson*.[1] Examining texts such as *Crimson*, Harvard's school newspaper, allows one to see how the university responded to the "negro problem" and the Mexican Revolution, for example. It seems that once political upheavals take place outside the University, the University responded with not only trying to research the problem further, but also trying to be more conscious of the plight of racial minorities by contributing to their possibilities for obtaining a higher education. However, the response to concerns related to Mexicans and African Americans was to create better educational opportunities in a segregated manner. At this time, segregated education was the rule. W.E.B. Dubois' presence in Harvard was an exception.

Thus, this portion of the book seeks to begin to break the silences in the historical approaches discussed thus far in relation to Composition Studies' early history (1862–1950). The goal is to recover the lost Chicanx/Latinx voices of Composition Studies in parallel consideration with African Americans. Noteworthy Compositionists who have begun to tread this historical ground are Jacqueline Jones-Royster, Jean C. Williams, Keith Gilyard, Victor Villanueva, Jaime Armin Mejía, Mariolina Rizzi Salvatori, Christina Ramírez, and Kathryn Fitzgerald.

---

[1] This publication can be found at http://www.thecrimson.com/article.aspx?ref=411931 ("Wanted: Americans to Study in Mexico"), http://www.thecrimson.com/article.aspx?ref=372660 ("The Negro Problem in Boston"), and http://www.thecrimson.com/article.aspx?ref=284404 ("A Statement of Southern Problems").

AFRICAN AMERICANS: IN/VISIBILITY IN NINETEENTH-AND EARLY-TWENTIETH-CENTURY COMPOSITION

Consistent with both post-positivist realist theory and a critical race counter-storytelling method outlined in Chap. 2, I seek to place race relations at the center of the analysis of the absence of alternative racial considerations in elite histories of Composition. Doing so allows one to better understand the absence of African Americans in educational institutions and, thus, represents the difficulty of finding a textual presence in written histories of Composition. Such a viewpoint is consistent with the aims of critical race theory. Royster and Williams, African American Compositionists, state:

> [C]omposition histories show that when we consistently ignore, peripheralize or reference rather than address non-officialized experiences, inadequate images continue to prevail and actually become increasingly resilient in supporting the mythologies and negative consequences for African American students and faculty, and also for their culturally defined scholarly interests, which in their own turn must inevitably push also against prime narratives. ("History" 582)

Thus, the need to place race at the center of examination of educational history to question the absence of African Americans from mainstream educational histories seems obvious and necessary to challenge primary narratives of both Education and Composition history. However, the absence of African Americans in Composition history contrasts vividly with the participation of African Americans in social activist projects and in alternative presses which represented African American social interests in the Reconstruction Era.

African Americans have a unique social position in that they were the victims of slavery and, later, gross Jim Crow racial discrimination. As more African Americans acquired literacy, their substandard position in American society became a major issue of contention. African American Compositionist and rhetorician, Geneva Smitherman, states that "[b]lacks were the first to force the moral and Constitutional questions of equality in this country [and] of all underclass groups in the U.S., blacks are pioneers in social protest and have waged the longest, politically principled struggle against exploitation" (25). Their struggle dates back to before the Civil War; however, the result of the Civil War and the nineteenth-century emancipation of African American slaves, was the first nationally recognized social gain for African Americans. This gain was their freedom to work, live, and learn as independent and legally sanctioned human beings. The right to freedom gained by blacks also encouraged other minority populations to struggle for human rights, such as suffrage for women. One of the rights fought for by African Americans was the right to become literate through formal education.

Royster, author of *Traces of a Stream: Literacy and Social Change Among African American Women*, claims that the importance of her study rests upon the claim that "[t]he presence of African American women writers of worth has typically been neutralized and their achievements devalued" (4). Royster claims to "know quite well that...the rights of agency, and the rights to an authority to make knowledge and to claim expertise have often not been extended...to African American women" (4). She argues that the absence of African American women's literacy history is a result of racism, sexism, ethnocentrism, and political and economic oppression. For Royster, these are barriers that have been constructed around the African American experience since emancipation, and the exclusion of their literate practices have led to the absence of African American women in historical accounts of literacy.

Royster's contribution to the elite history of Composition becomes interesting as she sheds light upon African American literate populations who were beginning to enter the schoolhouse doors before, during, and after the Civil War. Mariolina Salvotori, a pedagogy historian, confirms Royster's contributions concerning the creation and development of African American normal schools in the South and Midwest. She states that "[i]n all, some thirty colored schools were in successful operation at the close of 1865" (173). The reason for so many "colored" schools of this time has largely to do with the results of the Civil War. Royster states that

> [a]fter the Civil War, there was a tremendous need for teachers for both free-born and freed African American men, women, and children whose opportunities to learn had been denied by law in the South for well over a century and severely constrained by predominant practices throughout the nation. Fortunately, even before the Civil War, teaching was a type of work that was sanctioned as being appropriate for women, so African Americans [began] preparing themselves to fulfill the need. Atlanta and Fisk Universities offered normal school training, which would equip them well to teach. (178)

Thus, in addition to the African American presence of women in the field of teaching, there was the achievement of having black normal schools, institutions that were primarily pedagogical and relegated to the margins. Royster states that in 1874, "[t]he Normal Course was the teacher-training curriculum, which accounts in large part for the numbers of women enrolled" (197). These women were committed to becoming institutional leaders who recognized the needs of the African American community. They strived to create a community that could take care of itself, "rather than be dependent on the kindness of the white community. Teacher training, therefore, was a top priority, as indicated by an appeal [for teachers in every community of Atlanta in their] university catalog" (196).

Given the above available accounts of African American literacy projects found in locations such as black normal schools of the late nineteenth century, it is surprising that Compositionists haven't rewritten the field's histories to reflect this knowledge and research of African American literacy practices. This knowledge still exists in marginalized Composition and Rhetoric scholarship. A closer examination of these alternative sources and contributions, points to a reason, perhaps, for their exclusion: the racial focus of these institutions. It is their marginalization on the basis of race that largely explains their being absent from educational history and, more specifically, the history of Composition. As such, it is imperative that not only the contribution of normal school history to Composition be recognized, but also the contributions of African Americans to the practices and definitions of literacy be recognized.

In addition to the work of Royster, African American Compositionist Keith Gilyard has written on African American contributions to Composition in "African American Contributions to Composition Studies." For Gilyard, African American contributions consist of "various confluences inside African American intellectual and rhetorical traditions. Free Black churches, culturally specific jeremiads, slave narratives, secret schools, Black women's clubs, and Black colleges all represent an enriching merger of African American intellectual...concerns with writing instruction..." (626).

Gilyard cites various historical black figures as contributors to Composition's history as it is concerned with language using practices such as rhetorical prowess. Such figures as Frederick Douglass, W.E.B. Dubois, Ida B. Wells, and Hallie Quinn Brown are representative of a wide array of language uses, including writing pedagogy, educational theory, essay writing, speech delivery, and the scientific teaching of writing to adults (628–629).

Gilyard also cites Carter G. Woodson (1875–1950) as a complementary figure to W.E.B. Dubois' educational philosophy. In Woodson's manifesto, *The Miseducation of the Negro*, there is a section titled "The New Program" where Woodson advocates for a new language agenda for "Negroes":

> After Negro students have mastered the fundamentals of English, the principles of composition and the leading facts in the development of its literature, they should not spend all their time in advance work on Shakespeare, Chaucer and Anglo-Saxon. They should direct their attention also to the folklore of the African, to the philosophy in his proverbs, to the development of the Negro in the use of modern language, and to the works of Negro writers. (Woodson quoted in Gilyard 630)

This manifesto, written in 1933, is interesting to note because such a progressive writing pedagogy for African Americans existed 40 years before the adoption of the "Students' Right to Their Own Language" Resolution by the Conference on College Composition and Communication (CCCC) in 1972.[2]

Such an absence in elitist histories of Composition seems tied to the racial climate of the historical time period. In the 1930s, such a progressive pedagogy could not have been considered by professional organizations such as the National Council of Teachers of English (NCTE) and Modern Language Association (MLA) because at this time, African Americans were barred from full participation in these organizations (Gilyard 630–631). Furthermore, CCCC was not formed until 1949, and it was not until 1968 that CCCC responded to the marginal position of African Americans in its professional organization and, later, to the ways in which CCCC could respond to the unique linguistic circumstances of African American students. As such, Woodson's contribution to Dubois' educational philosophy and to the elitist history of Composition seems as if it was "manifested" before its time because of its attention to the specific literacy needs of African Americans. Woodson encouraged more than

---

[2] In 1972, the Executive Committee of the Conference on College Composition and Communication (CCCC) passed a resolution on "students' rights to their own patterns and varieties of language." Based on that resolution, CCCC created a position statement entitled "Students' Right to Their Own Language," which was adopted at the CCCC Annual Convention in April 1974. See http://www.ncte.org/library/NCTEFiles/Groups/CCCC/NewSRTOL.pdf

a common assimilation of American mores through American literature; instead, he encouraged African Americans to learn about their own history in American literacy.

The South is also a particularly interesting geographical location when looking at the history of African Americans in higher education because it is an area rampant with racist practices which sought to exclude African Americans from political participation and, more personally, from their human dignity. Grim confirms that "[w]ith the restoration of Southern political, conservative, and democratic power during the late 1870s, black men and women were excluded from participation in the dominant society's politico-jural sphere, and were denied access to authority" (123). Racial intimidation was also used as a strategy to ensure the powerlessness of Southern African Americans through violent acts such as lynching and the rape and sexual exploitation of black women. Thus, the South is an area that shows the racist practices Royster mentions above. It is important to note that racial intimidation and disenfranchisement hindered full participation in educational institutions or common schools of this location and time period for African Americans.

If I put late-nineteenth-century literary practices by women in dialogue with current Composition theory, I find African American women being oppositional critics of their culture ahead of their time and long before the theory of critical pedagogy became popularized in the field of Composition in the seventies. In the history of Composition, being an oppositional critic is conceptualized as beginning after the educational field's response to the Civil Rights Movement, which undoubtedly affected the practice and theory of Composition. However, upon closer analysis of the literary practices of African Americans, it becomes apparent that being in opposition to a culture was a literary practice evident in the late nineteenth century. In the next chapter, I will go into further detail to show how the field of Composition was affected by the Civil Rights Movement. For now, it is interesting to see the connections between the two periods and their critical agendas.

Now we will turn our gaze to the Mexican American, Chicano/a populations of the nineteenth and early twentieth century. Where were they in relation to African Americans at this time? What was similar and different about their educational struggles? How does their native language play into the differences experienced by them at this time?

MEXICAN AMERICANS: IN/VISIBILITY IN NINETEENTH- AND EARLY-TWENTIETH-CENTURY COMPOSITION

The situation of Mexican Americans in American history is quite different from that of African Americans for numerous reasons. The first of these is the manner in which they were colonized in their own land (Northern Mexico), which it is now considered the Southwest (Texas, California, New Mexico, Colorado, Arizona, Wyoming, and Nevada). The second reason is their geographical concentration (as a result of their internal colonial status), and third is their possession and persistent use of a "foreign" language. While social and educational circumstances and opportunities for African Americans changed quite drastically surrounding the events of the Civil War, the circumstances concerning education for Mexican Americans in the Southwest from 1846 to 1870 were quite dismal in comparison. Like African Americans, they are a displaced people. Reginald Horsman, historian of the University of Wisconsin, states that

> [f]or some, southern slavery taught that another route to free, prosperous society was the total subordination of the inferior to the superior race... Mexicans and others might not be enslaved, but they would be subordinated to the rule of a superior people...The United States would become a colonial power. (258)

Although Mexicans were not slaves in the same sense that African Americas were in the past, their lands, in the 1800s, were regarded as free and open territory to be taken by English, Anglo settlers, who in turn believed it was their Manifest Destiny to colonize and develop the Southwest and West, all the way to the Rio Grande. They also sought to deliver freedom to the Mexicans who were claimed to be under the reign of the oppressive Mexican government because it would not allow slavery. While some Europeans were present in the Southwest/West during the early 1800s, they were relegated to the strictures of the Mexican government and law. Many of the Europeans did not want to abide by the abolition law of Mexico, and they saw it as their right and their destiny to bring prosperity to this nation that had not been fully developed by the Mexicans and Spanish Criollos and Mestizos present in these territories.

This type of arrogant thinking was the reasoning behind the Anglo-American belief in "Manifest Destiny." Thus, since Mexico lost more than half of its territory due to the Mexican war with the U.S. territories, including the Alamo and the Battle at Saint Jacinto in the Southwestern region, it has repeatedly been argued that the plight of Mexican Americans today is one of continued internal colonialism in contrast to the transplanted plight of African Americans. In addition to differences between the manner in which Africans were brought to the U.S.A. and the way Mexicans were internally colonized on their own land, Mexican Americans never had the benefit of educational institutions equivalent to "Negro" colleges. Thus, the blind spot created by excluding Mexican Americans in both the history of education and Composition is huge. It is also, as a result, a more tedious contribution to recover.

Making the above arguments requires a keen awareness of the colonial history of mid-to late–nineteenth-century Mexican Americans (also referred to as Californios and Tejanos during this time period). The U.S.– Mexican War (1846–1848) occurred because of the USA's desire to conquer and expand into the northern regions of Mexico. Ranching was no longer desirable as a method of cultivating and using land, and the pre-1848 practice of farming would be replaced by agricultural interests more suited to the needs of a growing capitalist market's interests. As such, old systems of the Spanish government, religion, and property management as well as Mexicans were devalued and replaced by American governments, land management legislation, and Protestant religions, and became dominated by whites.

The Mexican population, like the African American population, also experienced displacement and, thus, transformations that were akin to those endured by the African slave populations. The California Land Claims Act of 1851,[3] which was passed after the Mexican American War and the signing of the Treaty of Guadalupe Hidalgo, caused many Mexican American landowners in the U.S. territory to lose their land at a discouraging pace to white Americans. Mexicans living in U.S. territories were often stripped of their rights to their land despite the Treaty's promise to ensure their property rights and recognize their legal property documents. Although the land act of 1851 recognized Spanish and Mexican land grants, only wealthy ranchers could afford the lengthy legal process

[3] In 1851, the U.S. Senate passed Gwin's Act to Ascertain the Land Claims in California. The Act mandated that three members appointed by the President rule on land claims. The proceedings were formal, and neither Mexicans nor Americans could appeal to the U.S. District Court and to the U.S. Supreme Court. However, only the wealthy could afford such proceedings, so dispossession of land became a common practice.

to prove their property rights. Thus, Mexican American hopes of equality under the California Land Claims Act were annihilated. Moreover, land-owners became the victims of American squatters, who would take their lands piece-by-piece through violent means. As such, the former economic status of Mexicans was lowered to the extent that they could not afford to send their children to school or secure rights to basic civil liberties, such as the right to have land claims recognized in order to own property.

Carlos Muñoz, Jr., in *Youth, Identity, Power: The Chicano Movement*, argues that during the years of transformation of the Southwestern region (1846–1930), few Mexican Americans gained access to college. The ones that did were from the small Mexican American middle class, located mostly in San Antonio and New Mexico. Churches also played a large part in providing help for Mexican Americans in these regions to attend school. Muñoz states that "[t]hose few [Chicanos] from the working class who were fortunate enough to attend college did so with the direct assistance of members of the Catholic and Protestant clergy, although the Mormon Church played a significant role in some areas" (127). Richard Griswold del Castillo and Arnoldo de León's, in *North to Aztlán: A History of Mexican Americans in the United States*, discuss the role of religious institutions, in the form of missions, in education. They write that "[i]n New Mexico (and Southern Colorado) the Protestants appeared to have had a special zeal for instruction; by the mid-1880s they had established some 33 missionary schools in New Mexico that tended to more than 1000 children" (55). These church schools shared another aspect of the black normal school and the Protestant mission school, namely the domi-nance of female teachers and a focus on the education of female students. Castillo and León claim that "[w]omen seemed especially determined to train Mexican American children, primarily girls, and transform them into productive members of society" (55).

Most schools, however, were not considerate of the language needs of Mexicans in this area. Schools were, as they always have been, instillers of the dominant American culture and English language. Griswold del Castillo and de León confirm that teachers introduced Mexican American children to the "American dream" in public schools as a means of cultural erasure and assimilation. Catholic Church instructors, many of them nuns, made it their commitment to replace Mexican customs with American ones (55). One of these customs was, of course, the primary use of the English language by these students, although, after the U.S.–Mexican War, the California state constitution of 1849 recognized Spanish-language rights and stipulated the bilingual publication of state laws. However, as the Gold Rush brought an overwhelming influx of non-Spanish-speaking immigrants into the new state, a series of anti-Californio (a Californio was a Californian of Mexican heritage when California was part of Mexico and shortly thereafter) laws—referred to collectively by the disapproving phrase "greaser laws"—were passed, including a law that ended Spanish-language schooling in 1855. This law was not discarded until 1966, and currently English is the official language of California.

However, despite English-only laws, Spanish is the second most frequently spoken language in the U.S.A. today. The 1990 U.S. Census Bureau cites 17,345,064 Spanish speakers in the U.S.A., with the third most frequent language, French, only reaching 1,930,404 (Sánchez 554). There is, nevertheless, a drastic difference in the circumstances of the Spanish-speaking populations in the U.S.A. More recently, the American Community Survey Reports for the U.S. Census of 2011 cite 37,579,787 people who speak Spanish in addition to English, and in 2010, 36,995,602 people spoke Spanish at home in addition to English. The trend of Spanish speakers in the U.S.A. is also projected to grow over the next decade. Furthermore, because of generational differences, some Chicanx/Latinx speakers speak both English and Spanish in varying contexts, and some are dominant English speakers. Some speak only Spanish, and some also speak Spanglish (a conglomeration of Spanish dialects and English dialects).

Today, the Latinx immigrant populations from both Mexico and Latin America have led to a dramatic growth of this population in the U.S.A. These immigrants now largely comprise Spanish-speaking populations. This situation is unlike that of the Black English/Ebonics controversy of African Americans. Latinxs and Chicanxs are a heterogeneous population. This linguistic patois is the subject matter of many Chicanx/Latinx writers and cultural critics today. Gloria Anzaldúa is one of the most popular queer, Chicana feminists who wrote about linguistic "mestizaje" and is well known for her notion of border theory and identity, even though she passed away in 2004. While I espouse border theory as a viable theory for composing pedagogy for multilingual writers, I notice that Anzaldúa is not regarded as an official rhetorician or Compositionist. I'm not sure why because she theorized a method of writing and communicating that is similar to the process of "negotiating academic literacies" and "code-switching." The crossing of borders that Anzaldúa spoke of is very much in line with contemporary Composition theories. I think it should be referred to and cited much more often by mainstream Composition scholars of the twenty-first century who work with students that negotiate many competing discourse communities as well as languages. Her theory is, of course, very suitable for scholars looking to implement and practice more effective writing instructional methods that accommodate Chicanx/ Latinx students.

In addition to the unique linguistic circumstances of Chicanxs/ Latinxs, segregated educational opportunities with divisive instruction and facilities are and have been similar to those found in the educational history of African Americans. The *Barrios*[4] located in segregated areas within urban areas developed with the urbanization of the Southwest. The schools associated with these barrios soon proved inadequate for preparing young Chicanxs to become more than industrial laborers. As a matter of fact, many Chicanxs did not see the benefit of receiving an education because of the inadequacies of educational opportunities. According to Griswold del Castillo and de León, Mexican citizens of the new regions saw little educational prospects even though all states and territories in the Southwest did order the establishment of public school systems. However, in the years following the cession of Mexico, few legislators made efforts to implement such opportunities for adequate schooling for this population (37).[5]

Furthermore, David Gutiérrez, a critical Chicano historian, argues that these dismal opportunities were largely due to the isolation of Chicano communities. Even the present-day Southwest is described as a colony by Rodolfo "Corky" Gonzáles, a key organizer of the Chicano Movement. Gonzáles noted that "the Southwest is very much like one of the colonies that have been colonized by England, by some of the European countries and those places that are economically colonized or militarily taken over by the United States" (Gonzáles quoted in Gutiérrez 288). Gutiérrez lists pertinent sources to look for the beginning of the historical presence of Chicanos: *The Los Angeles Barrio, 1850–1890: A Social History* (1979) by

---

[4] "[This] term derived from both the Iberian and Aztec traditions and applied to city districts inhabited by individuals having common familiar ties. In New Spain and its frontier settlements, the term referred to particular urban neighborhoods. After 1848, people used it to denote a discernible section of a town site inhabited by Mexicans" (Griswold de Castillo and de León 24).

[5] See also *Let All of Them Take Heed: Mexican Americans and the Campaign for Educational Equality in Texas, 1910–1981* by Guadalupe San Miguel, Jr.

Richard Griswold del Castillo and *Chicanos in a Changing Society: From Mexican Pueblos to American Barrios in Santa Barbara and Southern California, 1848–1930* (1979) by Albert Camarillo (290). These sources will undoubtedly contribute to understanding the circumstances of segregation for Chicanxs of the late nineteenth and early twentieth century. Interestingly, cultural isolation continues to be a contemporary phenomenon of both African Americans and Chicanxs in twenty-first-century U.S.A. Thus, it seems that looking to their earlier history for an explanation of the ghettoization of both populations can provide some possible educational interventions for current educational concerns regarding both minority populations.

The educational history of Chicanxs in the U.S.A., while quite different from that of African Americans, shows a similar trend of dismal opportunities for education and, thus, cultural assimilation into the U.S. mainstream. If Chicanxs were not visibly present in institutions of higher education, then it is not surprising that they were not present in the early history of Composition. What can be recovered, however, are the language traditions practiced by Chicanxs of this time.

In "Mapping the Spanish Language Along a Multiethnic and Multilingual Border," Rosaura Sánchez gives a detailed history of the Spanish language in the U.S.A. even before the U.S.A. existed. She states that written cultural productions such as newspapers, testimonials, theater, poetry, and narratives were still written in Spanish long after the U.S. invasion of the Southwest. Furthermore, Rosaura Sánchez and Beatrice Pita provide vivid archival data in the form of testimonies, political treatises, personal letters, and counter-travel narratives written by María Amparo Ruiz de Burton in their book *Conflicts of Interest: the Letters of María Amparo Ruiz de Burton.* They show a rich literary tradition that was indeed engaged in by the recently colonized Spanish and Mexican peoples of the early Southwest colonies such as California and Arizona in the mid-to-late nineteenth centuries.

Another source that contributes to the rich rhetorical history of Mexicans in the nineteenth century is *Hispanic Periodicals in the United States, Origins to 1960: A Brief History and Comprehensive Bibliography.* In this text, Hispanic newspaper owner, editor, and writer Francisco P. Ramírez is discussed. Ramírez, who was only 17 years old at the time, was initially a staunch supporter of learning the English language, statehood, and refinement in the new state. He was also a Republican. He first wrote for the Spanish section of *The Los Angeles Star* and later took over ownership of the newspaper *El Clamor Público* (The Public Clamor) 1855–1859 in the state of California shortly after the U.S.A. won over California as a result of the Mexican American War. In 1848, the Treaty of Guadelupe Hidalgo was a promise that was not kept for the people who had already inhabited the area before the war. The original status of the Spanish Californios and Hispanicized Indians (indigenous) who were already present was stripped away, and the promises of the treaty which dealt with the conquered people's right to maintain property and financial assets were often forfeited. Once the lowly status of non-English Europeans (Spaniards) became evident, he began to express disfavor with this new inferior status in the newspaper and often expressed and promoted ideas such as racial and cultural pride and the maintenance of the Spanish language for the colonized of the Southwest. He was the first to use the terms *Raza*, "biculturalism," and "this land is our land." In short, he was the first Mexican American journalist to use the press to fight for civil rights for his people.

Antonio Coronel was another writer for newspapers that were offshoots from Ramírez's original papers and he solidified an activist stance toward the preservation of the Spanish language in 1856. In 1877, *La Cronica* expressed disfavor with many Mexican Americans, who were losing their ability to speak Spanish. Language use was equated with cultural preservation, and since this time, we have seen the issue of language preservation and English-only laws come up again and again. Bilingual education is often a site of contestation when schools lose money, and it was not different back then. At this time, the press seemed an important vehicle from where to advocate for the preservation of culture and to express disfavor with the less-than-equal treatment for Mexican Americans, Spanish, and indigenous peoples of this historical time period. It is also important to note that the Civil War was not long over in 1877 and that many of the Californios had Afro-Mexican roots and sympathized with the Union as Mexico had abolished slavery in 1821. Their sense of racial inferiority was felt and was often expressed in these newspapers.

In an editorial for another early-twentieth-century Southwestern newspaper, *The Mexican Voice*, Consuelo Espinosa wrote the following in "The Constitution and the Fourteenth Amendment": "I am not afraid to say that some parents teach their children not to talk to or play with a Negro or a Mexican. This is un-Christian and un-American. We say that we have to teach the youth of German the way of Democracy. Let me tell you, Americans, we still have a great job ahead of us, especially against the same racial prejudice" (95). What these newspapers and their writers contribute to the literary and rhetorical traditions of the late-nineteenth-century history of Composition Studies when looking at the Southwest is that there was, indeed, a rich literary and rhetorically driven presence of Mexican Americans in this area that has been severely understudied. One only has to look at the book *Conflict of Interest* to see the richness of Maria Amparo Ruiz de Burton's letters to see the eloquence with which she wrote both in Spanish and in English.

All of these writers may have been of a literate class and had some form of literary and rhetorical training that was not only relegated within the walls of Eastern elite institutions or within the walls of the normal schools. Out of necessity, however, these rhetors were lively and active contributors to civil rights rhetoric of the late nineteenth century and were also important predecessors for what would later become known as the Chicano Movement. Ultimately, the Chicano Movement would be the climatic point of expression and advocacy for the preservation of language and culture for those who were internally colonized as a result of the U.S.–Mexican War. This war created a new class of dispossessed people who had no other choice but to use their voice in order to preserve their right to life, liberty, and the pursuit of happiness even if the land they occupied never changed location but only changed political rule and cultural annihilation.

Out of these early newspapers and letters, a new consciousness was being created that can be compared with W.E.B. Dubois' "double-consciousness" as a descriptor of one that is a keen observer of his/her surroundings even while one is considered alien to that environment. When one becomes inferior, alien, outside of what is considered the dominant culture, then one begins to take on the role of an observant cultural critic. Out of such a perspective, rhetoric comes alive to create advocacy and other types of genres that serve to express a common experience among a newly conquered or oppressed class. One such genre that was born as a result of Latinxs/Chicanxs becoming internally colonized through the war was the "counter-travel narrative," which is akin to what José Martí wrote in his treatise *Nuestra America*. Through the revisiting of political documents and narratives that discussed the politics of the time, one can see how many Latin Americans became cultural critics of their surroundings in the same way that those who were explorers came to narrate their surroundings upon arrival to the New World.

This "New World," while new to many, was old to more than these new arrivals. However, the new arrivals, such as the Spanish and the English, made the Old World new due to their remapping, reclassifying, and regent-rifying of peoples and spaces that were in their natural habitat. The result was that what was once familiar became strange, and thus, counter-travel narratives can serve two functions: (1) to preserve culture and preserve a worldview that existed before conquest, and (2) to describe and narrate the new oppressive circumstances that are composed of the new surroundings, now foreign and unfitting. Thus, a new genre would be born as it would be one that is naturally oppositional due to its counter-stance.

These counternarratives can also be seen as precursors to what are now considered "counter-stories" popular among critical race theorists, and they can also be seen as a sort of counter-historical narrative, as they are stories that complicate the dominant culture's accounts of history and conquest. For example, who said that the indigenous were savages? Who said that the indigenous were more civilized and more attuned with nature than the conquerors? Counter-narratives, in short, are akin to critical historical narratives as well. These examples, while largely absent from traditional and "radical" histories of Composition Studies, show somewhat of a parallel consideration of Latinx voices to the voices of African American women in Royster's work.

From an ahistorical standpoint, one sees that, currently, in academia, written cultural productions by Latinxs are largely written in English. Interestingly, the 1991 U.S. Census Bureau reports that "only about 10 percent of Latinxs complete four or more years of college, as compared to 22.3 percent of the non-Latinx population" (Sanchez 551). Thus, any amount of Latinx scholarship, even if written in English, is only representative of 10 % of the largest minority group in the U.S.A. This number is low considering that in some parts of the Southwest, Chicanxs comprise up to 80 % of the total college population (i.e., the University of Texas-Rio Grande Valley).

Although there are no specific connections made by scholars between Composition and Latinxs in the late nineteenth and early twentieth century, the Chicano Student Movement of the 1960s stressed education, admissions into institutions of higher learning, and Chicanx Studies content courses in high schools and colleges. The unique educational needs of Chicanx populations were a major concern of the movement and later of Compositionists who were interested in the language issues raised in documents such as "Students' Right to Their Own Language." Today, there are numerous people working in bilingual education who have struggled with the ideas of English-language immersion and genuine

bilingual/bicultural education. These educators work on analyzing the speaking and writing problems of Latinxs. As a matter of fact,
the University of California has its own research institute dedicated to
the research of linguistic minorities, called the University of California
Linguistic Minority Research Institute. These language-related issues as
well as the circumstances surrounding Chicanos/as educational attainment during the civil rights era will be explored in the following chapters. More specifically, the next chapter seeks to answer questions that
are crucial to develop a critical counter-story that includes the concerns
of Latinx students in the fairly young field of Composition Studies.
These questions are: Why is the scarcity of Latinx Compositionists more
pronounced than that of African American Compositionists? How has
Composition, as a field, responded to the history of the cultural and
linguistic circumstances of each of these groups? What is the current
thinking within Composition Studies on the specific needs of Chicanxs/
Latinxs regarding the educational barriers they face in institutions of
higher learning?

    In order to answer the above questions in the next chapter, I have
examined the archives of *College Composition and Communication*.
I have also sought to both analyze the pedagogical responses to the
inclusion of Latinx voices in the Composition classroom and determine the number of Latinxs who actually publish in the field on issues
of in/exclusion of Latinx voices. With a notable absence of Latinx
scholarship in Composition Studies, I turn to possible alternative considerations and locations in order to fill those gaps with what should
have been written about and what should receive its due attention.
Such considerations include rhetorical strategies that were used by
different segments of the Latinx population during political responses
to reconstructive historical moments that were effective at effecting
change and progress toward more inclusive, multicultural, and educational opportunities for Latinxs. When we look toward the Chicano/a
Movement as an important rhetorical component for change within
the University, we see that there is much to account for within our
field that, up until this point, has been virtually silenced. Currently,
the NCTE/CCCC Latinx Caucus is growing, and more attention
will be given to reconstructing and adding to this neglected history
over the coming years. As the current co-chair of the CCCC Latinx
Caucus, this is part of my mission as the leader of this relevant group
of notable Composition scholars.

CHAPTER 6

The Second Reconstruction: The Civil Rights Era and Composition's Response to the New "Egalitarian" University

Both the 1870s and the 1960s were times of innovation and change. The innovation of mass education beginning in the late nineteenth century during the reconstruction era was a direct response to the changes that our nation was experiencing at the time. During this era, slaves became free and, supposedly, "equal," and educational institutions became more formalized as our nation was securing its position as an industrialized capitalist nation that required skilled workers, technological development, and professionalization. The U.S.A. responded to these needs by stressing education and calling for the training of more teachers to teach new populations entering the schools. The preparation of skilled workers to man the new industries called for creative responses by universities and colleges all around the U.S.A. The nineteenth century is commonly referred to as the first civil rights era for this reason; the civil rights period of the 1960s is often referred to as the second reconstruction era by historians. Historian Eric Foner, for instance, notes that the changing character of historical scholarship has allowed for both the first and the second reconstruction to be seen in a more critical light. He states that

> [t]he "Second Reconstruction"—the civil rights movement—inspired a new conception of the first among historians, and as with the study of slavery, a revisionist wave broke over the field in the 1960's. [For example,] Andrew Johnson, yesterday's high-minded defender of constitutional principles, was revealed as a racist politician too stubborn to compromise with his critics [during the first reconstruction period]. (84)

© The Editor(s) (if applicable) and The Author(s) 2016   97
I.D. Ruiz, *Reclaiming Composition for Chicano/as and Other Ethnic Minorities*, DOI 10.1057/978-1-137-53673-0_6

Revisions to historical actors and to historical events are an important part of revisionist history as they serve the function of providing more than one account of a person or an event, and oftentimes, these perspectives are critical, as noted in the quotation above. To be deemed a racist is quite the contrary from being known as a defender of constitutional principles when the Constitution defends equal rights and treatment for all Americans.

Foner finds that such new historical interpretations of the first reconstruction era emerged out of the new political perspective that characterized the second reconstruction historical period. These new accounts of the past countered more traditional historical accounts written before the "new historical" movement, which challenged older notions of history. Foner explains that the failures of the first reconstruction era in achieving civil liberties for all made the changes witnessed in the sixties inevitable. He claims that

> [b]y the end of the 60s the old [historical] interpretation had been completely reversed. Most historians agreed that if reconstruction was a "tragic" era, it was so because change did not go far enough; it fell short especially in the failure to distribute land to the former slaves and thereby provide an economic base for their newly acquired political rights. (85)

The reconstruction of the 1860s, thus, did not live up to its promises to free slaves in a manner where they would realize true freedom and self-actualization in a country that prided itself on the many freedoms guaranteed by the Constitution of the U.S.A. Similarities between both of these Reconstructive periods are evident in Foner's juxtaposition of interpretations of the notion of "equal protection" of the law after massive unrest and national growth and change. It is this social change that, after the 1960s, impacted educational institutions as they responded to mass social movements with innovative ideologies, curricular change and a political policy which emphasized color blindness—at least at the discursive level, before the creation of critical race theory (CRT), which critiques color-blind rhetoric for perpetrating more subtle, but equally as damaging, forms of racism.

Furthermore, national changes and growth led to the creation of new bureaucratic institutions to help control and accommodate new exigencies from the public. For example, the social unrest of the 1960s that occurred all over the U.S.A. challenged a number of notions, including concepts of democracy. Such fundamental presuppositions had to be reinterpreted as they had been in the late nineteenth century. The meaning of equal opportunity was once again put center stage to be contested and realized to a greater extent than the past had afforded. The assassination of Martin Luther King, Jr. (MLK) after a series of social protests, boycotts, and civil rights reforms within the legal arena crystallized the identification of the continuous problem of racism. Racism could no longer go unnoticed by educational institutions and academic disciplines. While King's death is known as the climactic point of the second civil rights movement in the U.S.A., there were other social struggles occurring in the nation and abroad that led to global social unrest during and after the 1960s—revolutions were taking place in the Atlantic as well.

Not surprising, the turbulent 1960s spilled directly into Composition Studies, as noted by Compositionist Lester Faigley, when on April 4, 1968, during the annual Conference on College Composition and Communication (CCCC) meeting in Minneapolis, MLK was assassinated in Memphis. A letter, written by Richard Braddock on behalf of the CCCC was sent to Coretta Scott King, King's widow. In this letter, he laments that

> only recently we have realized that we have been hurting ourselves by not discovering and utilizing the rich resources of our Negro members we have not known well or of non-member Negro colleagues we have not known at all…After all these years, we are finally taking steps to identify and establish closer communication with all our colleagues and to broaden the representation on our Executive Committee and, very soon, among our officers. (quoted in Faigely 59)

One can discern in Braddock's words the language of remorse, regret, and hope for future change within a field that, from its beginning, dealt with and still deals with acculturation and accommodation to a white mainstream. However, it was not until this moment that the circumstances of other cultures began to be given serious consideration.

The delay in reconsidering racist practices came to an end, in part, as a reaction to the sixties and MLK's death. The outrage produced by his murder as well as the struggles within the legal sphere and educational institutions, where a critique of racial attitudes and unfair civil rights laws that discriminated against blacks and other non-whites, led to the formulation of new policies. Previously, as we all know, segregation was legal in society because of the "separate but equal" doctrine legalized in the Supreme Court case of *Plessy v. Ferguson*[1] (1896). The decade of the 1960s also saw the emergence of an antiwar movement; people in this country were unhappy with their nation's prolonged involvement in the Vietnam War. The time was ripe for mass social protest and for changes in civil rights laws. For example, the *Brown v. The Board of Education*[2] (1954) Supreme Court decision was a fundamental recognition that segregation in the schools meant unequal education. The country had to wait ten more years for Congress to recognize the needs of racial minorities as it did in the Civil Rights Act of 1964,[3] four years before MLK's assassination.

Faigley's discussion of the influence that MLK's death had on the field of Composition was continued in Ernese B. Kelly's essay "Murder of the American Dream," in which she vividly elucidates the problems with the field's inattention to blacks in Composition. It was at this time that Composition began to encourage Compositionists to critically engage both race and social status in the Composition classroom. Only recently, then, has the theoretical goal of becoming oppositional critics of one's culture become part of the critical pedagogical practices of Composition. By recently, I mean since the 1960s. At this time, race consciousness also

[1] "In 1896, the Supreme Court struck down the first set of federal civil rights laws enacted to protect blacks from exclusion and segregation in public facilities. Ignoring the systematic state-supported terror blacks were suffering at the hands of the whites in that post-reconstruction era, the Court said that the Fourteenth Amendment's equal protection clause did not apply to counter enforced separation of the races, as applied to the internal commerce of the State. This forced separation neither abridged the privileges or immunities of the colored man, deprived him of his property without due process of law, nor denied him the equal protection of the laws, within the meaning of the Fourteenth Amendment" (Bell *Race* 131).

[2] "There, a unanimous Supreme Court finally gave voice to Justice Harlan's color-blind constitutionalism by holding that separate education facilities for blacks and whites were inherently unequal. In so holding, the court recognized that de jure race consciousness in education proceeded from the same assumption as de jure segregation in railway transportation: black inferiority. Doctrinally, of course, *Brown*'s significance is that it dismantled the separate-but-equal doctrine that had been used to maintain dual school systems throughout the South. The central tenet of *Brown*, however, is not merely that race is an irrelevant variable in government decision making; rather, it is that racial classifications, when used for the specific purpose or subordinating individual members of a particular racial category, run counter to the equal protection guarantee in the Constitution" (Bell *Race* 147).

[3] "This act expressly prohibits overt acts of racial discrimination. Now, as a century ago, the ideal of equality embodied in the Constitution is being effectively emasculated through the strict application of color-blind constitutionalism in a society where color continues to have primary relevance" (Bell *Race* 134).

brought forth broader participation of other cultural groups in the field of Composition (i.e., Asian-Americans, Native Americans, and Chicanxs).

Donna Burns Phillips, Ruth Greenberg, and Sharon Gibson also discuss Composition as a changing field during the time period of 1965 through 1979 in response to social movements, social needs, and the assassination of MLK. They explain that

> [n]ot surprisingly, the political and social upheaval of this era had a direct effect on the composition scene: many CCC [*College Composition and Communication*] articles focused on social and educational concerns as they related to the teaching of writing—Martin Luther King's assassination, minorities and teaching correctness, remedial teaching, democratizing freshman English, students' right to their own language, ethnic literature, and sexism. Other trends can be noted during this period: the number of pieces addressing only literary concerns diminished, while articles addressing the pedagogical application of theory increased. At the same time, the core topics established during CCC's first fifteen years continued to engage conversants and readers: grammar, teaching composition, usage, teacher training, and the state of the discipline. New topics could be noted as well: tagmemics, sentence combining, cognition, rhetoric, invention, critical thinking, and synthesizing theory, for example. (457)

During this era, Compositionists began to encourage students to think critically about their current positions in society and to question the power structures that were largely responsible for their situation. This was the beginning of critical pedagogy.[4] However, it should be noted

[4] Consistent with the fear of a nonhumanitarian mission of the University characterized by Lester Faigley, critical educator Paulo Friere describes this type of nonhumanitarian education as "necrophilous". He states that such an education is nourished by love of death, not life (Friere 58). Furthermore, he calls this type of education "the banking concept of education," which is the exact opposite of the type of critical pedagogy referred to in this book. The banking concept of education is described as serving the interests of oppression. It is "[b]ased on a mechanistic, static, naturalistic, spatialized view of consciousness, it transforms students into receiving objects" (58). In short, it inhibits both men's and women's creative power. Instead of a dehumanizing method of education, Freire advocates a "humanizing pedagogy in which the revolutionary leadership establishes a permanent relationship of dialogue with the oppressed...it expresses the consciousness of the students themselves" (51). Furthermore, students are seen as subjects who can not only attain knowledge but also discover themselves as its permanent re-creators. In short, they become agents of their own knowledge acquisition, knowledge-making and, hence, their own education. Process pedagogy, expressionist rhetoric, and epistemic rhetoric movements are characteristic outcomes of critical pedagogy.

that Composition never shed its regulating function even while establishing a close relationship between ideology, politics, and pedagogy. Compositionists, however, began to realize, as Karen Spears notes, that

> [p]edagogy, itself a rhetorical process, is never innocent. The point here is to recognize that any approach to teaching writing is embedded in a host of rhetorical and ideological assumptions and that the more recent formulations attempt, more self-consciously than ever before, to foreground those assumptions for students and faculty alike. (327)

This transition to critical pedagogy, however, was not well received by everyone in the field. Maxine Hairston complained that everywhere she turned, she found Composition "faculty, both leaders in the profession and new voices, asserting that they have not only the right, but the duty, to put ideology and radical politics at the center of their teaching" (180). She obviously was not comfortable with this ideological shift taking place in the field.

This trend undoubtedly began in the sixties and has carried to the present day. However, voices such as those of Hairston are not very often heard in today's Composition Studies scholarship. This absence, however, does not mean that such a resistance to critical pedagogy does not exist. On the contrary, the absence becomes present when one sees the subject matter of the scholarship. While the subject matter might not outright show criticism of critical pedagogy, minority voices and the like of those inserting CRT in rhetorical considerations (see Aja Martinez) show trends and insights into what the field considers important.

Lester Faigley, an outright dissident of Hairston's view, has a chapter in his book *Fragments of Rationality* in which he describes the changing politics of Composition Studies. In this chapter, he discusses another form of dissatisfaction that many Americans were experiencing at this time. He explains that Americans were afraid that bureaucratic practices were making people lose their humanity. He claims that even

> [b]efore the Vietnam War and disruptions on college and universities during the Vietnam period, critics of education and society in general complained about uniformity and dehumanization and they used images similar to William H. Whyte's "organization man," a caricature of the thoroughly institutionalized bureaucrat with no identity apart from his niche in the organization, living a look-alike life in a look-alike house in a look-alike suburb [to demonstrate this problem] (56).

Before the 1960s, Americans were encouraged not to challenge existing bureaucratic structures and uphold the status quo to further technological development and to maintain white cultural supremacy, despite the civil rights laws of the late nineteenth century. Before this decade, minority populations were encouraged to assimilate to mainstream culture if they desired to gain success in the form of college degrees. Assimilation was really the only viable option for minority voices before the Civil Rights Movement if one wanted to be heard in any of the field's publications and panels.

Consistent with the claim above, Susan Miller claims that after World War II and during the 1950s, "American literary curricula became almost exclusively New Critical in orientation" (21). Thus, superior literary texts were said to be able to avert the decline of the West by placing literature against religious discourses in an increasingly secularized nation. Furthermore, by reading the Great Works of the American Literary Tradition, war-torn American souls could be saved. Adherence to a great literary tradition was needed to establish a national consciousness; thus, a literary canon, instead of official religious texts, was established as the true equipment of America's educated. As a result of this nationalist project, "nationalistic, abstract ideals of literary study soon dominated as both the goal of and the justification for writing instruction" (31). Like literary instruction and appreciation, writing instruction also became a vehicle for cultural maintenance and superiority. The likes of Ethnic Studies were not yet found, but there were classes in literatures of foreign languages. Often, however, these literatures were seen as exceptional, but authors were not interested in social critique as the basis for studying such literature. From the 1960s onward, however, Composition begins anew to reconsider many of the concerns previously raised in its history, albeit under new theoretical and political lenses. Literature as the foundation of education and, especially of writing, began to be questioned.

In 1949, the CCCC was founded; however, Stephen North dates modern composition and its new modes of inquiry back to 1963 in response to the reform movement associated with the Cold War and the National Defense Education Act of 1958[5] (North 11). In Kitzhaber's 1963 CCCC address, he cited studies and conferences that had taken place during Project English, a U.S. Department of Education effort involving a number

---

[5] It was prodded by early Soviet success in the Space Race, notably the launch of Sputnik, the year before.

of Curriculum Study Centers at locations throughout the country (Gage xvi). As such, Composition Studies as a field with a contemporary research agenda can be traced back to the early 1960s. These National Defense influence on the field of Composition and education in general led to curricular reactions to a growing emphasis on scientism and research in Composition. James Berlin explains some pedagogical responses to the restrictions placed upon Composition scholarship and practice.

In "Rhetoric and Ideology," Berlin discusses how in the 1960s and early 1970s, proponents of expressionist rhetoric (defined in Chap. 4) were highly critical of American society and politics, and saw the teaching of writing as a means of liberating students from that society (57). Current Compositionists who embrace the process movement[6] as a means to writing in first-year composition and beyond believe that writing can free the mind of individuals and can be done through going through the prewriting, writing, and revision stages of writing. This process also occurs through egalitarian collaboration in the writing classroom. This type of pedagogical practice in the writing classroom is credited by Faigley to the influence of the feminist movement of the 1960s and 1970s on theories of composing and communication. He states that

> [w]omen in consciousness raising groups explored alternatives to hierarchical and competitive male styles of discussion (Annas)...In the articles of the teaching of writing that appeared in *College Composition and Communication* and *College English* in the 1960s and 1970s there are few explicit connections made between the women's movement and the emerging process movement. But undoubtedly there was more mutual influence than one can find in the professional literature. (59)

Thus, the critical movements happening outside of the writing classroom undoubtedly influenced the ways curricula and pedagogical practices were imagined. They influenced the way writing was taught. From this point forward, Composition would be faced with the task of how to accommodate the cultural and linguistic circumstances of minority populations, both in theory and in practice.

The results have been varied due to the varying theories evident in the growing scholarship of Composition. The theories defined earlier by

---

[6] See Compositionists James Britton, Janet Emig, Peter Elbow, Linda Flower, Ken Macrorie, and Sondra Perl for more on process pedagogy.

Berlin are miniscule, although important, in comparison with the array of pedagogical theories associated with Composition. However, his theories are representative of the main pedagogical theories; other theories can be found to be related to Aristotelian rhetoric, expressionist rhetoric, and the New Rhetoric (aka epistemic rhetoric), which Berlin refers to and defines. Furthermore, because of the changing demographics of Composition classrooms, teachers are faced with the possibilities of creating and utilizing a combination of new and competing pedagogical theories and practices that emphasize or deemphasize the acculturating practice of teaching to write in Standard, grammatically correct English. An example of competing approaches would be those advanced by Lisa Delpit and Peter Elbow. While Delpit emphasizes acculturation for linguistic minorities as essential for success within the University, Elbow encourages writing that can be done without teachers. In this book, I contribute to this pedagogical spectrum while considering how to teach writing to Chicanxs/Latinxs in the twenty-first century. However, one cannot move on to the present in Composition without considering its past.

The sixties and its influence on Composition Studies can be seen as a time when the notions of democracy and equal rights were put to the test and, as a result, reinterpreted within educational institutions. The many social changes which occurred during this era caused educational institutions to be more inclusive of various populations in order to provide national stability. Universities and colleges were, again, opening their doors to previously excluded populations. A well-trained population of teachers was needed to fit the changing demographics of these institutions. Ideologies within institutions also mirrored the changes in broader society relating to inclusion and to the questioning of objective, positivistic ideologies which dominated up until the 1960s, as indicated above by Faigley. For example, walkouts, boycotts, and war protests influenced broad institutional innovation and change. In the next section, I consider the Chicano Movement and its influence on educational institutions and, as a result, on Composition Studies. The most obvious reason for making such a connection is that no one has made it as of yet, despite the fact that recent statistics indicate that the Chicanx/Latinx population in the U.S.A. is the largest minority population. It is still, however, not adequately represented in higher education and, as a result, in academic scholarship.

The goal of this book, after all, is to contribute to the growing body of scholarship on Composition pedagogies with a view toward helping Chicanx/Latinx populations in the Composition classroom as well as in the

University and community at large. While the following account does not focus on the participation of Chicanxs in the field of Composition Studies in the 1960s, it does deal with the impact of the Chicano Movement on educational institutions, and especially on curricula, and suggests that Composition Studies was, indeed, influenced by this educationally focused struggle. The goal of this next section is to provide a greater understanding of the Chicanx population and its desires for inclusion in both intellectual and physical realms of the University and in political society.

CHICANXS IN THE CIVIL RIGHTS ERA
AND IN COMPOSITION STUDIES

This section first seeks to give an overview of gains made by Chicanxs as a result of the Chicanx Movement, often represented largely in relation to its projection of the mythic Aztec homeland, Aztlán, also known as the Southwestern U.S.A. This 1960s and 1970s re-creation was "meant to legitimize one's roots in the region of one's residence..." (Sánchez and Pita 47). I see the use of Aztlán as a symbol of Chicanx cultural nationalism, a movement that instilled Chicanx cultural pride in the everyday lives of Chicanxs living in the U.S.A. Thus, we now turn our attention to the population most largely present in the Southwestern U.S.A.

In 1969, the Chicano Movement gained great momentum with the celebration of the National Chicano Youth Liberation Conference in Denver, Colorado. Activists from all over the country involved in both campus and community politics attended this conference, making the outcomes of this conference wide-ranging in terms of bridging community concerns with educational institutional concerns. While the majority of the students who attended this conference were student activists, many different walks of life were represented by youth of Mexican origin. The national forum brought together students as well as ex-convicts and militant youth from street gangs. The idea was that ethnic origin was what mattered, what brought cohesiveness to the group. The Chicano Movement had some similarities to black cultural movements of this time; the only difference, perhaps, was its awareness of its links to Latin America and Mexico and its acknowledgment of our ancient, indigenous past that was once part of the current U.S.A.

A nationalist ideology characterized by Chicanx self-determination and nonviolence was professed at this conference by Corky Gonzáles. During this week-long conference, Gonzáles and his followers emphasized revolutionary behavior on behalf of Chicanx students and youth in order to make the Chicanx Movement successful. They argued that earlier generations of Chicanx "had been Americanized by the schools, that they had been conditioned to accept the dominant values of American society, particularly individualism, at the expense of their Mexican identity. The result had been the psychological 'colonization' of Mexican American youth" (Muñoz 76). Out of these arguments which further emphasized the need for nationalist unity, a series of resolutions were approved by conference participants. These resolutions emphasized the need for Chicanxs to gain political and economic control of their own communities.

Special attention was to be given to community control of the schools. Chicano Studies,[7] thus, was born out of this need to connect community activism and educational reform, which would include previously ignored cultural and historical knowledge of Chicanxs in the U.S.A. These and other resolutions were compiled in a statement entitled "*El Plan Espiritual de Aztlán* or The Spiritual Plan of Aztlán" (Muñoz 77). The plan was prefaced by the following manifesto:

> In the spirit of a new people that is conscious not only of its proud historical heritage, but also of the brutal "Gringo" invasion of our territories, we, the Chicano inhabitants and civilizers of the northern land of Aztlán, from whence came our forefathers, reclaiming the land of their birth and consecrating the determination of our people of the sun, declare that the call of our blood is our power, our responsibility and our inevitable destiny... (78)

This plan was able to have a long-lasting impact when student leaders who had attended the conference in Denver were able to implement some of its resolutions at the Chicano Coordinating Council on Higher Education conference held at the University of California (UC), Santa Barbara. This conference became the founding convention of the Chicano Student Movement (79).

At this conference, the United Mexican American Students, the Mexican American Student Confederation, the Mexican American Youth Association, and the Mexican American Student Association became one unified Chicanx student movement called El Movimiento Estudiantil

---

[7]To see a more detailed treatment of the creation of Chicano Studies programs and the connection to bilingual education, refer to Rodolfo Acuña's *Occupied America: A History of Chicanos*.

Chicano de Aztlán (The Chicano Student Movement of Aztlán or MEChA) (79). Today, many strings of MEChA groups can be found across the country at community colleges, state colleges, and universities.

Such organizational achievements were long called for but were created in a moment of historical opportunity due to larger national attention to the Black Movement and to changing social demographics and needs. In *Brown-Eyed Children of the Sun: Lessons from the Chicano Movement, 1965–1975*, George Mariscal explains the low political profile of Mexican Americans up until this point:

> In the case of Mexican Americans in the late 1960s...the experience of being perceived as foreigners by dominant U.S. society, the result of over one hundred years of marginalization dating from the 1848 takeover of the Southwest, had driven many to adopt a low political profile in the hope of peacefully assimilating into the melting pot of middle-class comfort and cultural homogeneity. (25)

However, the assimilation model did not ensure success for this population, and cultural alienation was often the result of such a low political profile. Thus, seizing on the opportunity to become politically active, effective, and visible became the goal of the Chicanx Movement of the sixties.

One of the key results of this movement was the belief that the university was a means of becoming more politically effective and, thus, a means for Chicanxs to gain larger control over their own communities at a political and economic level. The community needed to view universities as "strategic agencies in any process of community development..." (81). MEChA's goal to establish itself as a power base on campus meant that more Chicanxs needed to be recruited in order to make this movement successful at creating a Chicanx consciousness at this critical historical moment. In the process, Chicanxs sought to change educational institutions in order to liberate Chicanxs from prejudice and oppression and from feeling a need to assimilate to escape their "degraded social status," which is explained in more depth in *"El Plan Espiritual de Atzlán"* (80). The way this power base manifested itself on college campuses was through Chicano Studies Programs. However, it was very important in the implementation of these programs to remain in constant dialogue with the community at large to ensure that Chicanx Studies programs would not be "put in the straightjacket of the usual, academic guidelines" (83).

Thus, strong emphasis was placed on dissolving the academy/community dichotomy in order to ensure that Chicanx Studies programs would serve the direct interests of the larger Chicanx community and not simply the academy's interests.

As a result of this conference at UC, Santa Barbara, Chicanx intellectuals "identified the institutions of higher education as strategic targets for political change" (84). Chicanx Studies programs were then instituted "at California community colleges located in areas with a substantial Mexican American community, at all the state colleges, and at virtually all of the campuses of the University of California" (84). Great gains were made in this era for the Chicanx community, especially in California.

One may wonder, as I do, how the gains made by Chicanxs during this historical era influenced and affected Composition. It is hard to say; part of the reason this question is hard to answer is due to the absence of any mention of the Chicano Movement in the scholarship representative of Composition during this historical time period (up until 1975 when the CCCC made a resolution statement titled "Students' Right to Their Own Language" [SRTOL]). During this time, there was no direct consideration of the ideologies of either the Black Movement or the Chicano Movement in Composition Studies. In Table 6.1, we see the breakdown of authors who wrote for the *College Composition and Communication* (CCC) journal, which, as its name indicates, focuses on issues that are important to the field at the time. This table is provided by Sandra Gibbs in "College Composition and Communication: Chronicling a Discipline's Genesis" by Donna Burns Phillips, Ruth Greenberg, and Sharon Gibson:

What does the table say of the field's attention to minorities? In my opinion, it says that the field of Composition was indeed changing, witnessed by the inclusion of Composition scholars such as Donald Murray, Sharon Crowley, Maxine Hairston, Linda Flower, and Mike Rose. These Compositionists were contributing to a changing discipline that was considering students' welfare over the states' interests (with the exception of Maxine Hairston, who was more of a critic of these changes while still calling attention to them). These Compositionists considered not only the backgrounds of students, but also the distance between these backgrounds and the expectations of the University.

The list of the most cited scholars within CCC also implies something else, however, as noted by the authors of this article: this implication is similar to Richard Delgado's claim that the most commonly cited scholars in a field's academic journals determine what is appropriate to discuss

Table 6.1   Most frequently published authors of major articles

1950–1964	1965–1979	1980–May 1993
H. Allen (4)	R. Larson (8)	R. Connors (6)
D. Lloyd	R. Lloyd-Jones (6)	A. Lunsford
R. Braddock (3)	F. D'Angelo	M. Rose
B. Kogan	R. de Beaugrande (5)	L. Faigley (5)
P. Wikelund	T. M. Sawyer (4)	L. Flower
H. Wilson	R. Gorrell (3)	M. Hairston
E. Steinberg (2)	E. Corbett	C. Berkenkotter (4)
V. Rivenbaugh	E. Suderman	D. Stewart
S. Radner	G. Sloan	S. Stotsky
	J. Lauer	S. Witte
	L. Odell	C. Anson (3)
	R. Hoover	L. Bridwell-Bowles
	R. Gebhardt	G. Brossell
	W. Ross Winterowd	E. Corbett
	W. Marqhardt	F. D'Angelo
	W. Pixton	R. Fulkerson
	G. Cannon	J. Hayes
	S. Crowley	J. Hoetker
	M. Sternglass	D. Murray
	A. M. Tibbetts	L. Peterson
	F. Christensen	L. Podis
		G. Sloan
		N. Sommers
		E. M. White

and who is appropriate to cite for these same discussions.[8] Quantitative measures of who is cited in a discipline largely determine what the field or discipline pays attention to and, thus, also determines a power base for that same field. Consider the following statement:

> Such quantitative measures help determine what can be considered within the community as common knowledge, and common knowledge is the power base. Writers will construct their discourse around what their audiences can be assumed to know and accept. Researchers will see the investigative techniques as models. Initiates will ingest this core as part of the membership rite. CCCC members will rely on name recognition and elections shaping the organization that molds the field. In sum, work associated with these names becomes the traditional paradigm, and all subsequent

[8] See Richard Delgado's "Imperial Scholar."

work moves toward its support, its enlargement, or its overthrow. (Gibson et al. 454)

In short, CCC was exclusive in the same way many scholarly journals were at this time. The minority voice was the exception and not the rule.

One CCCC scholarly document that sought to enlarge the field of Composition during this era was SRTOL. It was the beginning of an inclusive tradition of difference within Composition. However, Linda Brodkey, a critical Compositionist, explains that although SRTOL sought to enlarge the field of Composition, it still did not have a significant impact on the field's attention to difference and to minority concerns in general. She states:

> "Students' Right to Their Own Language," a resolution adopted by the 1974 Conference on College Composition and Communication and reaffirmed several times since, publicly denounces ill-informed and self-serving language policies as "false advice for speakers and writers, and immoral advice for humans" (see preface to "Students' Right to Their Own Language" 1974). The syllabus drafted for "Writing about Difference" at the University of Texas may not address precisely the same issues as the 1974 resolution, but opposition to the syllabus is curiously reminiscent of the political climate in which the resolution on language was drafted and ultimately adopted. Whether the controversy is about dialect or difference, it seems opponents just say no, perhaps because difference and dialect alike challenge "many long held and passionately cherished notions about language" (Students' Right 1974:1). (229)

I will discuss the specifics of the syllabus to be addressed below that Brodkey refers to above momentarily. My inclusion of the above quotation, however, is meant to show that public opposition and scholarly power, demonstrated by the "canon" of a discipline, largely influenced the dismissal of serious consideration and implementation of the tenets of SRTOL. The ideology of inclusion which served as the foundation of this resolution was not closely tied to Composition pedagogy as Burns et al. suggest above; instead, what one finds in the SRTOL resolution is a discussion of linguistic attributes that consider dialect and whether or not one dialect is superior to another. The ideologies of the sixties' movements and the tradition of the inclusion of differences in this resolution, however, are only alluded to in the consideration of difference and cultural attributes of language. The language imperative, however, is still evident.

The ultimate goal of SRTOL, then, is to acculturate students to eventually become proficient in grammatically correct Standard English. The long-held belief that Standard English is a superior dialect established the ultimate imperative of Composition, regardless of differences: to become a fluent and literate English speaker and writer.

Furthermore, English-only legislation[9] undoubtedly affected the practice of teaching Composition and currently influences new and creative responses to teaching students without forcing them to possibly lose part of their cultural dignity as professed through language. However, due to the institutional bureaucracy of higher education institutions, English is a force to be reckoned with. With this force comes confrontation with possible cultural and linguistic annihilation; this possibility seems unlikely when talking about the Chicanx/Latinx population due to continued migration to the U.S.A. Still, students must be able to read and write academic English in order to gain access to the academy. This is what I call the English literacy imperative and what Gloria Anzaldúa calls "linguistic terrorism."

Therefore, those academics committed to preserving the cultural and linguistic traditions of linguistic and cultural minorities have faced and still face a dilemma—how can we facilitate the political entrance of these students into the academy without asking them to negate part of themselves? This question becomes difficult to answer because of the linguistic variability of U.S. Chicanx/Latinx populations. For example, in "Mapping the Spanish Language Along a Multiethnic and Mulitlingual Border," Rosaura Sánchez gives a detailed history of the Spanish language in the U.S.A., even before the U.S.A. existed. She states that written cultural productions such as newspapers, testimonials, theater, poetry, and narratives were still written in Spanish after the U.S. invasion of the Southwest. However, currently, in academia, written cultural productions by Latinxs are largely written in English. The 1991 U.S. Bureau of the Census reported that "only about 10 percent of Latinxs complete four or more years of college, as compared to 22.3 percent of the non-Latino population" (Sánchez 551). These numbers are still accurate

---

[9] See *Gutiérrez v. Mun. Ct. of S.E. Judicial Dist.*: cite as 861 F.2d 1187 (9th Cir. 1988) and *Hector Garcia, etc., Plaintiff-Appellant v. Alton V. W. Gloor et al.*, Defendants-Appellees No. 77-2358, United States Court of Appeals, Fifth Circuit, May 22, 1980. Both of these cases demonstrate workplace discrimination against the speaking of Spanish at the employment site. Both judgments were against the speaking of Spanish in the workplace other than out of absolute necessity such as the use of Spanish by court interpreters.

today. The last U.S. Census report on educational attainment was reported in 2013. With the U.S. Hispanic population over the age of 18 totaling 29,673,441, only 2,831,183 have completed a Bachelor's degree, and only 140 have completed a PhD compared with 27,434 PhD completed by whites only.[10] This is a vast disparity that reaches over into the academic publication sphere, where these disparate numbers are also represented in terms of who publishes and what the subject matter of these publications are in Composition Studies. As such, any amount of Latinx scholarship, even if written in English, is only representative of less than 10 % of the largest minority group in the U.S.A. This number is generous since many undergraduates do not publish, and if they do, they are in venues that are marginalized in comparison with the most prestigious journals of any given field. We all know what journals these are, and the infographic above (Table 5.1) shows what those journals mean for our field. Nevertheless, this number is low considering that in some parts of the Southwest, Chicanos/as comprise up to 80 % of the total college population (i.e., the University of Texas Rio Grande Valley).

There are no specific connections between Composition and Latinxs in the late nineteenth and early twentieth century; however, the Chicano Student Movement of the 1960s stressed education and making institutions of higher education more aware of the unique educational needs of Chicano populations. Unlike the death of MLK and the Black Movement, the Chicano Movement has not received enough attention from Compositionists interested in the linguistic ideas which began with documents such as SRTOL. Recently, however, interest in historical rhetorics of Chicanxs/Latinxs has increased (see the works of Damián Baca).

The unique linguistic circumstances, however, of Chicanxs/Latinxs in the U.S.A. have a strong and rich textual history beginning with the education of new U.S. citizens after 1848 (some are accounted for in the previous chapter). The beginning of acculturation through education began with the English-only movements that soon followed the colonization of California, New Mexico, and Texas. Since then, bilingual education programs across the country have struggled back and forth with the ideas of English-language immersion and genuine bilingual/bicultural education.

[10] See: http://factfinder2.census.gov/faces/tableservices/jsf/pages/productview.xhtml?pid=ACS_13_1YR_B15002I&prodType=table

Social, cultural, institutional, and educational changes that began in the 1960s and impacted the field of Composition allowed me to perform a study of Mexican and Mexican American Generation 1.5 students. They demonstrated the educational dilemmas of both dominant Spanish-speaking and undocumented students striving to achieve the American Dream. The study is titled *Generation 1.5: A Border Culture in Ethnography* (2003). Studies such as this are now critical for informing the current field of Composition about the unique cultural, linguistic, and migratory circumstances of the multidimensional nature of Latinx students striving to attain a college education, while balancing two cultures, two languages, and two places to call home (various parts of Latin America and the U.S.A.).

Furthermore, because changes that occurred in the 1960s and resolution statements such as SRTOL, programs which facilitate the entrance of Chicanx/Latinx student populations into four-year institutions such as "Puente" have been made possible and have had beneficial consequences for both the educational achievements and the self-esteem of these students. Still, these programs are few and far between. What about at tier-one universities? What about at elite universities? Programs such as Puente are predominantly found in community colleges such as the one I attended (Fresno City College), where I was a Puente student. Thus, more studies need to be done at four-year universities, where students are expected to perform at a higher level because of pronounced competition. In tier-one universities, for example, Scholastic Aptitude Test (SAT) entrance scores are expected to be high, performance is expected to be granted with A's, and culture and background are not an immediate concern. However, the demand for high performance should not deny students opportunities to write at a tier-one level about subjects that deal with difference, diversity, and politics of power. I will discuss the specifics of such a course that I taught in the spring of 2006 at the University of California, San Diego (UCSD), in Chap. 7.

There is also a need to reconsider resolutions such as SRTOL which mainly concentrated upon the linguistic circumstances of Chicanxs/Latinxs and did not challenge the subject matter taught in the University. During the sixties, however, there were changes in institutions of higher education which went further than considering the linguistic circumstances of the Chicanx/Latinx population. These changes concentrated upon an education that would be suitable for Chicanx/Latinx and which challenge higher education as a mere acculturating tool. Chicanx Studies programs were implemented as well as programs that would help facilitate a greater admittance of Chicanxs/Latinxs into higher education, such as Educational Opportunity Program (EOP).

There are still questions that need to be answered, however, in the field of Composition Studies. This chapter seeks to answer questions that are meant to not only concentrate upon a lack in the field but, in addition, to complement what Composition has already researched and learned about Chicanxs/Latinxs in the field's scholarship. These questions are, in the nascent field of Composition Studies: First, why is the scarcity of Chicanxs/Latinxs Compositionists more pronounced than that of African American Compositionists? Second, how has Composition, as a field, responded to the history of the cultural and linguistic circumstances of each of these groups? Third, what is the current status of Composition Studies concerning the plight of Chicanxs/Latinxs and regarding the educational barriers impeding them from reaching the "top"?

While one obvious answer to these questions could be a dismissal of consideration of any of them, this answer is exactly the reason why one should want to investigate such questions further. As noted above, the conservative political climate which contributed to the Texas culture wars as well as the public's rejection and resistance to documents, such as the SRTOL, and to Composition classes, such as Brodkey's English 306 at the University of Texas at Austin (UT Austin), are two main reasons why serious consideration of issues of difference are not apparent in mainstream scholarship. Consideration and implementation of such considerations in Composition pedagogy become controversial and sometimes upsetting to a large segment of those committed to tradition, standards, and cultural maintenance. However, seeking an answer to the question on Composition Studies' stance on the teaching of Composition to Chicanxs/Latinxs is a good reason to continue to investigate why attention to difference is controversial. Is it simply because it runs against the grain of the status quo?

In her work, Paula Moya stresses the importance of textualizing experience, that is, difference, and I would suggest that this textualization needs to be considered by Composition teachers. I, myself, have had the experience of observing and teaching a class that ran against the grain of the mainstream, "imperial scholarship" of Composition (see Richard Delgado 1984) by incorporating the textualization of Chicanx/Latinx experiences. Clearly, it is important to shed light on why a particular political climate can shunt such experiences.

I am not suggesting that there are not any attempts at inclusion in the current scholarship of Composition Studies; obviously there have been many contributions, some of which I will discuss in the next chapter. However, in the current practice of Composition, there are still exclusions that need to be considered. As Lester Faigley states, "[r]ecognizing the sources of contradictory and incompatible discourses runs squarely against both the expressivist and rationalist traditions that posit a unified self in the teaching of writing that deny the role of language in constructing selves" (128). Tradition is not easily let go, especially when it represents the majority of a field's scholars and practitioners.

Upon examining minority scholarship, I have found that many minority-authored journal articles and books in the field are still tokenized, meaning that there are not many publication by scholars of color when compared with white counterparts and this is not reflective of truly inclusive efforts. For example, why not have a journal dominated by scholars of color sponsored by the CCCC? If genuine inclusion of colored pedagogy does not exist in the mainstream journals of Composition, then why do alternative journals not challenge this exclusivity of scholarly journals? Is it a matter of funding? These are questions to consider, especially in a continuously growing het-erogeneous America. There was once a special edition of *College English* that dealt with such issues pertaining to Chicanxs/Latinxs in the field: notice the "a" singular. It was *College English*, Vol. 71, No. 6, July 2009; while this is not Composition's main journal, it serves as an example of what an issue of JAC (*JAC: A Journal of Rhetoric, Culture, and Politics*) or CCC could look like. In short, it is not enough to call attention to our scholarly contribu-tions and concerns for our space in the field and the ways in which Chicanx/Latinx students are taught in our writing classrooms.

One reason could be that both historical moments, the late nineteenth century and the 1960s, were a time of change stemming from both resis-tance and backlash to existing structures and social relations. Both periods, however, provoked more backlash and counterchange: a counterresistance to the innovation and change of the prior time period—or better yet, what could be called the regulation and moderation of progressive innova-tion and change. More specifically, after the 1960s and 1970s, American citizens witnessed the decline of the Civil Rights Movement, and in the 1980s, there was a backlash to civil rights and equal opportunity rheto-ric common to the prior two decades. This backlash manifested itself as the heated response to "reverse-discrimination" and "color-blind" racism, as many Republican conservatives believed that no one should receive special or preferential treatment in the professional or academic arena. Derrick Bell confirms this political backlash in the following statement: "Notions of color-blindness were nurtured in the political campaigns of the early 1980s, when the Reagan administration, sensing that large numbers of whites were disgruntled by the attention paid to minority concerns, undertook to undermine the civil rights gains of the previous two decades" (134). Similar to the counterresistance that grew in response to many policy initiatives which began in the mid-1960s, in the late nineteenth century, after the implementation of policies that helped to ensure schools with a more integrated student body, reactions to curricula that reflected the experiences of the newly integrated students emerged. Part of the reaction manifested itself into meritocratic rhetoric. Meritocracy became a new method of assimilation and thrived off of color-blind rhetoric and equality rhetoric.

Along with the establishment of normal schools, which eventually became the state college university system, came the desire to be more like elitist educational institutions. The politics of change promoted by civil and educational institutions became diluted, as color-blind rhetoric and meritocratic ideology eventually devalued the concept and practice of defining civil rights. After the 1960s, educational policies which sought to transform the educational institution (see Lowe and Kantor) were likewise transformed into a desperate call for a more meritocratic system of education that would question the earlier rationales for the transformation of educational practices largely witnessed in the civil rights era. In both periods of reconstruction, those who gained access to a higher status desired to maintain their meritocratic position; in the late nineteenth century, those who were actually supposed to benefit from the initial democracy of education, for example, through normal schools, became disenfranchised. Similarly, those subjects that were supposed to be recognized by alternative studies programs, such as Chicano Studies and Ethnic Studies, found themselves in institutionalized programs that lapsed into meritocratic intellectual views. The initial purpose of these programs became lost in the primary function of the university—to maintain and contribute to America's ever-growing middle-class citizenry.

Both the media and the middle class responded with powerful opposition against what seemed to be revolutionary educational outcomes and against those who attempted to reintroduce major social concerns into academic rhetoric. For example, during the summer of 1990, at UT Austin, the director of lower-division English, Linda Brodkey, and a committee of faculty and graduate students wrote a revised syllabus for the required first-year composition course in response to heightened attention to a racially tense campus environment and, hence, the need for more attention to issues of difference and multiculturalism. English 306 would encourage students to write about important public debates on racial, sexual, and ethnic diversity. U.S. Supreme Court opinions and opinions from federal courts dealing with cases of racial discrimination would provide the textual material for the new syllabus and were to involve cases that would include at least three arguments (the plaintiff's, the defendant's, and the court's), providing a balance of opinions.

The subject matter to be discussed in this course was immediately met with resistance and, eventually, public disdain as some of the UT Austin faculty were publicly vocal about their dissatisfaction with the new course material. Richard Bernstein quotes Alan Gribben, who declared in the *Daily Texan*, UT Austin's student newspaper, for example, that "'without even pausing for a vote,' the English department 'will start explaining to presumably benighted UT students how they ought to feel about issues of ethnicity and feminism'" (324). However, on several occasions, Linda Brodkey, who was the writing program administrator of the program in which I taught at UCSD, noted that Gribben never looked at or examined the syllabus closely. Most of the criticism from the UT Austin faction that opposed the new English 306 curriculum was based on the subject matter of the text that was initially going to serve as a summer reading requirement for the graduate students who would teach the class in the fall. It would also be part of the course syllabus. This book was *Racism and Sexism: An Integrated Study* by Paula Rothenberg. However, because of the criticism, the book's inclusion was abandoned.

Bernstein also quotes James Duban, another one of Brodkey's critics, and a faculty member in the English Department at UT Austin at this time. Duban also disagreed with the aims of this course in the *Daily Texan*. He stated in his article titled "A Modest Proposal" that he "had come to feel that the various topics that motivate students to write should receive only passing attention from the instructor, whose primary obligation is to offer freshmen intensive feedback about grammar, style, tone, form, cogency, organization and audience" (307). What is interesting to note is that the approach to argumentation taught in the proposed course was to be based on Stephen Toulmin's *The Uses of Argument*, and the syllabus required the use of a handbook (texts characteristic of many first-year writing courses). So there was never any stated intent that the course would not cover the basics of argumentation or the basics of English grammar, style, tone, form, cogency, organization, and audience. The subject matter of the course, however, was the main point of contention.

Before the syllabus was even finished, it came under heavy attack, both on and off campus, causing its implementation to be eventually canceled. The main reason for the attack was that the class did not maintain the status quo which was consistent with the function of literacy at this time and location, namely the teaching of the classics and literary masterpieces to maintain cultural hegemony with the help of writing classrooms. When attention veered away from this status quo, most likely due to Brodkey's focus on argumentation and critical analysis, the middle class seemed to panic. Brodkey was accused of teaching a multiculturalism course that would indoctrinate students to adopt certain "critical" beliefs about society that would be an obvious challenge to traditional English department business as usual.

In 1992, Lillian Robinson published a transcript of an interview she conducted with Brodkey regarding this course and the process which ultimately led to the indefinite postponement of this class at UT Austin. She states that she believes Brodkey's story to be an important historical story in the history of Composition because she "know[s] that the Texas story belongs in any survey of the backlash against feminist and multicultural studies," in the 1990s (23). In an article which appeared in the *Texas Monthly* just before the syllabus was being changed at UT Austin under Brodkey's supervision, there was a paragraph that is representative of the sentiment of this time period and of public attitudes showing disdain for multicultural curricula. Robinson describes the paragraph as a sneer toward including

> Sandra Cisneros in a course in American literature [instead of] an acknowledged classic like *The Great Gatsby*—with Cisneros being characterized as a "currently trendy young Chicana writer." Nothing was said about her work except that she was "fashionable" among us, was young—that is, still living—and a Chicana, and that was supposed to be sufficiently damning in itself. (24)

Apparent at this time, evident in the quotation above, is a clear backlash to the gains made in the civil rights era and which were most visible in the late 1960s through the late 1970s.

With the Reagan administration clearly attacking many of the reforms of these decades, many middle-class, mainstream Americans began both a public and an intellectual backlash against progressive politics within universities around the country. Brodkey had a clear understanding of the connection between this conservative right-wing backlash against her course and the political motivation behind it that went above and beyond her syllabus for English 306. More specifically, she states:

> When you start looking at it on a national level, you ask yourself: why the attack not only on this course but on other efforts that faculty are making to reform the curriculum on a larger scale, why this moment? And why was it effective? Because it really shouldn't have been. It shouldn't have been that easy to get *Newsweek* to demean faculty efforts to include new texts in classes or to recognize that the demographics are slightly different in most universities than they were ten years ago. (24)

In discussions surrounding the circumstances of English 306, it is apparent that fears surrounding multicultural curricula fueled an effective, cogent backlash, which had far-reaching educational and political consequences.

Conservatives felt that the inclusion of minority voices within literature and writing classes signaled the reduction of standards and a growing disrespect for the old knowledges that comprised university curricula as a sort of religious canon. The inclusion of minority voices such as those of Chicanxs went counter to this traditional curriculum and was considered a form of affirmative action, and affirmative action was considered by counterrevolutionists as a threat to the old order. In short, any kind of curriculum that focused upon difference was also a threat to the old cultural artifacts that, likewise, ignored difference. Those who possessed the power to influence textual canons of scholarship for many mainstream disciplines were also careful about the amount of attention given to minority voices, as exemplified by the portrait of Composition scholarship provided by Sandra Gibbs above.

Robinson goes on to discuss the strong attachments right-wing conservative intellectuals and individuals held toward the traditional curriculum and traditional culture as sacred texts that become fetishized. Brodkey then responds to the comparison of tradition texts with religious texts by referring to a historical parallel which took place in the 1950s, another conservative era in which "William Buckley launched...some version of

God and Man at Yale" that has resurfaced in the nineties, "only in the secular version [where] there's no distinction between God and man, we just have man as god" (Robinson 24). This discussion between Robinson and Brodkey is quite telling of the era in which many of the gains in the revolutionary period of the 1960s were met with a vehement disdain during the "counterrevolutionary" period. Many of these gains were subjected to a political backlash that led to the breach of academic freedom that was, until then, supposedly protected within university's walls.

Referring to the reactionary counterrevolutionaries as "right-wingers," Robinson continues to lament the effects of such a limiting intellectual reaction, namely to stifle the ability of instructors to implement a pedagogy that would allow for opportunities to critique widely accepted and unquestioned ideas. She states that "[t]hese people think of education as the teaching of fundamental facts and truths, so that we end up with higher education as a series of techniques. You learn computer science, you learn how to be a functionary in an advanced technological society. But you don't learn to ask questions about it" (24). What is unfortunate about this backlash, exemplified by the elimination of English 306 at UT Austin, is that the critical pedagogical responses to the accommodationist and inclusionist practices prompted by revolutionary thought and change in the 1960s and MLK's death became suspect. Ultimately, they also became discredited to the point where such characteristics within pedagogy became akin to "brainwashing" and "indoctrination" at the expense of students learning how to become thinkers, questioners, and social analyzers.

Brodkey also laments that such a backlash challenged the very practice of democracy or the ability to see all people as equal and as able, participating civic citizens. She explains:

> We were saying that students here [at UT Austin] are expected to be critical thinkers and reasoners. Eighteen-year-olds are not just large children. They're young adults. If the society grants them the civic responsibilities of adults, the function of the university should be to help them apply the resources of the intellect to the problems that are plaguing our culture. A course like "Writing About Difference" [English 306] presumes students are capable and willing to assume that kind of citizenship, and the committee I chaired assumed that democracy can only work if teachers are willing to teach students to confront real issues. (24)

Looking at ways in which the intellect of individuals can be put to work in order to address problems plaguing our culture is one version of critical pedagogy. Looking at Supreme Court opinions, as the English 306 syllabus proposed, centered in part on racial discriminatory circumstances, might show individuals how legal processes work. It would encourage an analysis of court documents as texts that, up until then, had largely evaded them because of their relegation to the legal arena.

Such a pedagogical stance is consistent with CRT in that a major tenet of CRT is that race can impact the way legal cases are decided. Looking at legal opinions also allows for the critique of law as a construct that changes meaning; after the 1960s and 1970s, the English 306 course was seen as privileging previously disenfranchised races, but that changed with a manipulation of the new "equality rhetoric" associated with the 1980s. The precept behind such a pedagogical stance hinges on the ideal that textual interactions and publications have real material consequences. The ways these legal exchanges get decided says a great deal about how society views racial relations and cultural, historic, and national attitudes. Being aware of these exchanges and how they work can aid in the practice of participatory democracy.

As I mention above, this is one pedagogical response to instilling a greater social awareness in students. Unfortunately, this response was halted by a public which wholeheartedly believed that such practices constituted "brainwashing." It is ironic that the ability to think here is translated as "brainwashing," and that teaching the canons and traditional knowledge is considered what teaching should be because it is right and true for a select few with power. The point I am attempting to make here is that my suggestion for the incorporation of critical historiography in writing classes is a response to the counterrevolution of "right-wingers." They believe that their version of truth that is commonly accepted and included in canonical historical accounts is the only one. Traditional historiography, while now believed to be contingent and incomplete, has indeed ignored the history of large segments of the U.S. population and clearly needs to be questioned, reconstructed, and supplemented with new and previously unknown histories and experiences.

What I have emphasized in this chapter is the connection between the inclusive and changing 1870s, through the lens of the Eastern and Midwestern educational institutions, and the accommodationist and revolutionary 1960s, and its effect upon the field of Composition Studies. I have also considered the Chicano Movement as a possible missing historical contribution of the field to critical pedagogy. I looked at the conservative backlash of the 1990s as the cause of reversing any gains made in the intellectual arena and halting the efforts of minorities to gain equal access to education and equal consideration within a field's mainstream scholarship. I attempted to show the effects of this political climate upon Composition and the current need to counter conservative pedagogical trends with critical historical critique within the writing classroom.

I have done so by concentrating on the need to reconsider the Chicano Movement and its pedagogically critical attributes within the context of Composition Studies in the late 1960s and 1970s. This argument for the reconsideration of the history of Composition Studies as well as for a new pedagogical strategy that emphasizes the inclusion of historiographic texts will be argued for in the next chapter, which concentrates on the political climate of the 1990s and its effect on multicultural curricula. I provide some important statistics relating to the heterogeneous and growing Chicanx/Latinx population in the U.S.A. to establish the importance of providing appropriate pedagogical strategies to ensure their educational success and the opportunity for mainstream students to learn more about these populations. I then examine "brands" of muliticulturalism defined by Paula Moya and then consider the ways these "brands" of muliticulturalism are practiced at Hispanic-serving institutions.

CHAPTER 7

Multiculturalism's Conflict: A Nation's Quest for Accommodation and Excellence in Education

After the conservative backlash in the 1980s against multicultural curricula, as exemplified by the public reaction to English 306 at the University of Texas at Austin, there emerged counterresponses with the election of President Bill Clinton. He showed a commitment to increasing educational opportunities for minorities under the premise that greater educational opportunities enabled minority populations to contribute positively to the national economy. Thus, the rhetoric of race and culture gave way to the rhetoric of economics under Clinton's administration. The backlash of the 1980s was met with a new discourse from the Democratic Party that offered a new platform focused on convincing white working-class and middle-class Americans of both parties that new educational policies emphasizing universal curricula would improve educational systems for all students without singling out particular groups for benefits, as was said to have occurred under Affirmative Action. Multicultural education, thus, only became justified by the manner in which it could produce productive citizens who could fulfill a growing number of technical jobs and contribute to our world economic presence and status. Meritoractic rhetoric was, once again, revived as the end of Affirmative Action took place during the 1990s.

During the 1990s, what some called the divisive polices of Affirmative Action were ended; as a result, many of the gains made in the 1960s were overturned as being too concerned with achieving racial equity and with being "politically correct" at the expense of national standards. Civil rights gains were now seen as "outdated" and replaced with policies that stressed

© The Editor(s) (if applicable) and The Author(s) 2016   125
I.D. Ruiz, *Reclaiming Composition for Chicano/as and Other Ethnic Minorities*, DOI 10.1057/978-1-137-53673-0_7

"merit" at the expense of the goals of multicultural curricula. Affirmative Action was said to have led to lower standards due to the educational leniency of the 1970s and the multicultural, divisive educational admissions policies based upon identity politics. However, one has to wonder if such policies were eliminated because of the fear that the University would have to change to accommodate the growing racial, cultural, linguistic, and ethnic diversity within their institutions. In a sense, then, the political rhetoric changed in a manner that would, quite coincidentally, avoid further diversity in higher educational institutions by aiding minority admissions in a minimal sense.

In, *Racial Formation in the United States* (1994), Michael Omi and Howard Winant explain that political expedience led to a Democratic platform that focused upon universalism rather than divisive identity politics:

> The Democrats' approach…aspired to "universalistic" rather than "group specific" reforms. With their appeals firmly directed toward white suburban voters, and their emphasis on economic stagnation…rather than social and racial inequality, the Democrats went on to retake the presidency…In 1992, for the first time in almost half a century, the Democratic Party platform made no specific pledge to address racial injustices and inequalities. (147 and 151)

Clinton's appeal to universal policies that did not concentrate on racial divisiveness[1] or identity politics came largely out of the political climate of the 1990s. The conservative backlash of the 1980s heightened in the next decade when political struggles over education led to efforts by conservatives to deny all but the most basic kinds of education to members of groups they deemed unworthy (Moya 140–141). For example, voters in California passed (by a margin of 59–41 %) Proposition 187[2] in 1994, and Affirmative Action came under attack as more white Americans claimed that minority recipients of this redress program were gaining an unfair advantage (141).

---

[1] See also "The Racial Futility Component in Black Voting" (Bell 648–649). In this piece, Professor Paul Frymer "traces the party's move to the right, with emphasis on Clinton's call for welfare reform and for cutbacks on 'excessive' employment benefits, both widely perceived as benefiting 'undeserving blacks'" (648).

[2] That ballot measure, which was heavily funded by conservative political groups, sought to deny to the children of illegal immigrants (most of who are assumed to be Latinxs) the right to any free public education whatsoever.

Moya explains that in the decade of the 1990s, these policy initiatives from the culture wars of the 1980s made educational innovations in multiculturalism increasingly difficult for progressive educators to justify:

> The culture wars of the 1980s brought to the center of the American consciousness the link between politics and education. Faced with movements toward more inclusive and culturally sensitive educational curricula at the primary, secondary, and postsecondary levels—efforts brought about, in part, by the new social movements of the 1960s and early 1970s—political conservatives responded by decrying the decline of the national educational system. The chief targets of their attacks were multicultural education and ethnic studies, educational reform movements aimed at remedying discrimination in education. (139)

Faced with this conservative backlash, advocates of educational initiatives who support popular and curricular diversity in education have found themselves, since then, scrambling to respond adequately to the charges leveled against them. These charges alleged that they sacrificed standards in favor of "accommodationist" muliticultural pedagogies such as those based upon identity politics, often, but not solely, found in Ethnic Studies departments and classes (143).

Clinton's focus on universalism and the improvement of the economy made it possible for him to recognize those institutions already heavily populated by Hispanics as officially sanctioned Hispanic-serving institutions (referred to as HSIs from this point on). They became eligible for federal funds to improve their curricula, educational facilities, and outreach programs. Thus, the Hispanic population in the U.S.A. became recognized as a growing economic concern with an increasingly expanding population and as being a critical portion of the U.S. citizenry with real economic and voting power.

An example of this Democratic response is seen in Clinton's official recognition of educational institutions composed of 25% or more students of Latinx descent. In *Teaching Writing with Latino/a Students: Lessons Learned at Hispanic Serving Institutions* (2007), Cardenas et al. explain that "[i]n 1994, President Clinton signed the executive order, Educational Excellence for Hispanic Americans, under the reauthorization of the Higher Education Act. This act officially recognized the government designation of HSI's [Hispanic Serving Institutions]" (3).[3]

---

[3] Another organization which further recognized the importance and increasing presence of HSIs was the President's Advisory Commission on Educational Excellence for Hispanic

Furthermore, HSIs are "accredited, degree granting, public or private, non-profit colleges or universities with 25% or more total undergraduate full-time equivalent (FTE) Hispanic enrollment" (Laden 186).

While these institutions were long in operation before this recognition, the official status given to these institutions brought opportunities for more funding, curricular development, as well as recognition of the growing importance of an educated class of Latinx workers. These changes undoubtedly enabled the curricula at these schools to reflect a pedagogy that was more inclusive of the needs of the unique student populations found at these colleges. However, merely enabling an institution to reflect more diversity in its curricula does not necessarily mean that action will be taken to change curricula. Indeed, oftentimes, the curricula stay the same as it was prior to receiving HSI funds and recognition. I've experienced teaching at a couple of different HSIs and the curriculum does not reflect the needs of this population as far as being ethnically empowering or relevant to their cultural backgrounds. What needs the curriculum does reflect is a need for Latinxs to become literate in Standard English as consistent with one of the missions of the University and our field. The tenets then of multicultural education were all but discredited during this decade.

HSIs have become fruitful sites for further research in Education and in Composition Studies and should be considered in any discussion of the history of the teaching of Composition at teaching universities, including state universities that grew out of the normal school tradition discussed earlier in this book. The Cardenas et al. volume suggests an examination of HSIs curricula, including the teaching of Composition; this research initiates a study that allows for a comparison with Composition programs at other educational institutions. It is time for Composition needs of the Latinxs population to be considered in studies that focus on the way Composition is conceptualized and one way to begin this assessment is by examining how it is carried out at HSI locations. When we take a closer look at HSIs, we also see that there is a geographical concentration of them in the Southwest, a region ignored in traditional histories of Composition. Thus, taking a look at these institutions will enable the U.S.A. to further enrich the history of Composition and Pedagogy. In what follows, I take a

Americans (Commission) in 1994. Established by President Clinton's Executive Order 12900, and renewed by President George W. Bush, it issues a collective call to each executive agency to "increase Hispanic American participation in Federal education programs where Hispanic Americans currently are underserved" (Laden 190).

close look at these institutions by defining what they are and their educational mission, and examining how the populations present at these institutions have influenced the way Composition pedagogy is practiced there. This pedagogy clearly challenges traditional conceptions of Composition Pedagogy, such as current-traditional rhetoric and the Harvard model.

What follows here is a general description of the heterogeneous population of U.S. Latinxs that has become the largest minority population, as demonstrated by available statistics. I rely on Kirklighter et al.'s pathbreaking book *Teaching Writing with Latino/a Students: Lessons Learned at Hispanic Serving Institutions* to provide a snapshot of the type of pedagogical innovations taking place at these nontraditional institutions, changes not recorded in the official history of Composition. One of my initial findings reveals that there is a conflict between traditional multicultural pedagogies and more universal educational pedagogies among HSIs. In what follows, I first establish the population trends for Latinx populations. I then look more in depth into HSIs and their characteristics and provide an example of conflicting pedagogical approaches that cannot be easily classified as traditional or universal. In many cases, the attributes of the student populations make their classification difficult.

A GROWING POPULATION: THE HETEROGENEOUS LATINX PRESENCE

In a 2002 Pew report titled "U.S.-Born Hispanics Increasingly Drive Population Developments," the Latinx population is reported to "...defy simple characterizations." According to this study, this diversity of identity characteristics results from

> a diversity of groups that differ not only by country of origin but also by immigrant status and racial self-identification. Having grown rapidly through immigration, its future dynamics will increasingly be driven by today's young native born. Though concentrated in established urban areas, Latinos also retain a large rural presence and have recently spread to new areas of the country. (1)

My case study (presented hereafter) takes place in California, a state with one of the largest Latinx populations; here, I will address the rising Latinx population trends in California and in San Diego. The 2006 U.S. Census Bureau reports that California's population is composed of 35.9 % of Latinxs of any race. The San Diego population is composed of 30.1 % Latinxs, while 35.9 % of San Diego's population speaks a language other than English, and as the 2000 U.S. Census Bureau reports, the dominant language spoken by Americans other than English is Spanish. The fact that more than one-third of the state's population is of Latinx descent and that there is a growing Spanish-speaking population should have spurred interest in a bilingual curriculum. Yet, many of our educational institutions still practice English-only curricula and genuine bilingual programs can only be found at sparsely distributed "magnet" schools where educational experiments are being carried out. Instead of these ad hoc measures, the state needs to look more closely at what can make the Spanish-speaking or bilingual populations of California and, more specifically, San Diego, successful in their pursuit and path toward higher education.

Nationally, in states along the U.S.–Mexico border, the majority of public school students are ethnic minority students; in fact, people of Mesoamerican descent constitute the majority of Texas public school students. These demographic changes point to a need for the Composition profession to reconsider how we teach writing and the type of materials we use in courses serving these students. Chicano Compositionist, Jaime Mejía believes that current cross-cultural and multicultural readers Composition publishers are producing have yet to provide reasons for endorsement by the Latinx Caucus associated with the Conference on College Composition and Communication (CCCC). These publishers, according to Mejía, are committing gross oversights of current domestic realities associated with the growing, heterogeneous Latinx population. If this trend continues, not only the publishers, but also the scholarship associated with the field of Composition shall further increase cultural misunderstandings and racism which have plagued people of Mexican descent in the U.S.A. for over a century and a half. HSIs, however, are educational institutions which are continuously providing new insights into the pedagogical innovations that successfully contribute to a growing Latinx college-going and graduating population.

Hispanic-Serving Institutions

According to Cardenas et al., 50 % of Latinx students in higher education currently attend HSIs: "HSI's are among the most underserved and under-recognized sites for teaching, research, and educational activism. While Hispanic populations represent the largest and fastest-growing

minority group in the nation, the professional visibility and national prestige of HSI's have failed to keep pace" (ix). Cardenas et al. take a deeper
look at what is taking place at HSIs that, though mainly concentrated in
California and Texas, can actually be found in several U.S. states. The
following list shows which states have HSIs and how many HSIs each of
these states has:

> Arizona (19), California (109), Colorado (7), Florida (19), Illinois (11),
> Massachusetts (2), New Jersey (5), New Mexico (25), New York (21),
> Oklahoma (1), Oregon (1), Pennsylvania (1), Texas (54), and Washington
> (1). As might be expected, California, Texas, and New Mexico have the
> highest number of HSIs reflecting Latinos' deep historical roots in that
> region of the U.S. (Laden 191)

The 2004 list of HSIs provided by Laden reveal that California is the
state with the most HSIs, which are steadily growing in numbers. This
is the state I am currently teaching in. Thus, it seems appropriate for me
to consider these institutions, even though my previous institution, the
University of California, San Diego (UCSD), is not characterized as an
HSI. Many students who attend HSIs strive to gain admission into institutions such as UCSD. Latinx population demographics at UCSD are
actually quite disturbing when compared with the community's Latinx
population. Even more important to consider is that San Diego is composed of 30 % Latinx, yet UCSD is only composed of 8 % Chicanxs/
Latinxs. There is a significant disproportion in numbers. Pedagogical
practices and admissions policies utilized at HSIs and mainstream universities also differ, though how they differ is still a subject of debate.
What, then, can be gleaned from HSIs and their success in educating
Chicanxs/Latinxs.

HETEROGENEITY/PROBLEMS WITH TRADITIONAL MULTICULTURALISM/ANALYSIS OF WHAT IS HAPPENING AT HSIs

According to Laden, there is a reasonable explanation as to why there
are so few Latinxs at mainstream universities. She explains the situation in terms of accessibility, noting that "Latinos take advantage of
the educational offerings available to them, by enrolling in colleges
and universities in their communities" (188). Most Latinxs taking

advantage of higher educational opportunities are largely concentrated in HSIs. However, their presence at these institutions does not absolve mainstream institutions from the poor showing of Latinxs. In fact, the concentration of Latinxs at HSIs contributes to the segregationist pattern of education. Laden finds mainstream institutions at fault for not addressing the near absence of Latinxs in the University system. She states that

> [i]t is not enough to let HSIs do the majority of educating of this population; other higher education institutions must assume their share and play significant roles, too, in this process or Hispanics will be stratified within higher education to only HSIs and the like. (195)

The recurring argument for addressing the educational needs of Latinxs in the U.S.A. is generally linked to the growth of the population. This argument is well articulated by Margarita Benítez and Jessie DeAro in "Realizing Student Success at Hispanic-Serving Institutions." They make clear that the problem is more than an ethnic problem: "Given the increasingly diverse population in the U.S.A., and the national interest in fostering a skilled workforce and an educated and engaged citizenry, all educators must work to support these students; minority student success is no longer a minority issue" (35). However, they also lament the fact that there are no specific references to what is actually contributing to students' success at HSIs. Laden agrees that "[t]he enrollment and completion rates for students who attend HSIs tell the U.S.A. that something good is clearly going on. What the statistical data do not give us is a detailed picture of how this is happening within HSIs nor do they tell us how many Latinxs are still not doing well or why" (193). In what follows, I examine what has been reported about an institution of higher learning composed of a large Latinx population, namely an HSI: the University of Texas, Rio Grande Valley (UTRGV).

I am particularly interested in reports that attempt to gauge the degree of literacy success and access for students of Latinx origin at UTRGV. These reports are part of a study that appears in *Teaching Writing with Latino/a Students: Lessons Learned at Hispanic Serving Institutions.* This book looks at a variety of curricular programs implemented at HSIs and evaluates their contribution to success or struggle. What characterizes the curricula discussed is that most of the programs consider the students' individual cultural and linguistic circumstances. While statistics cannot give a detailed picture of how success is being measured at HSIs, an analysis of the curricula programmed for use at HSIs can give us an idea of what takes place. The curricula addressed in Cardenas et al.'s book range from those that concentrate specifically on Chicanx/Latinx issues within the nation (such as bilingualism and feelings of alienation or inadequacy) to those that are more mainstream and focus on practicing argumentation and writing narratives.

Before talking about the specifics of what reportedly takes place at one of these institutions, I would like to give the reader a way to classify the pedagogical approaches I discuss in terms of whether they are traditional or universal multicultural programs. I will also analyze the curricula discussed to determine whether the multiculturalist practice seems in line with the current political trend of universalist education that avoids divisive curricula.

Paula Moya advocates for universalist multicultural curricula. The universalism she refers to is a brand of multiculturalism that concentrates on the identity politics of the 1980s. While this may sound divisive at first glance and a bit out of touch with current post-structural and postmodern theories that dismiss the notion of identity, upon closer analysis, one sees the benefits and the necessity of studying groups of people that come from underrepresented groups such as Chicanxs/Latinxs and African Americans in relation to their specific needs and skills. Moya's *Leaning from Experience: Minority Identities, Multicultural Struggles* (2002) dedicates a chapter to defining and analyzing the most popular "brands" of multiculturalism that have been heavily attacked by the conservative factions in the wake of the culture wars. Although she does not agree one should completely do away with identity politics of ethnic groups, she does advocate a brand of multiculturalism based upon universalist premises because the benefits of doing so are actually quite similar to the benefits suggested by Clinton in his election to the presidency—everybody wins.

Moya states that one of the main goals of her book is to "provide a reconstructed universalist justification for the kind of work being done by myself and other ethnic studies scholars" (2). The work she is referring to justifies why studying specific ethnic groups is a practice of scholarly inquiry that can actually help the university become more universal by studying previously understudied groups and cultures. I quote her at length to show her rationale for such a curriculum:

I demonstrate that studying the texts and lived experiences of Chicana/os (and other marginalized people) is necessary to construct a more objective understanding of the (social and economic) world we live in. I show that while the experiences of Chicana/os are admittedly subjective and particular, the knowledge that is gained from a focused study of their lives can have general implications for all Americans. The texts and lived experiences of Chicana/os and other marginalized people are rich sources of frequently overlooked information about our shared world. [I]f there did not exist entire groups of people such as "Chicana/os" or "women" whose histories and accomplishments have been systematically ignored or distorted by previous generations of scholars, then there would be no reason for present-day scholars to devote themselves to a focused study of the histories, socioeconomic situations, political movements, or literary and cultural productions of those groups. (3)

Here, Moya offers her argument for a curriculum in response to right-wing conservative arguments against divisive multicultural curriculums. These arguments are based on the premise that divisive policies and curricula do nothing more than divide a nation of people that can only benefit from seeing their similarities and not their differences. This position is against quota systems that, for them, unfairly give advantages, such as college admissions, to people based on their group affiliation.

I agree with Moya's claim that schools need to advance multicultural curricula that concentrate upon what can be gained through studying specific groups of ethnic peoples. This view is contrary to multicultural pedagogies which concentrate on "victims" of society that can only be granted true equal opportunity to higher education when their victimized status is recognized. So instead of focusing on their victim status, this approach concentrates on what is different about them. In my assessment of the curricula described at UTRGV, I cannot provide a comprehensive taxonomy of what every multicultural curriculum looks like or classify each as universal or divisive. I can, however, provide comparisons of pedagogies found at alternative institutions with large populations of minorities such as HSIs with those at other institutions. The goal is to demonstrate that there are lessons to be learned from such institutions for mainstream institutions. Such was the goal of the Clinton administration by recognizing these institutions as an opportunity for Hispanics to receive the attention they have long deserved in comparison with the historically black colleges and tribal colleges in operation since the late nineteenth century. However, since the goal of both Clinton and Moya is universalism and not segregation-ist institutions or curricula, mainstream institutions can learn from HSIs. They are committed to implementing curricula that benefit all students and provide critical tools with which to become critics of their culture (one of the goals of Composition pedagogy for quite some time now).

Moya relies on her post-positivist realist theory of identity, explained in Chap. 2, in order to argue for a multicultural curriculum that considers identities of multicultural populations:

> [P]ost-positivist realist theory of identity posit[s] one way in which pro-gressive intellectuals might go about fostering the conditions conducive to working toward a better society. I argue that when we pay the right kind of attention to our own and others' particularity, we position our-selves to develop a more productive understanding of our universal human-ity. Working with a reconstructed notion of the human universal, I end by defending the value of cultural diversity on the basis of an understanding of multiculturalism as epistemic cooperation. (15)

Moya emphasizes that her theoretical position is "post-postivistic," not absolute or deterministic. She stresses that her notion of the human uni-versal is reconstructed and that identities are constructed in the same ways post-structuralists argue that knowledge is constructed, namely by the interaction between people, knowledges, and the discourses that produce those knowledges. Thus, there is no a priori identity or knowledge prior to individuals.

Instead, it is individuals who produce both identities and knowledges about what constitutes their experience. However, her theory encom-passes the realist theory of identity as part of her theoretical framework because she does not dismiss identity altogether as many post-modernists do. She further explains her theoretical position in the following way:

> Against postmodernist theorists, I show that the extreme linguistic con-structivism informing postmodernist conceptions of identity impedes rather than enables the achievement of the liberatory political goals they claim as their own. Through an elaboration of the postpositivist realist theory of identity, I demonstrate that effective political agency is best located in the project of examining and explaining, rather than dismissing or subverting, identity. (12)

Moya's theory provides a lens through which to analyze the uses of identity in the following pedagogies practiced in various classrooms at HSIs.

DESCRIPTION OF TWO PEDAGOGIES AT THE UNIVERSITY OF TEXAS, RIO GRANDE VALLEY

The essay I will first address from *Teaching Writing with Latino/a Students: Lessons Learned at Hispanic-Serving Institutions*, "Discovering a 'Proper Pedagogy': The Geography of Writing at the University of Texas-Pan American," is written by Dora Ramírez-Dhoore and Rebecca Jones. It discusses their attempts at finding a proper pedagogy for a university writing curriculum at a university made up of more than 80 % Latino/a students.

The first interesting characteristic of this study is that the two writing teachers involved in this study come from two very different backgrounds:

> Dora grew up in a farm-working, poverty-level household in a rural Oregon town and is now working as an assistant professor in American literature, focusing on Latina/o studies in her research. Rebecca grew up in a white middle-class family who owned their own business in a small town in North Carolina. She studied rhetoric and composition in her PhD program and now works as a writing program administrator. (64)

The different backgrounds situate these teachers in differing spaces as they approach the competing "political material space[s]" of this South Texas university, composed of 87 % Latino/a students who are border dwellers between the U.S.A. and Mexico. Some of the students in their classes are often Mexican Nationals who "drive across the border on a daily basis" (64). The other students often are coming from underfunded and overcrowded local high schools. Education for these students often comes second to family obligations and while being expected to compete with mainstream students who attend universities and are not burdened by familial responsibilities.

As far as these students' writing abilities are concerned, they vary across the board. For example, "in each course, professors have to address the needs of students at many different levels—challenging the advanced student while finding creative ways to help the basic writer catch up. Correlating to these various levels of ability is the retention and graduate rates of students.

In 1999, for example, UTRGV only graduated 8.4 percent of their students in four years and 21 percent in five years" (Cárdenas et al. 66). Mejía, a Composition scholar who once taught at UTRGV, believes that the ability to change these retention rates, given the population demographics of this university, lies in implementing a proper pedagogy (66).[4]

Mejía believes that such a pedagogy is one that includes ethnic literatures and that also "focus[es] on the literacy of not just Latino/as but also of the indigenous folk in the United States" (52). Focusing on these literacies would challenge older notions of literacy and colonialism that often ignore the literacy practices of these populations and their efforts in challenging assimilationist perspectives by retaining their own culture and language. Implementing pedagogical practices at HSIs that are cognizant of students' backgrounds is the goal. The student demographics at HSIs correlate to Mejía's call for such pedagogical application because he believes that such a curriculum would speak directly to the needs and interests of the students. Mejía's proposal encompasses a consideration of Anzaldúa's pedagogical suggestions that ask that we take into account "other ethnicities...races...cultures...and histories' alongside the demands of both scholars and university students to perform particular standards that mark success[.] Even more importantly in this political educational space, what are our options for best practices for teaching?" (67).[5] Like Mejía, Ramírez-Dhoore and Jones also explain that a "stock" pedagogy that is based on the premise of difference does not go far enough in addressing the local circumstances of the "political educational space" in question. They state that "we must examine the particular things within a political and educational space that necessitate differences in practice and theory" (68).

RAMÍREZ-DHOORE'S CLASS

In Ramírez-Dhoore's upper-division writing class, there was a mix of students "who spoke Spanish (in a both fluent and bilingual capacity) and others who knew only English, having been 'taught out of my language,'

---

[4] See Mejía's "Bridging Rhetoric and Composition Studies with Chicano and Chicana Studies: A Turn to Critical Pedagogy," found in *Latino/a Discourses: On Language, Identity, and Literacy Education*, edited by Michelle Hall Kells, Valerie Balester, and Victor Villanueva.

[5] For a more specific discussion on the controversial role between race and literacy, see *Literacy and Racial Justice: The Politics of Learning After* Brown v. Board of Education, by Catherine Prendergast. Carbondale: Southern Illinois UP, 2003.

as one student [said]" (Cárdena et al. 68). For Ramírez-Dhoore, the students' mixed language abilities constituted what Anzaldúa refers to as a linguistic nightmare, aberration, and mestizaje. Ramírez-Dhoore explains that these varying language characteristics often result from what Anzaldúa has called "linguistic terrorism"[6] because the mixtures of language abilities are in a sense "orphaned" because they are recognized as nonofficial, nonstandard discourses and are, of course, marked by the students' Spanish in/abilities. Ramírez-Dhoore notes that, because of these linguistic characteristics, the students struggle with constructing their identity in Standard American English.

With this struggle in mind, Ramírez-Dhoore implemented readings that would allow students to identify with the authors' experiences as well. These readings included *Attending to the Margins*, edited by Michelle Hall Kells and Valerie M. Balester. This book examines the benefits of embracing the border as a myth of identity and asks whether embracing this position allows students to feel comfortable "within or against academic discourse" (69). Ramírez-Dhoore states that in the class, students find their voices for the first time. However, the students do not initially view the essay "as a format that can incorporate anything besides academic discourse written in Standard American English. Perfecting this is what they desire and expect to achieve in the traditional classroom" (70). They desire to know the rules of the game in their quest for educational and professional success. They know that their current linguistic abilities are not representative of the standards of academic discourse.

In this class, students wrote essays that elucidated "the ways students equate success with moving out of poverty, learning English well, and rising to middle-class status" (71). Thus, education for these students closely related to upward mobility. Ramírez-Dhoore states that [t]heir writing shows a clear understanding of the need to 'fit into' academic discourse. There is a struggle here and one that reflects a power dynamic where one dominant group regulates and thereby influences the language and linguistic identity of another group" (70). Interestingly, these students are very aware that there are rules to the "game" of academia. These rules also indicate what is counted as academic expression and academically acceptable. Thus, it seems that there is an implied negation of these students'

---

[6] Chicana poet Gloria Anzaldua wrote of "linguistic terrorism" in *Borderlands: La Frontera*: "So, if you really want to hurt me, talk badly about my language. I am my language" (80–81).

culture, language, and identity, and the students play into it as if it were part of a game to be mastered. Ramírez-Dhoore confirms that these students view education as a game and "re-create" the rules that regulate when they can and cannot speak their "foreign tongue." As a result of this apparent struggle, Ramírez-Dhoore believes that it is her duty to reveal how linguistic terrorism plays a part in the students' fear of expressing themselves in a "foreign" language and in their hesitancy to write in a language other than English in the academic essay format.

Through reading the students' essays and seeing their hesitancy to write in a nonstandard form, Ramírez-Dhoore sees that her students are aware of their ambiguous positions in the Academy. Thus, her pedagogical approach "allows students to articulate what they already know through experience" (72). Ramírez-Dhoore justifies her pedagogy as she frowns upon the idea that students be asked to negate their cultural and linguistic voices and, instead, adorn a Standard American English "mask." She states that "[t]his game is tiring" and that educators need "to critically analyze how this ambiguity can move educators and students forward into that third space, the liminal space of possibility" (79).

Upon analysis, I would, at first glance, characterize Ramírez-Dhoore's pedagogical practice as somewhat divisive. However, what Ramírez-Dhoore offers is valuable because she is intimately aware of these students' home backgrounds and has experienced many of the hardships that they have. Her pedagogical practice might be interpreted as being divisive in that it relies on essentialist beliefs about students and their identities. I would not characterized her pedagogical approach as universalist because of references to "masks of identity" and to "playing academic games." While it is not enough to classify a pedagogy as divisive by simply having a racial and linguistic focus/component, it is the ways in which this focus is implemented and the rationale that lies behind. Perhaps, she is still working toward that third-space pedagogy where liminal spaces bring mutual respect for cultural and linguistic diversity.

Consideration of the multicultural curricula taxonomy provided by Moya above shows the influence of the political rights and the basis of their success in terminating racial programs, which, for Moya, informs an inclusive multicultural pedagogy. It is not enough for students to simply learn about themselves, especially if they are of a "minority population," according to Moya. Students have to learn about each other in a constructive, inclusive, and critical manner. However, the course just discussed is an upper-division course.

I would, however, suggest some changes to this class if it was taught as a first-year composition course. I would suggest changes to the current structure so that it more appropriately sets a goal that is able to accommodate students from other cultures and backgrounds. As an upper-division course, it does have clear objectives, relies on a clear pedagogical rationale, and serves the student population well at this institution.

Jones' Class

Jones' class is similar to Ramírez-Dhoore's class and both teachers share students. The students are aware that they have to master academic discourse to pass the class and eventually graduate. Jones relies on the stance taken by Lisa Delpit as well as criticism of her stance to negotiate her position in the classroom. Jones takes Lisa Delpit's warning seriously. She says of Lisa Delpit, "She admonishes white middle-class professors for not recognizing their own position of power and especially for not sharing their knowledge of the discursive strategies of this position, explicitly, with their students who are not part of the 'culture of power'" (72). She also believes that "it is fine to '[t]ell [students] that their language and cultural style is unique and wonderful but that there is a political power game that is also being played, and if they want to be in on that game there are certain games that they too must play'" (73). Thus, Jones sees it as her duty to divulge her privileged position as the teacher in relation to the students while trying to negotiate her perceived "outsider" position because she is white.

She provides excerpts from several of her student essays from a Composition class in which they wrote about their literacy experiences. She is particularly struck by the students' linguistic position, perhaps because she has only dealt with white and African American students who had to worry about dialect issues in the South. She realizes that not being able to express oneself in a comprehensible manner (in English) "leaves scars that follow students into college, scars that affect their confidence" (73). After providing these excerpts, she also offers her "tentative theorizing." She explains that the reason for assigning the literacy essays is because she wanted to "allow the students to express their past concerns with learning and to help [her] understand where these students begin when they walk into [her] classes in South Texas" (76). The unique linguistic circumstances of the students in Jones' class make the outcome of assigning this essay more useful to her than it has ever been in the past.

Jones chose literacy as the theme of her class. Her students were encouraged to juxtapose "different visions of literacy with their own narratives"

(80). They read essays by Anna Quindlen and Judith Ortiz Cofer, whose essays demonstrate both privileged and deprived literacy experiences. These students also read David Bartholomae's "Inventing the University" and Deborah Brandt's "Sponsors of Literacy" to discuss what professors expect of their students. Jones also teaches the ethnographic essay that allows students to experiment with academic and personal prose. These essays allow her to plan her graduate course, which focuses on preparing high school English teachers, according to her students' experiences.

What is interesting about this class, then, is that dialogue is taking place between the students' experiences and the teacher's manner of utilizing them to teach even more students (her upper-division students). As a result, Jones implemented lessons she learned in a graduate class she taught where they discussed how by doing so, they could perhaps change these experiences for other students. There is a more inclusive approach at play here in that the literacy essay is one Jones has taught in very different geographical areas: the South and the Southwest. Different outcomes from these essays produce different results for her in terms of her pedagogy and understanding of her students' needs. Unlike Ramírez-Dhoore's class which asks students to focus on their individual differences in order to express themselves in a linguistically unhindered manner without any further consequences, Jones' class has breadth.

While I see the importance of classes such as the one taught by Ramírez-Dhoore, my argument, here, is to advocate for multicultural curricula that are more inclusive of a broader spectrum of populations for the purpose of having dialogue between different types of students with different life experiences. In this case, the dialogue taking place between the teacher and the student is very important in producing new goals and directions for teaching. Jones' graduate students become very interested in bilingual education, and it is a goal of the class for students to be able to gain the skills to "combat through more respectful pedagogies, the damaging misconceptions about bilingual students (in America) as being less intelligent and less willing to learn" (76). Jones says that her graduate students "... want to avoid, for their students, the pitfalls [her] freshman students have written about in their literacy essays" (Cárdenas et al. 76).

Both of these pedagogical experiences took place at UTRGV, an HSI. They demonstrate the desire for both teachers to allow their students to be "able to talk about past literacy practices and to reconcile them with current expectations and to change those expectations through this interrogation" (Cárdenas et al. 82). However, the ways these teachers envisioned reaching this goal were different. I am struck by the way these teachers characterized their different approaches as being influenced by their own literacy backgrounds. Ramírez-Dhoore, for example, is described as being a student who learned academic discourse by "mimicking (while learning to subvert) the discourse taught to her in the academic space" (81). Jones, on the other hand, describes employing a discourse born out of her white privileged status. These competing experiences as well as the upper-division class designation seem to have influenced the different pedagogies implemented to reach the same goal at UTRGV. Is it possible that these two teachers were influenced by both exclusionist and inclusionist experiences?

Ramírez-Dhoore states that she had problems, for example, with learning the concept of argument. For her, argument meant not agreeing with another's position instead of a type of scholarly prose. It seems then that Ramírez-Dhoore experience is marked by an ambiguous relationship to the academy, as is the case for many Latinxs in the U.S.A. However, I argue that the way to approach this ambiguity is by implementing an inclusionist muliticultural pedagogy that all students can learn from—a pedagogy in which students can learn about others' experiences similar to the ways Ramírez-Dhoore and Jones learned about one another and their position in relation to the Academy.

Experiences of exclusion, however, are not only found in multicultural practices and in mainstream pedagogies. In a paper delivered at the 2006 CCCC in New York, Mejía told his audience of an incident that demonstrates outright exclusionist practice that still plagues those of Latinx descent, daily. He stated:

> On November 17th, 2006, MALDEF, the Mexican American Legal Defense and Educational Fund, the Mexican American counterpart to the NAACP [National Association for the Advancement of Colored People], issued a press release announcing their victory in a lawsuit against the principal of an elementary school in the Dallas Independent School District. The principal at Preston Hollow Elementary School, Teresa Parker, segregated English-speaking Latino and African American minority students on the basis of their race, in violation of the U.S. Constitution. The federal judge in the case ordered the principal to stop the segregation and pay $20,000 in punitive damages to injured plaintiff students. In this case, the Court found that the plaintiff students "were assigned in a grossly disproportionate manner to ESL-designated classes, while their Anglo peers were assigned, with few exceptions, to General Education classes, also known as neighborhood classes, which were predominantly Anglo" (MALDEF). MALDEF's press release further stated that "The Court was 'baffled that in this day and

age, Defendants [relied] on what is, essentially, a 'separate but equal' argument'" (MALDEF). The elementary school's principal apparently instituted this intentional segregation in order to prevent white flight from the Anglo neighborhood where this school was located. (CCCC 2006)

In the face of such current exclusionary practices in educational institutions, Composition scholars should still strive to create pedagogies that might take these types of exclusionary practices into consideration. If linguistic, racial, and social segregationist practices still exist, then how can we, as front-line Composition teachers and scholars combat such practices? Some would say that we cannot because all we do is teach writing as was part of the argument against the implementation against Brodkey's English 306. However, the experiences of these students at UTRGV show just how much of a difference one teacher can make. If teachers decide to do something else besides the stock curricula or the assigned curricula, what might be the result? Ramírez-Dhoore's and Jones' three classes are just three examples of the differences a more "respectful pedagogy" could make.

Mejía also notes that in *The Shame of the Nation: The Restoration of Apartheid Schooling in America*, Jonathan Kozol argues that racial segregation still exists in our nation and that there are negative effects affecting our nation's students as a result of these practices. One such practice is the monolingual imperative present in America's curricula. Guadelupe San Miguel Jr., scholar of U.S. history who specializes in Mexican American education, comments on English-only rhetoric that still appears in the twenty-first century:

> English-only rhetoric reminded Mexican Americans of the 1950s, when they were excluded from the public schools, provided a separate and inferior education, force-fed an assimilationist curriculum, culturally demeaned in the classrooms, and punished for speaking Spanish in school. In other words, it suggested a return to the Cold War era of official racism, institutional discrimination, cultural suppression, and structural exclusion. (50)

This type of exclusionist practice is exactly the experience discussed by both Ramírez-Dhoore's and Jones' students above. They have been scarred, as Jones realizes, in a manner that could have been prevented if exclusionist pedagogies and practices were reexamined in the context of the needs of international cooperation and linguistic pluralism.

Mejía further reveals that there is a "virtual absence of Rhetoric and Composition graduate programs in Texas which can serve the needs of Texas Mexicans [that] is coupled by the complete absence of existent programs elsewhere which are directly focusing on our needs" (CCCC 2006). I share this sentiment with Mejía. In preparation for this talk by Mejía, he came across an e-mail I wrote as a response to a query sent by Cristina Kirklighter who sought information from the 4-C's Latinx Caucus for the 4-C's Executive Committee about what writing classes should include. Here's what I stated about Latinos working within our field:

There is no marked entry point or recognition of Latinxs in Composition. Our group has been one that has been largely ignored, yet called upon when it seems expert opinions and experiences are needed in order to understand the "bilingual problem" or the limited English speakers. We [in the Latinx Caucus] are not akin to the African American caucus in that our brands of English are not the only "dilemma" that we must deal with; we have to deal with an actual language being torn away and denigrated on a daily basis because it is [deemed] substandard. So, what seems to be a catch-22 for Latinxs in Composition is that instead of fighting to retain our language and culture, we actually aid in the constant erasure and denigration of our own language in the name of an "official discourse." We might come to Composition as one means of finding a respect for and an addition to that "official discourse"; however, oftentimes this does not happen. We become committee members whose goal it is to let the strange become familiar with the intent to know and perhaps annihilate those differences. I know this sounds harsh but this is the current state of our professional participation in the professional associations affiliated with Composition Studies.

When does a writing class become something else? A writing class is already something else when it is an attempt at denigrating the many at the expense of the few. Composition is involved in creating, maintaining and devaluing culture. It validates and negates at the same time. Therefore, one cannot say that simply teaching grammar in composition is what makes it a writing class, or teaching the five paragraph theme is what makes it a writing class, or teaching rhetoric is what makes it a disciplined writing class—because teaching all of these things inherently involves teaching and disseminating culture. Therefore, compositionists are almost always political actors, and the way that I see my group's role in acting politically is to tell the students ahead of time that this is what is going to happen to them; otherwise, my group will have participated in what they have experienced in painful numbers. Therefore, maybe I see my group's role as one of the demystifiers who realize that the institution is always larger than they are. However, Composition Studies, as a field, needs to realize the unique position that my group has [and has had] in [the] negotiation of identity and language, as we have probably the longest history in negotiating bicultural, bilingual, and multi-dialectical associations that have been comprehensively chronicled—just not in Composition. (Ruiz e-mail)

I will comment briefly on what I meant by this compact e-mail and connect this opinion with the purpose of this book, which is to argue for a Critical Historiographic writing curriculum in Composition classrooms. For the moment, I would like to demonstrate that other Latinx Compositionists share my sentiments about the role of Latinxs in Composition.

As stated earlier, we do occupy a marginal position. This marginal position, discussed by Richard Delgado, a critical race theorist, places Latinx scholarship in the realm of the ambiguous and substandard, and these labels are unjustified. However, given the demographics for the future trends for the Latinx populations, it is imperative that Compositionists begin paying more attention to the needs of growing, diverse students such as those Ramírez-Dhoore and Jones write about. Mejía also agrees with my sentiment about the lack of disciplinary respect within Rhetoric and Composition. He states,

What Iris Ruiz audaciously touches upon that I find so incisively compelling is that, as practitioners within the field of Rhetoric and Composition Studies, Latinxs have typically not been allowed to bring an important part of our culture or identity into writing classes. We have not been allowed nor have we been successful in creating an entry point into this field. Moreover, we will indeed be complicit in furthering the erasure of important parts of our ethnic identity. This complicity in furthering our ethnic cultural demise is something I have labored over for many years, both as a teacher and as a scholar within our field. Yet, as Ruiz informs us, Latinxs for centuries have been extremely talented negotiators of language and identity in the United States. As bilingual and bicultural negotiators, we have sought not to compromise our identity nor our proficiencies in more than one language, in more than one culture. Such negotiating skills should be the rhetorical coin of the national realm, yet the little value that the mainstream has recognized of such rhetorical skills all too often gets diminished throughout all of academia. At the crossroads of ambiguity, we're told to leave behind what we value most in the safe houses of our ethnic identity. (CCCC 2006)

A New Vision for Multicultural Inclusionist Curriculums

Mejía has a vision that many before have had. Unfortunately, this vision has not become a reality even when the reality of our nation's U.S.–Mexico border states is that ethnic minorities are the majority of public school students today: people of Mesoamerican descent, for example, constitute the majority of Texas public school students. This vision of bilingualism includes the possible placement of Anglo school children in bilingual classes where these students study both languages and our many Latinx cultures. Mejía asks,

> What if these same Anglo students had these two languages as centers of their academic study throughout their public schooling and then entered into our first-year college composition classes as bicultural bilinguals? Where would our field be then? Would Latinxs then have the kind of entry point into our profession that Ruiz and Linda Brodkey envision? (CCCC "English's 'Other' 2006).

He asks some interesting questions in relation to our shared vision. The vision is one that is consistent with a multicultural inclusive pedagogy that asks students to learn from one another. Instead, a more colonial relationship asks many students to negate a very, important part of themselves at the cost of the exclusionary pedagogical practices of the academy, including some of those practiced in Composition.

As Latinxs continue to grow and participate in the electoral process, will Composition respond to this growing population and the reality of its linguistic and cultural circumstances in relation to the University? If we continue to marginalize this population and call for their acculturation instead of a greater understanding of them, cultural misunderstandings and racism will continue to exist. Instead of marginalization and tokenization of Latinxs in Composition Studies, Mejía noted at the end of his talk that "we can create and facilitate the culturally based rhetorical changes in how we communicate with each other in the future, much as we've endeavored to do in the past" (CCCC 2006). We can build upon our strengths for the benefit of our current local, global, and diverse linguistic reality.

CRITICISM OF MULTICULTURALISM

There are, however, some strong arguments against any type of multicultural curriculum. The main argument against multicultural curricula is that because these curricula tend to focus on difference, they unfairly "coddle" minority students and aid in the divisive recognition of "us versus them" social relationships. However, cultural traditionalists such as "[t]hose who call for a return to the study of the Western tradition argue that a curriculum focusing on the 'great books' transcends ideology because such works are intrinsically more valuable than the works that historically have not been taught" (Moya 140). This view, however, is also divisive in that it negates other great books not considered part of the traditional Western canon. This point should be obvious by now, but current debates about the inclusion of Mexican American studies in high school classes in Arizona and California, both border states, show that traditionalist pedagogical ideologies still control most public school systems.

In the face of such a conservative backlash that current intellectual circles are now experiencing, it is imperative for multicultural educators such as those in ethnic studies "to have sound intellectual and *universalist* justifications for their programs, as well as for the salience of the identities around which such programs are organized" (Moya 144). While traditionalists argue for a divisive stance, this stance is consistent with arguments that multicultural curricula decrease standards and unfairly give "preferential treatment" to minorities. However, those of us committed to an enduring multicultural understanding of our society realize the importance of incorporating a variety of voices into the classroom. This is my rationale for embracing Moya's position on universalist multicultural curricula. Such curricula cannot be easily dismissed as "coddling" or divisive. How, then, can all students learn from one another in an engaging and critical manner?

Moya suggests a universalist multicultural curriculum that "should be structured to give greater emphasis to the cultures and views of non-dominant groups" because doing so will allow all students to study subordinated cultures "as containing a potential resource of alternative ways of living in and relating to the world" (170). At first glance, this may sound divisive in that it focuses upon difference. However, the fact that traditional curricula naturalize dominant experience as normal provides the imperative for dominant students to learn about minority cultures. Furthermore, these cultures are by definition subordinated and are not "naturally" learned about through normal channels of cultural transmission. While it may sound like the classroom is used as a space to "compensate" those who have been previously denied a place in the conversation, it is not. Instead, the classroom becomes a space to facilitate the emergence of alternative perspectives and provide students with the ability to offer more objective accounts of their experiences.

To support her argument, Moya refers to an ethnographic study of three teachers who were attempting to teach a multicultural version of history; the study was conducted by John Wills at a predominantly white middle school in Southern California. The outcome of his study led him to suggest a "'multiperspectival, truly multicultural history' of the United States [that] has the potential to provide *all* students with the tools that they will need to deal effectively as active citizens with issues of structural (and especially racial) inequality" (158). His suggestion stems from his observation of the multicultural history classes which claimed to teach a multicultural approach. He observed that the only time subordinate cultures were focused upon was in relation to how they contributed or related to European cultures. Specifically, Wills states that African Americans are "discussed only in relation to the Civil War or the Civil Rights movement, Asian Americans are discussed only in relation to the building of the railroads, and Native Americans are remembered only as the friends of the early English colonists" (157). These cultures were never focused upon for their own sake or from their own perspective.

Wills' position is closely related to the perspective of a "New History" referred to Chap.1 and explicated by Eric Foner. This type of "New History" is also found in books like Howard Zinn's and James Loewen's histories, which are meant to be revisionist histories that complement traditional "watered-down" history textbooks given out by the thousands and taught from in public schools facilities. A Critical Historiographic approach would take this "New History" approach a step further in that it would ask students to engage their own historical research. It would also ask them to complicate those traditional historical accounts with their own personal cultural knowledge and academic research into primary documents and alternative scholarly research practices such as ethnography and interviews.

INCLUSIONIST, UNIVERSAL MULTICULTURAL PEDAGOGY: CRITICAL HISTORIOGRAPHY IN FIRST-YEAR COMPOSITION

As I mentioned in the section before, I want to briefly elaborate on what I meant in the e-mail to which Mejía refers. I believe Latinxs are still marginalized in the field of Composition, not only within scholarly Composition Studies but also in terms of pedagogies considered for dealing with linguistic minorities in the writing classroom. However, interesting pedagogical responses to the needs of this growing population are emerging. My specific pedagogical proposal in this book is the incorporation of Critical Historiography within Composition pedagogies. Critical Historiography allows for both an investigation into historical circumstances and current political debates. It can lead students to construct arguments which consider the ways history is constructed and how perspectivism and politics influence historical positions, narrations, and effects. Historiography also enables students to integrate previously ignored histories into their current understanding of inclusions and exclusions of populations to which they themselves may belong. The inclusion of Chicano Studies and Black Studies programs in institutions of higher education in the civil rights era is a good example of the impact that the incorporation of "new histories" can have. By looking back to previously excluded histories of these programs, one can learn how they contributed to the "cultural pride" of students. One can also learn of the purpose and intended effect of the creation of Ethnic Studies programs in the 1970s. As a matter of fact, Foner reminds us that it is because of the changes that occurred in the civil rights era and that sought to include previously excluded experiences and knowledges that a "new" historiography exists. The implementation of Critical Historiography in the writing classroom would continue this tradition of questioning and rewriting history.

Our own field has shown how histories get rewritten for the benefit of all that are involved in a discipline such as Composition Studies. And as Royster and Williams remind us,

> Composition histories show that when we consistently ignore, peripheralize or reference rather than address non-officialized experiences, inadequate images continue to prevail and actually become increasingly resilient in supporting the mythologies and negative consequences for African American students and faculty, and also for their culturally defined scholarly interests,

which in their own turn must inevitably push also against prime narratives. ("History" 582)

Royster and Williams' call to address nonofficialized experiences in the above passage is a recognition of the value of implementing a historiographic perspective in the writing classroom. But one obvious question that arises out of this book is: Why historiography? While I agree with Royster and Williams's intent to contribute minority experiences to the traditional history of Composition, I also find that we need to go beyond present-day experiences by examining our participation in history. I suggest creating a curriculum that periodizes history and allows for a study of the intervention of various previously disenfranchised or excluded populations such as African Americans and Chicanxs/Latinxs in U.S. history. Thus, in addition to adding historical minority experiences to the traditional history of Composition, I also argue for including critical writing exercises in Composition classes that address the writing of history, the exclusion of histories, and the need to recover the past.

A critical analysis of history calls for examining previously excluded historical accounts, or, rather, a historiographic perspective which considers historical accounts of particular populations, preferably those not focused upon traditional histories. This approach should also look at historical accounts as a series of narratives that often capture only part of a historical moment. Thus, I am proposing a historiographic method which, at its start, searches for the silences or the blind spots in the narration of past events and asks, "what is missing?" Specific historiographic theories that help me implement such a historiographic method in the writing classroom as well as write Critical Historiography are outlined earlier in this book. Specifically, I rely on Eric Foner's "new historical method" and Rolph-Trouillot's social contructivist historical method as well as Moya's theory of post-postivist realist theory, which attempts to recover unofficialized experiences of people of color. Recognizing that experience is constructed and made accessible to the U.S.A. through texts will allow the U.S.A. to begin to see what is textualized in some versions of history and what is left out, what is presented from the perspective of the majority population and what considers the perspective of nondominant populations.

Recovering excluded histories is akin to recovering identities in that the histories not previously considered are a necessary part of what constitutes identity formation. As such, the notion of identity also becomes one of interrogation in the same instance that history is questioned. The title of this book was originally *Shattering Glass Mirrors: A Case for Critical Historiography in the Composition Classroom*. This would be one possible way to see the mirror being shattered from without as well as from within. Once one begins to question history, one's identity can become shattered and disrupted over and over. The notion of identity, however, is still salient for trying to understand how various experiences are constructed as majority and minority. For example, in *Learning from Experience: Minority Identities, Multicultural Struggles*, Moya states that claiming an alternative experience in the form of identity grants one the ability to challenge traditional labels and imposed identities. I include the following extended passage because it also offers an example of a critical historical exercise in questioning terminology and identity labels. Moya states,

> I want to consider now the possibility that my identity as a "Chicana" can grant me a knowledge about the world that is "truer" and more "objective" than an alternative identity I might claim as a "Mexican American," a "Hispanic," or an "American" (who happens to be of Mexican descent). When I refer to a Mexican American, I am referring to a person of Mexican heritage born and/or raised in the United States whose nationality is U.S. American. The term for me is descriptive, rather than political. The term Hispanic is generally used to refer to a person of Spanish, Mexican, Puerto Rican, Dominican, Cuban, Chilean, Peruvian, and so on, heritage who may or may not have a Spanish surname, who may or may not speak Spanish, who can be of any racial extraction, and who resides in the United States. As it is currently deployed, the term [Hispanic] is so general as to be virtually useless as a descriptive or analytical tool. Moreover, the term has been shunned by progressive intellectuals for its overt privileging of the "Spanish" part of what for many of the people it claims to describe is a racially and culturally mixed heritage. A Chicana, according to the usage of women who identify that way, is a politically aware woman of Mexican heritage who is at least partially descended from the indigenous people of Mesoamerica and who was born and/or raised in the United States. What distinguishes a Chicana from a Mexican American, a Hispanic, or an American of Mexican descent is not her ancestry or her cultural upbringing. Rather it is her political awareness; her recognition of her disadvantaged position in a hierarchically organized society arranged according to categories of class, race, gender, and sexuality; and her propensity to engage in a political struggle aimed at subverting and changing those structures. (41–42)

Each identity marker referred to above stresses the post-structural aspect of identity. There are many identities that can be claimed by a woman of

Mexican descent. Each one of these markers has a historical story behind its creation. The imposition of any of these terms upon one woman can affect the way she is viewed and also the way she views her experience in the world. By adopting her own identity marker and knowing the history behind that marker, she is able to practice a type of agency that is based on a rejection of imposed identities and a historical knowledge of an alternative experience and identity. Teaching Critical Historiography in the writing classroom is one method of being able to bring about this agency while teaching critical writing skills.

Identity markers are sometimes tied to oppressive social realities but can be transformed into a form of personal and cultural agency through a Critical Historiographic pedagogy. As a woman of color who wishes to know the consequences of embracing any identity marker, whether it is adorned with negative or positive social perceptions, Critical Historiography allows me to study each term and the potential uses I can take advantage of for my own entry into an academic field of discourse. An identity marker can also provide access into certain social groups and can allow me to take it on as a positive label and use it to affirm myself as a Chicana feminist, for example. However, without the historical awareness of what each individual term means and its historical roots, I am left with a meaningless label or just a word that others will use to classify me with. I can be labeled or I can choose to assert my agency. I can also challenge derogatory and oppressive terms that can produce oppressive material realities such as refusal to listen or to take seriously. In short, a Critical Historiographic approach, if used to problematize my own identity and the history tied to it, allows me to formulate my own agency, positively and assertively.

Again, the problem of essential identities and experience arises when one talks of identity and experience as that which can be textualized and known. But I would like to remind the reader here that the position I embrace is similar to Moya's when she states that "I nevertheless contend that *some* forms of identity politics that are undertaken by members of marginalized groups in the service of creating economic, social, and political equity between different groups are epistemically and morally justifiable" (130). She adds, "Since identities are indexical—since they refer outward to social structures and embody social relations—they are a potentially rich source of information about the world we share" (135).

As far as the benefits of implementing such pedagogy in a writing classroom composed of mostly nonminority students or a percentage of both minority and nonminority students are concerned, it is clear that looking at and writing about subordinate experiences

> when shared with people who have not been oppressed or have not lived in the same way allows oppressor and oppressed alike to have a more complex and adequate understanding of their shared world than either of them could have by themselves. I argued that as long as certain identities are devalued, those identities will be epistemically valuable and politically salient. (Moya 132)

A second obvious question that arises is: Why should this critical notion of historiography be implemented in the Composition classroom in lieu of traditional multicultural theories? The answer is obviously multifaceted, and I touched on some of the problems I see with traditional multicultural curriculums in my discussion of HSIs earlier in this chapter. However, my interest in the recent conservative backlash against minority inclusion in higher education as seen in the Anti-Affirmative Action era recognizes the importance of students turning back to histories of inclusiveness to question what has caused such a backlash.

Foner sees a similar connection between race relations today and those central to the debates of Reconstruction (1870s). He states that "[t]he issues that agitate race relations today—Affirmative Action, the role of federal government in enforcing the rights of citizens, the possibility of interracial political coalitions, the relationship between economic and political equality..." were also common during the late nineteenth century (18). He thus also supports a historical connection between the present and the past regarding race relations and inequality (18). What one learns by looking at these time periods in a critical manner is that pubic political backlashes are not uncommon and are not immune to change and challenge. Students also learn to see that in times of social upheaval, many learn and witness events that are not represented in mainstream history, but might be embedded in a collective social memory in either primary texts or in the brains of those old enough to recollect the historical moment in question. This is why interviews can be part of the process in searching for primary documentation for evidence in critical historical essays.

For example, the following was found as a comment in a response to a short online news article written by Rudy Acuña titled "Massacre at Tlatelolco." Acuña discussed the perils that go along with all of the excitement of global sports events such as the Olympics and the World Cup. He mentioned the 1968 Olympics in which Jon Carlos and Tommy Smith were stripped of their gold medals. This historical event is well known to most historians and it is one that is telling of the tense race relations of the time. But the inclusion of Tlateloco is quite interesting in that no one really knows about the massacre, and no one really remembers it. Acuña remembers it, however, and, while he is well into his 70s, he remembers this important historical moment. These are the types of historical events that need to be written about, discovered, and included in discussions of civil rights. While civil rights were on display at the 1968 Olympics, the massacre was overlooked. The following comment shows a reaction from a reader that was also at a ripe adult age during this important historical moment. This is important history, though it might be dismissed as just another comment on a web article that has no significance. I include it at length, however, here because I think it is important. It is one step closer to putting this neglected experience into language to provide a more complete and complex picture of that day in Mexico City:

> I was watching these 1968 Olympics from army barracks at Fort Meade, Maryland. Knowing nothing of what was going on at Tlatelolco, I was nonetheless transformed when I witnessed the Black power salute on the podium during these games. Americans living in 1968 could not escape the reality of racism, governmental genocide, political assassinations. When flying home from 'in country', April of that year, I was detained at Kansas City Airport because of reports of roving bands of vigilantes armed with shotguns patrolling the ASB bridge as angry African Americans reacting to the assassination of MLK were setting their part of town on fire. It was the same year that I watched Bobby Kennedy's hearst pass on its way to Arlington cemetery. It was the year that I spent many weekends in the Baltimore Row House Ghetto, with an African American friend on Thanksgiving, discovering a love for pickled herring and fried fish. In 1969, when I became a college student, well, my life's work as a Chicano activist was set and continues to govern my public life. Rodolfo Acuña continues writing material that is relevant to many of our American lives especially in the 60s when our generation of Chicanos indeed changed the American experience, paving, plowing the way for the waves of Raza that continue to sweep onto our shores, empowering our continued presence that shows no sign of retreat. (Anonymous comment on Acuña's "Massacre")

This comment was written by a Latino: it is vivid, historical, local, personalized, and important. Here we have someone who discusses his own experience during this time period. What was he doing, what was he thinking, who was he with, and what were the results of his experiences? He tells the reader that he became a college student shortly thereafter and became a Chicano activist. He takes the term and uses it as a form of agency situated in a historical moment that shows what his surrounding circumstances were. As mentioned earlier, this was a time when Chicano Studies was formed. The surrounding circumstances of empowerment, acceptance, accommodation, social change, and inclusionary practices made it possible for him to become an activist and reflect on this moment some 45 years later. What a great historical moment! One can also read within his comments how he envisions himself as someone who defines himself as a Chicano activist for life. He realizes the importance of writing all of this down and sharing the experiences of their past for those who are now in another era of conservative immigrant policy. At the end, he notes that "Raza" show no signs of retreat. This is fruitful commentary for dialogue and for reflection on the second Civil Rights Movement in terms of a personal, local, and, otherwise, unknown historical memory.

I have provided two minor examples of what Critical Historiography might look like and what its aims are for writers, critical thinkers, and even for those who browse the web in thirst for knowledge, historical or not. In the next chapter, I seek to provide a rationale for what comes in the last chapter and a specific case study which took place over the course of a quarter in the spring of 2007 at UCSD. I hope it provides a useful way to look at how a Critical Historiographic writing class might function and how it can vary from class to class, instructor to instructor and institution to institution. Next is a consideration of how Critical Historiography functions as a unique "brand" of multiculturalism.

CHAPTER 8

Historiography in the Writing Classroom: A Case for Teaching Chicanx/Latinx History as an Alternative to Traditional Multicultural Pedagogies

The example of Brodkey's English 306, representative of the 1980s culture wars and the universalist response of President Bill Clinton, provides rhetorical justifications for the cultural mission of diverse educational institutions, such as Hispanic-serving institutions (HSIs). The Brodkey example points to the fear of political conservatives of changing pedagogies that stray from the classics, and it seems that Clinton's universalist rhetoric would be more effective in calming these fears and garner more support from Republican factions. The conservatives' fear of difference did lead to a verbal attack on an individual professor at the University of Texas at Austin, when the class she and her students designed departed from a focus on the classics but met the needs for understanding argumentation for a diverse student body. Brodkey's class was a direct threat to common, traditional English curricula and was met with a controversial and public debate that weakened the defense of this class and led to its demise.

On the other hand, the Clinton example shows an effective response to those afraid of difference and multiculturalism. He successfully used the rhetorical appeal of universalist justifications, which were based on economic well-being. Universalist rhetoric allowed institutions such as HSIs to continue to receive federal support despite the prevalence of multicultural pedagogies and curricula at these institutions. Implicit in this funding is a recognition of the need for institutions of higher education that can meet the needs of Latinxs. In addition, the contributions of Latinxs to the U.S. economy and current

© The Editor(s) (if applicable) and The Author(s) 2016
I.D. Ruiz, *Reclaiming Composition for Chicano/as and Other Ethnic Minorities*, DOI 10.1057/978-1-137-53673-0_8

demographics justify support for these HSIs, especially in areas that have large concentrations of Latinxs. We can learn from Clinton's effective rhetorical stance. Universalism meets economic appeals that are so important to sway Republicans to support educational initiatives for diverse populations.

However, the continued survival of these HSIs, despite threats to end critical multicultural gains brought forth by the social movements of the 1960s, has not been easy. Multiculturalism has been blamed, much like Ethnic Studies departments, for causing a decline in educational and civic standards by political conservatives. With the nation currently experiencing high unemployment rates and decreasing support for Humanities disciplines, the legitimacy of these programs is again being challenged by conservatives. Threats of cutting Ethnic Studies programs from academic curricula continue. In this moment of disarray, it has become very important for educators who are committed to multicultural education to learn how to defend their pedagogical stance by appealing to universalist justifications. *Multicultural curricula do not just benefit the multicultural segments of society; they also benefit those who have been accused of having no culture, namely "white" people.*[1]

Education, whether multicultural or not, implies the dissemination of both culture and ideology in the guise of practical skills. The intimate relationship between education and ideology has been discussed by Althusser[2] and some critical Composition scholars who see the first-year composition (FYC) class as one critical educational space where middle-class, white, male ideology is practiced and taught. In close connection to this idea, Lynn Bloom, Sharon Crowley, and Susan Miller also recognize the FYC classroom to be a critical educational space which focuses

---

[1] "Whiteness exercises such political force despite its thorough discrediting as a 'cultural color,' despite its having become the fair game of standup comics who reflect on the vacuity of 'white culture' in a nation in which so much that is new, stirring, excellent and genuinely popular—in music, fashion, oratory, dance, vernacular speech, sport and increasingly in literature, film and nonfictions writing—comes from African American, Asian American and Latino communities" (Roediger 6).

[2] In "Ideology and Ideological State Apparatuses (Notes Towards an Investigation)," Louis Althusser states, "in other words, the school (but also other State institutions like the Church, or other apparatuses like the Army) teaches 'know-how,' but in forms which ensure *subjection to the ruling ideology* or the mastery of its 'practice'" (Gupta and Sharma 88), from *The Anthropology of the State: A Reader* by Aradhana Sharma and Akhil Gupta.

on both creating and maintaining us, white, middle-class, male cultural values (see Chap. 3).

Given this inseparable connection between education and ideology, I view the Composition classroom as one location where educational theory, also known as writing pedagogy in the field, is directly involved in cultural practices. I am an avid practitioner of multicultural Composition pedagogy and believe in teaching a multicultural curriculum based on a kind of historiography that benefits all students. The cultural practice emphasized in such a classroom is to learn both about one another and from each other. My commitment to such an approach is a response to the counterrevolution of political conservatives who believe that their version of truth is the commonly accepted one and is often characterized as the norm or standard up against which everyone should be measured. *I posit that "traditional" texts such as the Western canon or Western historical accounts need to be questioned, reconstructed, and supplemented with new and previously unknown histories and experiences.* However, as mentioned in the Introduction, I am concentrating on a multicultural curriculum that will serve a universalist purpose, serving the needs of all students, including students from the largest minority population in the U.S.A., namely Latinxs.

According to the U.S. Census Bureau, from 2000 to 2006, the "Hispanic"[3] population accounted for one-half of the nation's growth, and as of July 1, 2006, there are 44.3 million "Hispanics," 14.8% of the total population of 299 million. Most Latinxs are born in the U.S.A.; however, our educational attainment trails that of the total population. For example, approximately 26% of the U.S nation's total female population has achieved an educational attainment of at least a bachelor's degree, but only approximately 13% of Latinxs have achieved the same level of education.

Given these statistics and recent trends regarding the population growth and density of Latinxs, I would like to consider the way a multicultural writing curriculum based on a post-positivist realist theory of identity differs from a traditional multicultural pedagogy, harshly criticized in the "culture wars" of the 1980s. In her work, Moya notes that political conservatives who are also opponents of multiculturalism often criticize curricula that are based on their belief that difference is divisive and unfairly accommodating to minority students. These same critics question the epistemic

---

[3] The term "Hispanic" refers to people of Latin American descent such as Mexican, Puerto Rican, Cuban, Dominican, Central American, South American, and "Other Hispanic". (US Census Bureau)

value of multicultural curricula. They do not value what could be gained from learning about a culture that is not the dominant one. *To counter these critiques, educators must reconceptualize, define, and practice multicultural curricula so that all can come to see its value.*

In discussing the various "brands" of multicultural curricula that have been practiced since the 1970s, Moya presents a taxonomy of various types of multicultural curricula. The fifth item on the taxonomy is titled "Education that is multicultural and social reconstructionist" (145–46). Of all the items in her taxonomy, this one offers a curriculum that is universal, as is evident in its objective of imparting critical thinking skills to all students, regardless of their race/ethnicity. This curriculum asks them to look at the social structures that create inequalities, such as racial, gender, and class disparities, in an effort to better understand the dynamics of social relationships and possibly alter them. Thus, this brand of multiculturalism seems to be representative of a critical universal, multicultural pedagogy or curriculum. Moya describes this curriculum as follows:

> [Education that is multicultural and social reconstructionist] thus explicitly concerns itself with developing pedagogical practices that will help students to understand the causes of oppression and inequality, and to develop strategies by which they can use power for collective betterment. The advantages of this approach are that it gives more consistent attention to issues of gender and social class than other approaches. (Moya 146)

However critical the above proposal may be, it does not come with instructional models. Because of this lack, I would like to provide the following pedagogical example of an instructional model that can be applied in a Composition class. I will label it as Moya did because it is a universalist-based curriculum: "Education that is multicultural and social reconstructionist." With this particular method, the classroom is viewed as a space where a critical engagement of the course material from a socially aware perspective is encouraged. Such a perspective allows one to critically analyze the social structures in place that ensure certain social relations that are inextricably linked to positions of power and prestige in U.S. society.

HISTORIOGRAPHY AND COMPOSITION STUDIES

In Chap. 2, I provided a theoretical framework for this study, including critical historical theory, critical race theory, and critical educational theory. However, my role as a Composition Studies scholar necessitates a contextualizing of historiography within Composition Studies and its use as a writing tool.

Writing about historical omissions and analyzing historical narratives are not new scholarly tasks or critical pedagogical tools within the field of Composition. The field has an established scholarly and pedagogical commitment to examining the writing process behind various disciplines that communicate official knowledge through writing such as Science and History. Furthermore, writing across the curriculum programs are formed at many universities that specifically associate modes of writing with various disciplines; these programs are closely associated with Composition and Rhetoric programs at these same universities. As such, implementing historical writing as a cross-disciplinary approach for FYC is not a new task for the field of Composition Studies.

In addition to the association of writing across the curriculum programs and Composition Studies, there are two important events that point to the commitment within Composition Studies to intellectual discussions regarding the writing of history, or historiography. These events are Octalogs I and II.[4] Both Octalogs I and II provide numerous methodological explanations as to the purpose and function of historical writing. These roundtable discussions took place at two different (4 C's) College Conference on Composition and Communication conferences. In both Octologs, various scholars, including James Berlin in Octolog I, came to a roundtable discussion to discuss the politics behind the writing of history or, more specifically, histories of rhetoric. In this discussion, there is evidence of a critical stance toward the writing of histories of rhetoric and of writing history in general.

The following quotation by James Berlin shows how the participants in this Octolog are considering the contingent nature of history and its various and competing purposes:

> There are no definitive histories since no historian's ruling perceptual network can ever account for the entire historical field, or even for the field it itself has selected. Thus, there must be multiple histories of rhetoric, each identifying its unique standing place—its grounds for seeing—and the terrain made available from its perspective. Most important, each history endorses an ideology, a conception of economic, social, political, and cultural arrangements that is privileged in its interpretation. These must be

---

[4] Octalog I. "The Politics of Historiography." Rhetoric Review, 7 (1988): 5–49.
Octolog II: "The (Continuing) Politics of Historiography." *Rhetoric Review* 16.1 (1997): 2244.

made self-reflexively available to scrutiny. In brief, historians must become aware of the rhetoricity of their own enterprise, rhetoric here being the designated uses of language in the play of power. ("Octolog I" 6)

This quote demonstrates that, close to 20 years ago, Compositionists and Rhetoricians were considering how the writing of history and the study of it might be incorporated in the field of Composition and Rhetoric. The way history is conveyed through language has been a concern of the field for some time now.

An example of a Composition textbook which has a unit dedicated to the analysis of official historical stories specifically geared toward first-year writing classrooms is Gary Colombo et al.'s *Framework: Culture, Storytelling, and College Writing*, which analyzes both the "The Discovery of America" story and the Rosa Parks story (it is currently out of print). I have utilized this text before, and during my sixth year of teaching, I designed a writing course that centered around the process of historical production involved in the Spanish Conquest.

The rationale for designing my Critical Historiography course is both scholarly and personal. The scholarly motivation was to implement a version of critical multicultural pedagogy that did not solely concentrate upon differences between populations of people, as is common with many multicultural writing curricula which center on identity politics. The personal reason is my personal engagement with "memoria," which is a rationale for implementing critical historiography in the writing classroom by critical educators who invite memoria in the classroom as Victor Villanueva suggests. As a scholar of color, specifically a Latina Compositionist, I wanted to live and breathe history. Thus, my race was enough of a personal reason to engage in self-discovery: an encounter with *memoria*.

Victor Villanueva has also written on *memoria* and Composition Studies in *"Memoria* Is a Friend of Ours: On the Discourse of Color". Engaging in *memoria* for scholars of color is sometimes a tricky scholarly endeavor because it seems that this sort of scholarly work is too personal and cannot provide pertinent scholarly knowledge to an objective body of knowledge. However, studying the history of the largest minority population in the U.S.A. hardly seems inconsequential for any student to study. In a recent e-mail conversation, Villanueva commented:

What struck me about the brown-on-brown stuff (which is what researchers used to say to us [Latinxs] when we studied our own histories, without ever thinking that there's nothing superior about white or whatever): anyway, what strikes me about this is that most of us on this continent with Spanish ancestry are the victims of their conquests, while students think we're being pro-Spanish (and we're more likely to be pro-indigenous). (Villanueva's E-mail)

This cultural confusion that Villanueva describes seems common among the experiences of Latinx scholars. We are oftentimes grossly misunderstood in terms of our historical roots. An engagement with Latinx *memoria* is a productive site for teaching writing for any scholar/student and is consistent with Moya's critical educational theory, post-postivist realist theory. An engagement with *memoria* departs from traditional multicultural pedagogy in that it is an attempt at prompting universal learning experience that do not solely concentrate on the victimized status of minorities. Instead, they provide opportunities for minorities and mainstream students to learn from one another and also to learn about the process of writing history in a universal sense. For me, engaging in *memoria* was also an opportunity to learn about my own history. Thus, the following is my engagement with *memoria* in the Composition classroom; however, it reads like a heavily annotated syllabus and is meant to be a glimpse into the processes and products that were a part of one engagement with Critical Historical Writing pedagogy at the University of California, San Diego (UCSD) in 2007.

From the Bottom Up and From the Start: The Classroom and Critical Historiography

A Composition class premised on the teaching of critical historiography as one method of universalist multicultural curricula starts out with a basic question: What is the purpose of history? I am familiar with this debate as it has been discussed historically in the field of Composition Studies which I outlined above. I use my knowledge and research to present quotations such as the one below to begin discussions regarding possible answers to the question above as we discuss possible interpretations of the meaning and function of history in U.S. society:

[H]istorians can differ widely about the efficient causality of their craft when they clearly differ so widely about the "why" of what they are doing. These differings are essentially disagreements about the "why" of what they are doing. These differings are essentially disagreements about the nature of the common good for the *polis*, which in turn lead to disagreements about ways and means. (Octalog I 5)

This quotation, for example, taken from a very popular journal of Composition Studies, *Rhetoric Review*, encapsulates the complexity of both the writing and the discipline of history. There are "differing" purposes of history, and the answer to the question of "why" write history largely determines the way the question "What is history?" is answered.

CRITICAL HISTORIOGRAPHY WRITING COURSE: PART I

Thus, as a class, we examine the various purposes for the writing of history in the first half of the course by discussing the following premises and questions.

The discipline of history has been heralded as one of the leading social sciences serving various humanistic purposes such as promoting a sense of patriotism and rationalism, instilling morality, providing lessons from the past, and representing us with role models in the form of heroes so we might be drawn to be like them. Oftentimes, these purposes are conveyed with no critical stance as to who gets to decide which historical events get written and disseminated and for what humanistic purpose. [5] This was the specific brand of history that is the antithesis of Howard Zinn's *A People's History of the United States*. There, he shows a critical understanding of history as one that largely glosses over the social processes at work in the production of "official history." Like Zinn, with the investigative purpose of interrogating the social aspects involved in the process of historical production, I would like FYC students to consider and interrogate responses to such questions as:

---

[5] Howard Zinn's *A People's History of the United States* features critical historical stories such as the massacre of Filipino villagers, features historical figures who are in danger of becoming erased from history books in Texas and the rest of the us, and includes voices from nontraditional historical figures such as Frederick Douglas. Quoting Zinn, "My history... describes the inspiring struggle of those who have fought slavery and racism, of the labor organizers who have led strikes for the rights of working people, of the socialists and others who have protested war and militarism My hero is not Theodore Roosevelt, who loved war and congratulated a general after a massacre of Filipino villagers at the turn of the century, but Mark Twain, who denounced the massacre and satirized imperialism." "Making History", letter from Howard Zinn to *The New York Times*, July 1, 2007. Also see: "A Radical Treasure," *The New York Times* by Bob Herbert, January 29, 2010: http://www.nytimes.com/2010/01/30/opinion/30herbert.html?ref=howard_zinn

1. What exactly is history?
2. Why is history taught?
3. Who does history benefit?
4. What processes go into the creation of historical texts?
5. How does history account for various indigenous accounts in the realm of American and World History?
6. What does power have to do with historical production? How is it hidden? How is it revealed?
7. What are the issues with current dominant models of historical production such as empiricism and relativism discussed by Michel-Rolph Trouillot?
8. How much of history is based on fact? Fiction? Point of view?

After determining the many possible functions of history, another question I present students in addition to "What is history?" is "How does teaching a critical perspective of the function and practice of history fit into the current debates about the purpose of multicultural education?" Through this discussion, we come to discover that "[h]istory is important, not just in terms of who writes it and what gets included or excluded, but also because history, by the very nature of its inscription as history, has social, political, and cultural consequences" (Royster and Williams 563). As such, the next step is to look at a historical moment which may be a contested story or absent story altogether in the U.S. history curriculum at the high-school level. The story we decided to study and look at from a critical historiography perspective was the Spanish Conquest of Mexico.

CRITICAL HISTORIOGRAPHY CASE STUDY: THE SPANISH CONQUEST (PART II OF THE COURSE)

The purpose of the second half of the course is to put knowledge gained about specific problems with historical production into practice. We look at some primary sources that deal with the Spanish Conquest of Mexico, written by Hernán Cortés in the form of letters to King Charles V providing first-person accounts of his meeting with Montezuma, the Aztec emperor of Tenochititlan, the Aztec empire, and the Aztec people. We also read first-person accounts recorded by the Aztecs and translated by Miguel Leon-Portillo. However, it should be noted that any contested historical event could be used as an example in this section of the course, even with the same introductory material used for the first half of the course. After an examination of primary sources, we look at secondary sources that have drawn upon these primary sources for the purpose of creating a seamless historical account of the Spanish Conquest of Mexico (or "The Fall of Tenochititlan") and see how the process of historical production works. We perform these tasks with a critical eye gained from the first half of the class, where we discuss the various purposes of history and the problems associated with them.

The Spanish Conquest of Mexico is an interesting historical story to look at because this story provides the genesis of the Mesoamerican people; however, its importance in terms of understanding the first "Americans" and the first incidents in "American Encounters" is tantamount to understanding what the "The Discovery of America" has been predicated upon. The Spanish Conquest took place in 1519, just 27 years after Columbus sailed the ocean blue and "discovered" America. Here, in this historical account, we have one of the first recorded incidents of the sixteenth-century imperialism/colonialism of a native culture close to home (Atzlan).

Now I turn to the practical and pedagogical portion of my project which actually served as the initial stage of research for this project. As mentioned earlier, this Composition class concentrated upon my teaching a critical historiographic approach to the Spanish Conquest of Mexico. Through the description and analysis of this course, I make the case that critical historiography in the Composition classroom allows one to teach a multicultural curriculum that is universal and not exclusive, following Moya's universal multicultural educational theory called post-positivist realist theory (see Chap. 2). A critical historical approach to a minority experience provides universal critical thinking skills while also enabling the study of minority history. In this case, what is salient is a Mexican American historical background that is tapped by looking at critical accounts of the Spanish Conquest of Mexico. This approach affirms the history connected with the current Latinxs experiences and correlating identities in the U.S.A.

Critical Historiography and Memoria as Universal Multicultural Pedagogy

After many of my own encounters with memoria—the kind Elena Garro writes about in her short story "It's the Fault of the Tlaxcaltecas" (Manguel 159–78), I listen to histories now with an inclination toward inquiry. Through my scholarly experiences, it has recently come to my attention that to study historical production is to discern the contingent nature of these narratives. It is an important personal discovery for me because it has allowed me to identify one possible discourse that defines who we are as individuals and what our role is in the current social structure. In Señora Laura's case, the protagonist of Garro's short story, memories come back to disrupt what she currently perceives to be her present reality: the traditional subservient Mexican woman married to a Mexican man. His/story,[6] however, comes back to haunt her or even to relieve her and to enlighten her to the circumstances that created her current reality: her unhappy marriage to a Mexican man. His/story, for Laura, comes back in the form of an Aztec lover (living, breathing history): a lover that comes at moments of Laura's hallucinations and daydreams.

This historical figure captures Laura and takes her back in time. He takes her back to the bloody battle between the Spanish and the Aztec in Tenochititlán. She sees the battle from a distance, but her Aztec lover is involved in the actual battle; her lover always comes back after shedding blood in battle to take her back to her present life. In the morning, she awakes with blood on her dress from the night before. History has haunted her and she will never be the same. She wonders, "Who is this man?" She comes to long for his presence and love. So she ultimately starts reading history books of the Spanish Conquest to recover the memory of her lover while he is back in time. Her present reality would never be the same because it has become so unbearable and so disrupted that she can no longer live in it. The last time her lover comes to enlighten her, she stays in the past forever. The history she thought she knew was destroyed—her reality destroyed—her comfort destroyed—and her purpose transformed. Of course, the story of Laura is an extreme version of the effects of discovering lost secrets related to one's identity, which can cause mental turmoil in individuals if those secrets challenge one's current self-conception and place in the world.

The first part of the original title of this book was "Shattering Glass Mirrors". Laura's story is a direct reflection of the meaning of that phrase, as her reality becomes shattered to never come back together in its previous state. The outcomes of my FYC class discussed in this chapter are not as dramatic as Laura's; however, my class did encourage students to engage historical texts with a critical eye toward omissions. The goal of this class was to question the official status of history and, hence, better understand the constructed and contingent nature of historical narratives. The pedagogical tasks in this class immediately called upon students to become aware of the social conditions under which histories

---

[6]His/story is used to imply the patriarchal nature and influence on traditional historical narratives, since most traditional histories have been written by men.

are produced. The assignments asked students to find possible reasons for why certain historical textual accounts had omitted events that were revealed in other historical texts about the same event. "The Discovery of America," which deals with the Spanish Conquest of Mexico, is a rich site for this pedagogical task. The diversity of readings allowed for no opportunity to engage in writing tasks that assumed one historical story total, justified, and correct.

In this quarter-long course (10 weeks), students read a variety of historical texts and criticism in the form of primary historical documents, such as "Manifest Destiny," *The Letters of Hernan Cortes*, Miguel León Portilla's *The Broken Spears*, and secondary historical sources that claimed to offer official historical accounts of the Spanish Conquest of Mexico. The bibliographic list of readings for this class is included in Appendix A. One of the restraints of this course was the 100-page limit to the class reader, and this limitation affected my decision to include only the most common and accessible texts that showed two primary accounts of the Spanish Conquest from the perspective of both "sides" involved in this bloody encounter.

The discussion of these influential, but not always widely read, historical texts was framed in a general discussion of what the purpose and function of history has been argued to be. We did not read Foucault, but my understanding of his analysis of rationality and the purpose and process of historical production and subject formation helped to inform the readings chosen for this course. Thus, the authority which provided initial understandings of the purpose and function of history was derived from historians who claimed authoritative explanations from Greco-Roman viewpoints. Starting from such arguments was an interesting place to begin because Greece and Rome are often claimed to be the genesis of all great thoughts and knowledge. Foucault lets his readers know that this claim is a myth of history. Students were directed toward more contemporary revisionist/critical historical explanations of "Manifest Destiny" and the Spanish Conquest of Mexico which challenged earlier traditional arguments. While earlier accounts claim that history is written and distributed strictly to impart values, morality, heroic examples, and lessons from the past, the latter seek to expose why silences in history often have a political agenda behind them such as building a national political consciousness and creating structures of power through historical production.

Programmatic Context

The programmatic context in which I taught this course is closely related to the basic aims of the Warren College Writing program, at UCSD, which can be found on the University website.[7] For the purposes here, I want to shed light on the following goals of this FYC program:

> Students are urged to move beyond merely agreeing or disagreeing with a given position. Instead, the emphasis is on understanding the underlying logic of an argument and on enhancing the quality of the arguments students make in their own writing. Despite their considerable intrinsic interest, the articles and essays assigned as readings are secondary to the goals of the course; the primary focus is always on student writing. (UCSD Warren College Writing Program Website)

The "individual and society" is the underlying theme of Warren Writing; the Toulmin Model is the argumentative structure used to guide students through the writing process. However, a deeper and perhaps more interesting (to most of us in Composition) theoretical basis of the goals can be attributed to the theoretical/pedagogical leanings of Linda Brodkey, the former director of Warren Writing.

Brodkey has written in "Transvaluing Difference" that

> words constitute worldview…; any attempts to describe reality are necessarily partial accounts…; they are limited by what can be seen and understood from a particular vantage point…the theory that language constructs reality—that what we know of reality is dependent on language, argues that the language used to register the most violent objections to difference thrives in part because of our desire to ignore differences and hence our own complicity in the very political inequities that African Americans, feminists, lesbians, gays and progressives on the University of Pennsylvania campus have been attempting to rectify…the negative valuing of difference—*not* white, *not* male, *not* heterosexual, *not* middle class—is socially constructed and can therefore be socially reconstructed and positively revalued. (159).

---

[7] Earl Warren College is one of the six undergraduate colleges at the University of California, San Diego and is named after the three-term California Governor and former Chief Justice of the US Supreme Court, Earl Warren.

Brodkey provides the theoretical foundation that supports the idea that the ways students construct arguments reflect directly on society and have real and tangible consequences: language constructs a version of reality. For Brodkey, the ways students use language reflect directly on the realities those languages create: "in the same way that cabinet makers make furniture and musicians make music, writers animate words, and these words are as much a part of the material world as tables and records and concerts" (161). Thus, students have to be accountable for the arguments they make. To see the underlying motives of any argument is to begin to question the underlying assumptions that inform one's own argument, while allowing one to see who is both included and excluded from that same argument.

Institutional Context

Since the end of affirmative action and Proposition 209 (a California legislative initiative that makes the process of considering race in admissions decisions illegal), the UC system has increasingly been criticized for its lack of a diverse student body. Even with affirmative action policies in place before the passage of Proposition 209, the number of Chicanx students at UCSD never surpassed 10% of the total student population. As a matter of fact, The Concilio (A community of Chicanx/Latinx faculty, staff, and students at UCSD) attributes the lack of underrepresented students at UCSD to factors such as a hostile campus environment, lack of critical mass of *Raza* (Chicano/Latino faculty, staff, and students), low numbers of Chicanx faculty, and limited visibility for Chicanx issues in the curriculum. They argue that this lack of representation is particularly unacceptable because some areas of San Diego County are over 30% Chicanx/Latinx. Even worse, the African American student body on the UCSD campus is virtually invisible ("Report Card on the University of California, San Diego: A Legacy of Institutional Neglect").

The Class

Given the admissions, demographics, and diversity characteristics of UCSD,
   I taught "Revisiting the American Past: The Spanish Conquest" in the spring of 2007 to a fairly privileged group of students (see Appendix A).

In my classroom, I promoted a universal multicultural curriculum that, as noted by Moya, concentrates on the lived experiences of minority students in a critical manner. However, the ways Moya's proposed curriculum differs from traditional multicultural curriculum are unclear. The following section serves to show that unlike traditional multicultural curricula, for which the content is the sole focus, a universal multicultural pedagogy focuses more on the teaching methods involved in teaching critical multicultural content. While the content is important, the way the content is presented, taught, and negotiated is even more important. This is because the goal of a universalist multicultural pedagogy is for all students to benefit from critically analyzing both multicultural and minority texts which concentrate on their experiences. Those experiences are always seen as socially and historically located. Thus, looking at minority experiences from a critical historical standpoint is one way to critically analyze the current status of minority populations in the U.S.A. For example, we discovered that the current experiences of Latinxs may well be tied to their history, even if this history is over 500 years old. However, the process of this critical discovery is not one that altogether avoids personal discomforts with the material or with the person providing the material, as will become evident in the remainder of this chapter. However, this conflict is demonstrative of the ways the content becomes secondary to the manner in which it is consumed by the students, taught to them, and negotiated by them.

Latina Composition Scholar at the Forefront: My Counter-Story

According to bell hooks, "For most women, the first knowledge of racism as institutionalized oppression is engendered either by direct personal experience or through information gleaned from conversations, books, television, or movies" (119). I am a woman of color with a PhD in Literature focused on Composition and Rhetorical history. I have experienced racist behavior while teaching this class, behavior that I think is important to discuss as I continue in the pedagogical description of this particular class.

My professional and academic accomplishments exhibit a strong commitment to educating ethnically and culturally diverse populations in each tier of the California higher education system. I wrote my Master's thesis on Generation 1.5 students. My research interests inform my desire to stay currently informed concerning "cutting-edge" teaching methods and theories focusing on linguistically diverse students, further revealing my dedication to promoting and supporting diversity initiatives and populations in higher education.

While I may not focus on my race/ethnicity in my teaching practice, I have to admit that the pedagogical moments discussed herein made me more aware of how others situate me as a colored female (more so than I would have liked to acknowledge myself). Nonetheless, regardless of my colored body, on the surface, I negotiate the classroom as many other Composition instructors would. I utilize the classroom as an intimate space where students (14 of them per section) share their work with one another and have a chance to bond with one another in a manner not possible in any of their other classes. Undergraduates at UCSD take other required courses that have 200 students or more in one classroom.

Thus, the intimate classroom setting I teach in often reveals that students are not particularly fond of being required to take two quarters of Composition. They voice this opinion on the first day of class. When students realize the sheer impossibility of getting an "A" in Warren Writing, they often search for flaws with the writing program or the teacher (you will read about one such complaint about me below). Furthermore, UCSD's admissions policy rewards students who have taken many Advanced Placement (AP) courses. Often, these students start off the class saying, "I passed the AP writing test and AP literature with flying colors." It seems as if they are attempting to establish their credibility with me as an "A" student; however, I was an experienced teaching assistant (TA) well-versed in the fact that an "A" in high school does not equate to an "A" in college. Every teaching faculty in Warren Writing knows this. Many college writing instructors know this.

Interestingly, although many A's are not given in FYC classes associated with the UCSD Warren Writing Program, I have had students write in my end-of-the-quarter evaluations that I make learning to write and the subject matter that goes with it virtually "painless". Such comments put a smile on my face because I consciously try to make pedagogy fun and interesting—I feel confident about my pedagogical abilities and I am not afraid to get to know my students and their opinions and engage them in intellectual conversations outside of the classroom and during office hours. Since I was still a graduate student at the time of this study, I also did not mind sharing my academic interests with them; however, I tried not to let these conversations cloud my vision of what the individual student's writing and analytical abilities are. I pride myself on keeping grading separate from the day-to-day, albeit very interesting and stimulating, conversations about student backgrounds, attitudes about the class, attitudes about history, and certain insightful comments about the readings do develop. Students are sometimes, unfortunately, misled by the friendly rapport I build with them and the grade they earn.

Keeping the evaluative process as consistent and objective as possible allows me to remain a credible instructor while being able to teach students critical historical writing skills that I think could be of use to them in the future. Because this is my professional persona, classroom discussions and workshop interactions can sometimes become very heated, stimulating, and often venture off topic. These discussions become especially engaging and often result in conversations about whether or not the students enjoy both the course and the subject matter.

In the reading and writing workshop groups where students read and comment on each other's papers, I sometimes let students choose who they would like to read and comment on their papers; interestingly, the "safehouses" that Mary Louise Pratt[8] identifies seem to be created when students choose with whom they will share their work and ideas. It is not common for students to immediately gravitate toward people with whom they have obvious differences in terms of identity, race, dorm room, age, and gender. The power of subjectivity and accompanying classification schemas is strong.

The following is a description of what I would label a "universalist" consequence of multicultural education that departs from focusing on the experiences of the "Other." Immediately, before the introduction and reading of Samir Amin's *Eurocentrism*, a group of three white students, two female and one male, decided they would be "pro-Eurocentric" in all of their writing engagements when the writing assignments themselves solicited no polarizing positions. In an assignment that asked students to apply one of the explanations of the function of history to the text of "Manifest Destiny," it was automatically assumed that the task was whether to justify the colonial actions that stemmed from this text.[9]

[8] Mary Louise Pratt (1991). "Arts of the Contact Zone" (pdf). *Profession* (New York: MLA) **91**: 33–40. http://www.class.uidaho.edu/thomas/English_506/Arts_of_the_Contact_Zone.pdf. Archived at University of Idaho, English 506, Rhetoric and Composition: History, Theory, and Research.

[9] The actual assignment reads as follows: Summarize Calcott and Starnes in relationship to one another paying particular attention to the various purposes of history presented in both articles. What claims are they making? How does Starnes specifically elaborate on the various

Interestingly, one particular white male student's paper argued that "Manifest Destiny" was justified and correct in its claims to civilize the beasts that currently occupied the land. His response was unsolicited because the writing prompt asked students to expose the various appeals that were used to justify the colonial projects evident in the text of "Manifest Destiny."[10] I spoke with the student after and he revealed that he "misunderstood" the assignment, and he revised his paper so that it addressed the assignment more appropriately. Nonetheless, it is interesting to note how the task, for this particular student, became a call for his personal stance regarding the controversial political nature of the text.[11]

Carnival: Inverse Subject Positions

Carnivalesque[12] moments happen when subjectivities and the powers that are associated with them become inverted: the powerless temporarily become the powerful, the dominant—the vantage point from which history is viewed. In this class, I assumed a double subjectivity—as teacher and as a Latina. My *Latinidad* is not easily shed. For example, I had a total of five Latinx students out of 28 in the two classes. These students participated and often went beyond what was asked of them in class. They took notes from the board for my own research purposes when the help was not solicited. They provided me with pertinent information about taking field trips to museums which discussed the history of the Americas.

---

purposes of history presented by Calcott? Is there a critical stance toward history present in either of the two articles? After engaging with the various purposes evident in the Calcott's and Starnes' articles, using O'Sullivan's "Manifest Destiny" excerpt, apply one or more of the purposes of history to the position made herein.

[10] Such appeals could have been but are not limited to an appeal to a deity, an appeal to lessons from the past, an appeal to the monarchy of England.

[11] The specific wording of "Manifest Destiny" and the excerpt referred to in this student's paper are as follows:

For this blessed mission to the nations of the world, which are shut out from the life-giving light of truth, has America been chosen; and her high example shall smite unto death the tyranny of kings, hierarchs, and oligarchs, and carry the glad tidings of peace and good will where myriads now endure an existence scarcely more enviable than that of beasts of the field. Who, then, can doubt that our country is destined to be the great nation of futurity? (241)

[12] My understanding of the "Carnival" stems from M.M. Bakhtin's *The Dialogic Imagination*.

They volunteered their time to be interviewed and surveyed for this study. Finally, they spoke out in class in order to provide help with translating some of the Spanish found in some of the texts we read and to critically engage in discussions that involved their own history.

The students discussed above saw the stories of their ancestors as the dominant subject of debate during the second-half of this class. They witnessed the ways dominant narratives of the Spanish Conquest become constructed from primary texts and eventually become construed as "the truth." They had the opportunity to confront arguments by critics who challenged not only Eurocentric perspectives of history, but also Eurocentric claims of Europe as the source of all relevant knowledge as well as the center with which to compare all other nations (given our discussion of Amin's *Eurocentrism*). As a result, they were able to make claims that allowed them to challenge the historical stories that they were exposed to in high school that portrayed the indigenous tribes as savages and to see how when distinct cultures come into contact with one another and battle, the winners tell the stories. In other words, these students were able to regain a sense of self-pride through the material they were writing about in an intimate way. They became interested in why their ancestors had been portrayed as the bad guys for so long and discovered that the meaning of "bad" derives from the social construction of one as being "bad" for a specific political function. *This pedagogical experience is a clear departure from a traditional multicultural pedagogy which concentrates upon "difference."*

While it might be controversial to admit, many times in classroom settings located in the conservative, privileged space of a tier-one university such as UCSD, the "minority" is perceived as the less powerful, less fortunate, and (perhaps most interesting for the purposes of this essay) less knowledgeable. However, in this particular class, those that had a more intimate connection to the historical moment were the students who were Chicanx/Latinx. These students became the more knowledgeable and, perhaps, the more acknowledged in the subject matter and in the classroom. Thus, this class provided some carnivalesque moments in which students saw the various productive forces at play in constructing historical accounts of the same historical event: the Spanish Conquest of Mexico. These carnivalesque moments contributed to the "pedagogical arts" of the "contact zone" in that they caused inverse instances of "shame and confrontation."

Interestingly, my subject positions, as well as the status of my authority in these particular classrooms, varied for each group of students. While these positions could be felt by any female academic educator in any class, this particular class brought a different kind of challenge in that I was teaching my "own history" as a subject interrogated for writing and analyzing. In this class I sometimes felt myself to be "The Nameless/Faceless Mexican Woman" with no authority or right to teach what I was teaching. Other times I felt myself to be "The Mexican Teacher" with authority and power for that group of students who felt empowered by the subject matter I was teaching (I occupied a privileged subject position). But for most of the students, I felt I was "The Faceless, Nameless, Bodiless Teacher with Power" (with authority to teach whatever I wanted, no matter who I was because I was giving the grades).

Regarding the first subject position where my authority was challenged, it must be remembered that I am a female of color teaching a writing course that deals with part of my history. In such a case, it becomes easy to assume that I am personally invested in the viewpoints that will be discussed in the course of the quarter. However, this particular historical event happens to be the one with which I am familiar in terms of scholarly breadth and exposure. Beverly Moss, another female Compositionist of color, states,

> I speak of scholarship and teaching together because how and why I do both come from the same source and are inextricably linked. In the scholarship that I do, mainly through ethnographic means, I seek to make my scholarly life and where I come from compatible; I seek a way for the public and the private to enrich each other. I seek a way to establish my place in the academy without giving up myself. (162)

According to Moss, making subject positions compatible is not impossible. The particular historical event discussed herein proves to be a ripe location for scholarly interest and for the teaching of writing. There also exists much scholarship focused on the relationship between the body of the teacher and the body of knowledge being taught (Freedman and Holmes 2003). It is easy in this particular situation to claim that my body was easily related to the historical subject matter, so therefore, my personal politics became suspect and my authority questionable.

I imagine that it was difficult for some students to see the relevance of looking back to a history that does not match their own when I seemingly had a more intimate connection to it. I also experienced moments of anguish, confrontation, and unsolicited responses to my pedagogy. While success is measured in varied increments, the fact that the majority of the students in this class responded positively and learned something critically is the measure of the success attributed herein. However, conflicts are sometimes inevitable when the class curriculum departs from the traditional content many mainstream students are accustomed to. Furthermore, to challenge dominant ideology and teaching practices during the first year of students' college education can be tricky when they have never encountered challenges to their current set of beliefs and comfort zones.

Thus, I offer an example of such a challenge to a critical historical curriculum which focused on the history of a minority population. I remember being surprised by the following incident which challenged both my pedagogy and authority. A white, female student in the same group as the student who attempted to justify "Manifest Destiny" in an earlier essay assignment began to express dissatisfaction with her grade. Her complaint resulted in limiting discussions about both the content of the course and the appropriate response to the writing assignments. However, somehow, my "politics" became a subject of interrogation. When I was informed of this student's complaint and the fact that she claimed my politics did not match hers, I was very confused. I was not sure what she actually meant by "my politics."

However, within the context of this first-year writing course that concentrated largely on Mexican History, my politics clearly had to be related to the course material because these course texts were the basis for what our verbal interactions and written interactions consisted. What other politics could she be referring to? I am Chicana, I am a female, I have intimate connections to the material, and she claimed that she did not agree with my politics, although I never discussed politics in the classroom. I never revealed my political associations. Therefore, I have no other choice but to deduce that I can be assumed to be "pro-Mexican." However, this class centered on the contingent nature of historical narratives. We looked at the course material as a case study with universalist intentions in mind, not for the sole purpose of simply admiring or promoting "Mexicans" or "Mexicanness." If she would have referred to the above description of the goals of Warren Writing, she would have noticed that "[d]espite their considerable intrinsic interest, the articles and essays assigned as readings are secondary to the goals of the course; the primary focus is always on student writing" (Warren College Writing). My pedagogical focus, however, was overlooked because of my colored body and association to the class material. My supposed "political bias" allowed her to question the grade I gave her in my class, although she was clearly a "C" writer. In short, she wanted an "A," but her work did not reflect "A" writing. She received a grade of C+ because that was what her writing reflected. I provided the appropriate evidence that her grade was accurate and that it was not personal or because my "politics" did not match hers.

Although it seems like wasted time, I am finding more and more that, as a Latina academic, I should be prepared to defend my actions at any given moment, especially when teaching scholarly matters that I have intimate connections with, such as Mexican History. (I also have intimate connections with my gender, but that does not mean I give males "C's" because they are not female.) I have developed somewhat of a defensive stance. But as many other "colored" Compositionists have admitted, academics of color struggle against assumptions about our qualifications, confront others who feel we have no right to be in the academy, and are consistently caught up in a battle to prove ourselves worthy, to show our loyalty, never letting our guard down for a second. This experience provides another reason why adhering to universalist justifications for multicultural pedagogy is important. The benefits have to accrue for all students, not just a select few.

Recently, as I mention above, I have developed a keen sense of my own subjectivity, sometimes wondering if I have become neurotic about it. Fortunately, the "colored" scholarship in our field reassures me that I am not alone in my insecurities. Victor Villanueva, a Puerto Rican Compositionist and personal mentor, admitted: "I read Anzaldúa or hooks or the poetry of Espada or Cruz or Esteves or any other writing of color, and I know I haven't become clinically paranoid. I know that I've been poked by one of the demons" (*"Memoria"*).

Yet, given this isolated and somewhat common experience, I have decided to continue to teach history as an appropriate subject for writing and analysis, despite political challenges that may arise as attacks on academic freedom. Susan Searls Giroux speaks of this assault on academic freedom that has become more pronounced since 9/11. Revolutionary nonconservative views have increasingly come under attack, and now more than ever the university has become a targeted institution for continued surveillance. Susan Giroux states:

> Organized around a kind of patriotic correctness, the current assault routinely blacklists professors and administrators perceived to be critical of the current Bush administration's policies, or those of its allies, as it seeks state and federal legislative and judicial aid in efforts to render the university classroom and utterly instrumentalized space devoid of critical thought, self-reflection, and moral accountability. (Giroux 14)

The academic freedom I am referring to is one that focuses on differ-ence that is determined to make a difference—not to suppress and oppress opinions and identities as David Horowitz would have it.

Some readers might wonder if I was trying to impose one historical story. Was I trying to condemn those who wrote Manifest Destiny? Do I not agree with a Eurocentric perspective (maybe not, but remember, Latinas are part European)? One of the most interesting and baffling aspects of the dynamics that took place during the course of this particular quarter is that these three students often tried to claim being "pro-Eurocentric" and that, therefore, I was probably "pro-Indigenous." But they never stopped to think that I, as a Latina, am both European and indigenous. As I see it, this confusion is all the more reason why this course should continue to be taught, as Villanueva would confirm. The conflicts that arose in this class, while not the prescription for such a class, may be one consequence of a universalist multicultural pedagogy. However, as one can see, there is a visible level of tolerance by all who participated in the class despite moments of discomfort with the material (Pratt would say this discom-fort is good, no?). Those who did not previously understand the role of the Spanish Conquest of Mexico in the process of identity formation of current Latinxs in the U.S.A. learned that Latinxs have a very complex history that is not often taught in traditional historical accounts of U.S. minority populations.

On that same note, those whose history was taught in these classrooms benefitted from a deeper historical understanding of their own identity and experience as a U.S. minority. These goals are, indeed, consistent with Moya's discussion of an "[e]ducation that is multicultural and social reconstructionist" (*Learning from Experience* 147) as *students had the opportunity to see that Latinxs in the U.S.A. are more than just a problem (as we are currently often conceived as)*. The students begin to understand the complex historical past of many of these populations, and this under-standing allows them to historically situate their current minority status and challenge derogatory descriptions of minorities as "less able," "less intelligent," "illiterate," "dirty," "unmotivated," and, thus, question how it is that this population has been described in this way. It asks students to begin to look at the social structures that create inequalities such as racial, gender, and class disparities in an effort to better understand the dynamics of social relationships and possibly alter them. Thus, critical historiography in the Composition classroom is representative of a criti-cal universal multicultural pedagogy or curriculum that rests upon post-positivist realist theory.

CHAPTER 9

Guatemala as a Site for Critical Historiography

In this book, I have argued that writing pedagogies should be inclusive of the histories of underrepresented populations. These inclusive pedagogies must entail inclusion on two levels: first, the curricula should include contested histories as a source for critical thinking and analysis through writing. Second, the curricula should present opportunities for those students previously underrepresented in "official histories" taught in public high schools[1] to see themselves represented in alternative histories in writing classrooms.

James Berlin reminds us, however, that suggestions for the implementation of such "[c]urricula[r] decisions are, however, often negotiated responses to larger economic, social, political and cultural events in a society" (184). Sociopolitical concerns, thus, determine curricular choices and even admissions policies. For example, the elimination of affirmative action in California shows that there is a move away from inclusion if the state has decided that race is no longer a factor in considering who gets admitted. For example, whether the struggling Watts High School student gets admission into the University of California, Los Angeles (UCLA) or the high-achieving honors student from Orange County receives admission for the same spot is based upon his/her merits and not necessarily his/her unique experiences or struggles in achieving scholastic success.

[1] *The Wall Street Journal* "The Culture Wars' New Front: U.S. History Classes in Texas," July 14, 2009.

© The Editor(s) (if applicable) and The Author(s) 2016   181
I.D. Ruiz, *Reclaiming Composition for Chicano/as and Other Ethnic Minorities*, DOI 10.1057/978-1-137-53673-0_9

When one thinks about these disparities, it is important to note that Watts' local secondary public school, David Starr Jordan High School, has a student body of 76.5 % Latinos, 23 % African Americans, and 5 % other, and is located in a high-crime area. These statistics reveal that, most likely, the student applicant from Watts will be either Chicanx/Latinx or African American. However, given the location of the school, this particular student has had fewer college preparation courses, less support, and more distractions. The racial aspect may be secondary to the education experience; however, this student will most likely be overlooked by an admissions policy that is heavily focused upon merit and does not consider race.

Curricula, like admissions policies, also lean toward the representation of the politics of larger society (as seen in the case of the University of Texas at Austin). Although disguised as politically neutral, curricula may be biased, ignoring minority views while representing the political views of the larger political majority of the state as well as the views of the universities' administration. In the University of California system, racial topics and critical perspectives are not easily implemented in writing course curriculum. Often students and parents react to such curricula as indoctrination, as was mentioned earlier in this book when I discussed the conservative backlash experienced by Linda Brodkey. Why is there so much controversy with the content of what is being taught in writing classrooms in today's twenty-first century? This answer calls for a brief reminder of the history of the discipline, which is also extremely political. Berlin reminds us that the history of "writing instruction has been a...scene of struggle over competing claims about the purposes of education, more specifically about the society the school and college should advocate and the kind of individuals they should encourage" and that "no classroom pedagogy can long survive without in some way responding to its historical conditions..." (*Rhetoric and Reality* 184–85).

While it is apparent that Berlin recognizes that pedagogies and rhetorics alike cannot be separated from politics, this simple recognition does not go far enough in addressing the specific populations that become excluded as a result of pedagogical implementations that serve the political interests of a dominant society. One sees this same "struggle over competing claims" in the multicultural debate of the twenty-first century which spans all over the map when considering whether multicultural curriculum should be part of public school curricula or not and for what reason and in what manner (i.e. Ethnic Studies Now initiatives in California and HB 2281 in Arizona). However, there have been recent developments that have shown greater support and attention to pedagogies similar to the one I advocate here. For example, UCLA has recently passed a diversity graduation requirement for all of their undergraduates, Arizona has rescinded their ban on Mexican American Studies in the Tucson Unified School District (HB 2281), although the faculty associated with the first Mexican American Studies program have not been rehired. And El Rancho Unified School District becomes the first school district in the state of California requiring Ethnic Studies for high school graduation, followed by Los Angeles Unified School District and San Francisco Unified School District.[2]

We do need to pay attention to the specific Latinxs population associated with the Southwest, represented by the changes in California and Arizona. However, we also need to pay attention to the growing number of other Latinxs in the U.S.A.. My argument for the consideration and inclusion of all Latinxs in Composition pedagogy and scholarship stems in part from demographic imperatives, as we consider the number of Latinxs students in high school and in college in many states across the country. According to a Pew Hispanic Center report completed in December 2009, one in every five school children is Hispanic and at least 1.2 million college students are Hispanic.[3] These numbers are important to consider when thinking about maintaining the strength and productivity of the U.S. workforce. Furthermore, the educational progress of Latinxs should be of particular interest because it is expected that between the years of 2000 and 2025, the white working age population will decline "by five million workers, as baby boomers retire from the labor force. According to the U.S. Census Bureau, the number of working age Latinos is projected to increase by 18 million."[4] Thus,

[2] Three Sonorans, "CA school district makes Ethnic Studies a Grad Requirement" Three Sonorans News & Analysis. June 27, 2014. http://threesonorans.com/2014/06/27/ca-school-district-makes-ethnic-studies-a-gradrequirement/?utm_content=bufferecad0&utm_medium=social&utm_source=facebook.com&utm_campaign=buffer

Schallart, Amanda, "Faculty Executive Committee approves diversity requirement proposal." UCLADailyBruin.May30,2014 http://dailybruin.com/2014/05/30/faculty-executive-committee-approves-diversity-requirement-proposal/

[3] Pew Hispanic Center Report, "Between Two Worlds: How Young Latinos Come of Age in America" http://pewhispanic.org/reports/report.php?ReportID=117

[4] Pew Hispanic Center Report, "Latino High School Graduates Enroll in College at Higher Rates than Whites, Yet Too Few Graduate" http://www.pewhispanic.org

there needs to be more attention to "[e]fforts to increase the numbers of Latino college graduates [that] will raise the economic prospects, social well-being and civic engagement of the fast-growing U.S. Hispanic population" (Pew Hispanic Report "Latino High School Graduates"), similar to the argument Clinton made during his presidency.

Furthermore, it is important to note that while Spanish is the dominant language spoken by many Latinos in the U.S.A., as there are more than 28 million Spanish speakers in the U.S.A., there are also indigenous languages associated with Latinx populations in the U.S.A.. Such a linguistic variety raises questions about the proposed homogenous status often applied to U.S. Latinx populations. Latinxs are heterogeneous not only in their linguistic competencies, but are also varied in their immigrant status, their generational status, their class status (income level), and their geographical locations within the U.S.A. For example, while the population of El Paso, Texas, is 75% "Hispanic," in Alabama, this same population only constitutes 3% of the total population.[5] However, the Hispanic presence is growing across the country. As of the 2008 census, Hispanics comprise 46.9 million, and by 2050, Hispanics are expected to constitute 30 % of the population, reaching close to 150 million.[6] Clearly, there is a need for Composition scholars to consider the implications of this population growth within our country.

Latinx Compositionists are well aware of the history of the field of Composition and the pedagogies that have emerged from its exclusionist scholarship. As discussed earlier in this book, much of the Composition scholarship of people of color has been marginalized. The pedagogical needs of African American students, for example, are not central to Composition Studies. Latinx scholarship in this area is fairly recent in the field. *As the number of Latinx students in higher education increases, there is a clear need for the field of Composition to more readily and seriously consider scholarship specifically devoted to the writing needs of this growing Latinx student population.*

If, as noted by Composition theorists, writing curricula have been inherently political and exclusive, it is time, as Mejía and I argue, for theories of writing to be inclusive. The question, of course, is how to design a Composition curriculum that is inclusive. There are undoubtedly many ways to do it. Here,

/2013/05/09/hispanic-high-school-graduates-pass-whites-in-rate-of-college-enrollment/

[5] Pew Hispanic Center report, "Demographic Profile of Hispanics in Alabama, 2008" http://pewhispanic.org/states/?stateid=AL

[6] http://www.census.gov/Press-Release/www/releases/archives/facts_for_features_special_editions/013984.html

I am proposing the incorporation of critical history in Composition classes as a way of addressing the needs of excluded students, like Latinxs.

Our changing demographics require all students to learn more about the histories attached to the various Latinx populations in the U.S.A. and for Latinxs to know about their connections to their intimate identities. Learning about this history and the way it is constructed enables students to challenge dominant cultural labels and categories that have led to mis-understandings and miscommunications across racial lines. It is time to go beyond preordained categories that assign certain traits and character-istics that are not inherently tied to the word/label itself, also known as stereotypes.

For example, the experience of being Latin American within the U.S.A. is not monolithic, it is not common, and it is not easily conveyed in main-stream historical texts. As Sánchez and Pita note, the term "Latino" "can-not operate as a simple ethnic designation because we cannot claim one national origin. Our origin is multinational and multiracial. Our Latinxs identity is trans-American, linked to the continents of the Americas and more specifically to Latin America" (30). However, the status of many Latinxs within the U.S.A. is often depicted as the common immigrant story without paying close attention to the varied populations, genera-tions, linguistic associations, and political histories of each individual of the Latinx population within varied regions in the U.S.A.. Therefore, looking at a few of these populations closely will allow one to begin to understand these variations and the apparent problems associated with grouping all Latin Americans together.

The goal of a Critical Historiographic course is to enfranchise histo-ries that have been kept out of mainstream history textbooks. However, the lessons taught should also strive to be pedagogically informed in a way that includes students intellectually, culturally, linguistically, histori-cally, and even locally. Here, the localities that I would like to address are Latin American populations. The goal of this chapter, then, is to bring to light critical histories associated with Latinx populations; here, con-sider Guatemalans as a specific case study for the creation of a Critical Historiographic course. As I have stated earlier, there is both a great need and a great demand for Composition pedagogies that address Latinxs in today's increasingly diverse postsecondary institutions.

The learning experiences I am advocating herein are those tied to histories associated with a variety of U.S. Latinx populations. These his-tories are inextricably tied to the histories of the Conquest commemo-rated two decades ago. The history referred to previously in this book specifically addresses the historical event of the Spanish Conquest of Mexico, also known as the Mexican Conquest, as a case study which demonstrates the actual implementation of a Critical Historical Pedagogy for which this book argues. However, the histories I touch upon in this chapter will be more recent and will, hopefully, give the reader historical breadth. These histories become important to look at when thinking about implementing a writing pedagogy in a class that is composed of students who identify as Latinxs.

A good part of the information about Latin Americans is taken from *Politics of Latin America: The Power Game* and from Sánchez' and Pita's "Theses on the Latino Bloc: A Critical Perspective." The editors, Harry E. Vanden and Gary Prevost, argue that each nation in Latin America has a political history characterized as having moments of dictatorship and democracy. Historically, struggle has characterized the socioeconomic structures of each nation, while traditional economic and capitalistic practices have concentrated most of the land in these countries "in a few families and left the vast majority of citizens with no or little land or means of adequately sustaining themselves" (xviii). As such, the basic struggle to subsist and maintain is one common factor which seems to unite the poor of Latin America, albeit at different points in history and with common instigators, such as the U.S.A. and dictators with particular economic and political interests. Furthermore, Prevost and Vanden state that "Latin America has experienced more revolutions than any other part of the world, yet the conditions for the lower classes in most countries are arguably not much better than they were at the end of the colonial period in the early 1800s" (xviii).

My purpose here is not to offer a synthesis of Latin American history but to point to a variety of periods and problems that one could address in a Composition classroom. What is important is to understand the nuances of the Latinx population now present within the U.S.A.[7] The political variations have been numerous, and "one must equally study the particular historical evolution of each country to comprehend its own brand of politics and see how it conforms to and diverges from general political

---

[7] See Rosaura Sánchez' and Beatrice Pita's "Theses on the Latino Bloc" abstract. This essay proposes the need to forge strategic political alliances by constructing this population as a bloc, a nexus of diverse groups that differ at the level of national origin, race, residential status, class, gender, and political views. Only in full awareness of our multiple contradictions and commonalities, presented in this essay as 11 theses, can we as Latinxs come together, construct our own fluid identities, and more effectively address the hostile political environment and polemics of the current moment.

trends and practices in the region" (Prevost and Vanden xix). Each nation of Latin America could be its own case study and provide fruitful information for historical inquiry and academic writing.

However, while Sánchez and Pita would agree that it is important to understand the variations within and among Latin American countries, it is also important to realize that in the U.S.A., there exists a "hostile political environment and polemic of the current moment" (Pita and Sánchez 25) with respect to immigrants, especially Latin American immigrants. One only has to see the dire situation of the many immigrant children being detained in warehouses until they can either find their families here in the U.S.A. or see a judge who can then send them back home. These children, however, are often dropped off at the borders of Honduras, El Salvador, or Mexico with no hope for any changes or a life free from crime and danger. Therefore, I would like to briefly elaborate on both of these points before going into specifics about the contested history of Guatemala.

Sánchez and Pita argue that because the U.S. Latinxation has now reached between 41 and 50 million (depending on whether one chooses to count undocumented workers), xenophobes, such as Harvard University professor Samuel Huntington, are concerned about the implications of the increasing presence of U.S. Latinxs. This concern is warranted due to the projected increase of Latinxs by 2050, which is estimated to reach 102.6 million (as per the Bureau of the Census 2004). While recognizing that this presence will bring changes, Sanchez and Pita also see Huntington's concern as xenophobic. They also see the importance of seeing this population as heterogeneous, recognizing that "[w]e are a composite, made up of multiple positionings—that is, of concrete social locations—and assuming multiple ideological perspectives and identities. We are U.S. citizens and noncitizens, documented and undocumented" (30). We are also a composite made up of various historical circumstances that have contributed to our current presence in the U.S.A. as both welcome and unwelcome immigrants.

Sánchez and Pita inform us that currently, U.S. Latinx groups' growing presence within the U.S.A. is more commonly due to twentieth-century U.S. interventions in the Caribbean and Central America as well as to the mid- to late-century military hostility to liberal or left-leaning governments, from Guatemala in the 1950s to Chile in the 1970s. US-backed military coups and reigns of terror in Argentina, Uruguay, and Chile have led to the emigration of thousands of Latin Americans to the U.S.A., other parts of Latin America, and Europe. More recently, neoliberal policies throughout

Latin America, enforced through trade agreements and conditions on loans from international financial institutions, have increased unemployment and imposed austerity measures that have spurred millions to emigrate in search of jobs and subsistence. As a secondary consequence, this constant emigration has enabled the U.S.A. to continually replenish its internal labor reserve through successive waves of Latin American immigration (29–30).

Thus, according to Sánchez and Pita, since the 1950s, an era commonly associated with the Cold War, there has been U.S. military intervention in various regions in Latin America, whether out of fear of socialist tendencies in Latin America or done to impose and defend U.S. interests in Latin America. I will elaborate on the specifics of such historical interventions relating specifically to Guatemala below. However, for the moment, it seems important to note that there is a range of historical factors, such as military and political interventions, that have contributed to the current presence of various Latin American populations within the U.S.A. As Prevost and Vanden confirm, "[g]lobal economic forces are driving people off their land in record numbers" (12).

It is important that educators become aware of these histories, especially educators at postsecondary institutions serving Latinx students who come from areas ridden with political, economic, and militaristic turmoil. While Latrants share many commonalities at a political and economic level, there are also many differences between and among Latinxs in the U.S.A. An important question arises, then, for Sánchez and Pita, which is, why then seek an umbrella identification such as the "Latino Bloc" if we are divided by so many differences? Their answer is that "[t]he rationale is fundamentally political. We need an identification that will interpellate us to participate in collective action, like the recent nationwide pro-immigrant marches; in this regard strict national origin identity could prove to be divisive and counterproductive" (32). Thus, it seems as if the rationale is political. If we can unite under a single identifying category, then we can more forcefully work together on changing educational policy and on countering xenophobic attitudes toward immigrants of Latinx heritage which have political, social, and economic consequences.

Part of our unification under the category of the Latino Bloc, however, can also encompass the desire for public educational institutions to pay attention to not only our critical mass, but also to our varied and contested histories that have contributed to our presence in the U.S.A. For example, how many public high school history textbooks include the reality of genocide in Guatemala committed against the large numbers of Mayas that reside there? How many of these textbooks discuss the histories of these sites under neocolonial control that has contributed to the constant influx of Latin American populations? It is not common knowledge that the historical circumstances that have contributed to the large numbers of Latinxs in the U.S.A. stem back to histories of the Conquest. More specifically, it is not common knowledge that

> [t]he internal economies of the indigenous societies were totally disrupted by the conquest and the imposition of economic systems designed to export wealth to Europe and thus incorporate the Americas into the international system on terms favorable to Europe. Economic power was seized by the European elite. Thereafter, the structure and functioning of Latin American nations would be heavily influenced by their trade and commercial relations with more economically developed areas; their economies, societies, and political institutions would also be transformed by the external orientation. Latin America was to fit into the international system as a producer of primary (unfinished) goods such as sugar, tin, tobacco, copper, coffee, and bananas. (Prevost and Vanden xix)

Given the intimate relationship between politics, economics, and social well-being, it is important to note that one dominant analytic that discusses this intimate relationship is dependency theory. While it is beyond the scope of my book to discuss the specifics of this theory, I would just like to briefly note that this theory views the economic situation of Latin America in relation to the increased dependence on developed nations, such as the U.S.A., for revenue that would allow them to stay competitive and afloat in the global capitalistic, also known as the neoliberal, economic market. When "scholars of Latin America and other social scientists studied the full implication of this phenomenon, they arrived at a theory that explained the continuing underdevelopment and dependency of Latin America" (Prevost and Vanden xx).

While dependency is a major issue to consider in any discussion of Latin America, so is the impact of the military. The military has a very strong influence on political and economic decisions throughout Latin America. As Prevost and Vanden note, "the military can often veto policy decisions by a civilian government, as was the case in El Salvador and Guatemala for many years; the oligarchy can threaten to mobilize their friends in the military on their behalf" (xxiii). It is also important to note that in Latin America, "politics are dictated by power and the powerful" and that the "constitution is often best described as an ideal to strive for rather than a basis for the rule of law" (xxiii). The complex histories of Latin American nations and the role of the U.S.A. in their political and economic affairs is one area of study that can be examined critically in the composition classroom. Guatemala is one such nation.

GUATEMALA

A total of 1.3 million Hispanics of Guatemalan origin resided in the U.S.A. in 2013,[8] according to the Census Bureau's American Community Survey. Seven out of every ten Guatemalans in the U.S.A. are foreign-born or immigrants. While few in relation to the total Latinx population in the U.S.A., they represent a sizeable population in particular cities, like Los Angeles, where they are 80% of the Central American population,[9] which is the second largest Latinx group of this metropolitan area, composed of 50% Latinxs.[10] The study of this particular population provides us with an example of issues, problems, and cultural differences important to consider in Composition classes (see Appendix A).

As of 2005, the population of Guatemala, as recorded by Francisco Lizcano Fernandez, is 11,385,000, and the breakdown of ethnic makeup is 53% indigenous. Since the late 1970s, Guatemalans and other Central Americans have been immigrating to the U.S.A. because of political upheavals and related economic crises throughout the region, including inflation, the reduction of social programs to guarantee decent living standards, political turmoil and violence, unemployment, low wages, land scarcity due to inequitable land allocation, and the population explosion, especially among indigenous people. All of these issues precipitated the mass internal and external displacement of Guatemalan *campesino* peasants, *indigenas/os*, and professionals. In February 1976, an earthquake destroyed much of Guatemala City, causing many to emigrate. The vast majority of the Guatemalan American population has arrived in the U.S.A. since 1980. Official immigration statistics do not reflect the true numbers of immigrants from Guatemala since most arrivals are undocumented refugees.

[8] Pew Hispanic Center Fact Sheet, "Hispanics of Guatemalan Origin in the United States, 2008." April 22, 2010. http://pewhispanic.org/files/factsheets/63.pdf
[9] Hamilton, Nora, 1935- *Seeking community in a global city: Guatemalans and Salvadorans in Los Angeles* / Nora Hamilton and Norma Stoltz Chinchilla Published Philadelphia : Temple UP, 2001.
[10] http://quickfacts.census.gov/qfd/states/06/06037.html

After 1980, large numbers of indigenous people and *campesinos* fled to the U.S.A. from counterinsurgency campaigns in the western highland areas. Significant numbers of school teachers, student activists, journalists, and other professionals accused of being guerrilla sympathizers also emigrated for political reasons. More than 300,000 Guatemalans have entered the U.S.A. illegally since 1980. In 1984, there were an estimated 1 million Guatemalan refugees, with many displaced within Guatemala and hundreds of thousands fleeing to Mexico and the U.S.A. Thousands also escaped to neighboring Belize, Costa Rica, Nicaragua, and Honduras. The 1990 Census also listed 225,739 foreign-born persons from Guatemala, reflecting the large portion of recent immigrants among Guatemalan Americans. However, the actual number of Guatemalan Americans is higher than the census figures, since many are migratory and/or undocumented and thus reluctant to have contact with officials. In reality, there are close to a million Guatemalan Americans, the second largest group among Central Americans after Salvadorans. Guatemalan Americans have settled primarily in cities with large existing Latinx communities. The greatest number is in Los Angeles, where the biggest concentration of Central Americans in the U.S.A. resides. There are also significant numbers of Guatemalan Americans in Houston, Chicago, New York City, Washington, D.C., southern Florida, and San Francisco. Smaller enclaves are found in Miami, New Orleans, Phoenix/Tucson, and other cities in Texas and North Carolina.

While Spanish is the official language of Guatemala, 21 ethno-linguistic Mayan groups have kept their ancestral languages alive. Garífuna and Xinca are also spoken. As first and second language, Spanish is spoken by 93% of the population.[11] English is spoken in all main tourist centers. These linguistic attributes challenge Guatemalans' classification as they are often mistaken for Chicanxs or illegal immigrants from Mexico. Obviously, given this brief presentation of their demographics, Guatemalans are a Latinx population with its own history, identity, linguistic attributes, problems, and position within the U.S.A. However, they also share similarities with many Latinx populations in the U.S.A. They are mestizos and are working class; they suffer racism, xenophobic attitudes, familial separations, financial insecurity, and the threat of deportation.

[11] http://en.wikipedia.org/wiki/Guatemala#Language

POSSIBILITIES FOR HISTORIOGRAPHIC MATERIAL

The current immigrant status of Guatemalans in the U.S.A. can be further understood when looking at an important critical historical document written in efforts to try to understand the complex impact of war on Latin American countries; it is the *Report of the Commission for Historical Clarification*. This document is a very interesting primary historical document because of its purpose and its proposed implementation. The commission that contributed to creating this document is referred to as the "Truth Commission" but is most commonly known as the "Historical Clarification Commission," which was mediated by the Guatemalan Peace Accords. The commission released a far-reaching report in February 1999, based on 9000 interviews. Interestingly, the report attributed 93% of the human rights crimes committed during the war in Guatemala to the army and its paramilitary units and only 3 percent to the insurgent *Unidad Nacional Revolucionaria Guatemalteca*. Most surprisingly, the report included accusations that, during the 1980s, the Guatemalan government committed "acts of genocide" through some of its actions and policies (Jonas 291). The report revealed that the state, through paramilitary and military forces, exercises much control over the insurgencies in a way that is "death"-trimental to Guatemalans (including Mayas and other indigenous Guatemalans), who are outright opposed to the land seizures that have increasingly taken place with the nation-state's increased involvement in the global capitalist economy power play.

As Susanne Jonas notes in her chapter, although indigenous populations are acknowledged through the discourse and rhetoric of public policy, actual inclusion of these populations in the governmental bodies of Guatemala has yet to be realized through real action. As such, it follows that much of the information found in the report of the Historical Clarification Commission report has not produced much action or change within political and educational institutions. Jonas states, "[m]ajor assassinations and crimes from the 36-year war, remained unsolved and unpunished" (291). This lack of punishment is most likely due to the state-sponsored violence that went unreported because of its questionable political justifications. Furthermore, as much of the memories of the indigenous populations can be found within the report, the inclusion of these memories in historical texts would be one manner to ensure that the memories of those massacred or classified as belonging to groups of the disappeared would not be lost. Jonas further states that "[t]he actual implementation of the Truth

Commission's follow-up recommendations would require new battles" (292). Sadly, even after 42 years of war with peace accords signed, conflict is still pervasive in Guatemala and "institutionalized justice remained a distant goal in Guatemala as impunity reigned supreme and honest judges continued to be killed, threatened, or forced into exile" (293).

Looking more closely at the historical circumstances leading up to the increasing presence of Guatemalans in the U.S.A. challenges conservative views of immigrants as coming to America to share a piece of the American pie. Upon closer examination, it is apparent that Guatemalan immigrants fled to escape political persecution and unstable living conditions, as their lands were often burned-out, forcing the indigenous populations to continually migrate to different parts of their mountainous terrain. They had to seek life elsewhere because life seemed impossible where they lived. Thus, a critical historical view of current Guatemalans in the U.S.A., whether documented or undocumented, can be gained when looking at documents that make known political and economic relations of Guatemala with the U.S.A. and the political turmoil that often results from economic and market interests of capitalists in both Guatemala and the U.S.A., ultimately causing many Guatemalans to immigrate here.

Furthermore, by taking a closer look at the specific social conditions in the homeland of immigrants within the U.S.A., students will be able to formulate contextual and historical explanations for the current status of Latinxs in the U.S.A.. Analyzing such global rhetorics begins to address contradictions and complications of cultural representations in history. Furthermore, as this book is dedicated to the use of critical history as a pedagogical writing tool that teaches rhetorical analysis of cultural texts, the goal of this is to stress the importance of providing a more thorough understanding of the historical conditions associated with immigrant populations present in the U.S.A. and to suggest ideas on possible materials for implementation in a Critical Historiographic course within Composition courses.

The Guatemalan example I have briefly reviewed would not only allow for student appreciation of the heterogeneous character of Latinxs in the U.S.A. today, but also serve to compare and contrast different versions of recent history through the reading of various texts, reports, documentaries, and testimonies, while allowing for the raising of questions, the comparison of different Latinx backgrounds, the formulation of issues, and the development of arguments in the classroom.

Given this inseparable connection between education and ideology, I view the Composition classroom as one location where educational theory, also known as writing pedagogy in the field, is directly involved in cultural practices. I am an avid practitioner of multicultural Composition pedagogy in my own classroom. I believe in teaching a multicultural curriculum in contrast to the subject matter most favored by political conservatives, namely the traditional set of canonical texts written by Europeans. I value and am committed to a multicultural writing curriculum based upon historiography that benefits all students and allows them to learn about both one another and others from each other. My commitment to such an approach is a response to the counterrevolution of political conservatives who believe that their version of truth is the commonly accepted one and characterized as the norm or standard against which everyone should be measured. I posit that "traditional" texts such as the Western canon or Western historical accounts need to be questioned, reconstructed, and supplemented with new and previously unknown histories and experiences. However, as mentioned in the Introduction, I am concentrating on a multicultural curriculum that will not only serve a universalist purpose but also enfranchise the largest minority population in the U.S.A., namely Latinxs.

CHAPTER 10

Conclusion

In this book, I have shown my familiarity and understanding of mainstream Composition history, scholarship, and writing theories in order to place the needs of Latinxs in Composition classrooms in a larger context so as to contribute to the implementation of curricular programs that will help them attain educational success. In this study, I employ the term "critical historiography" to mark the need for developing alternative Composition histories, as it is apparent in mainstream Composition that there are clear geographical and cultural group omissions which are part of the "lost histories of Composition." These histories are inextricably tied to black normal schools as well as to schools that serve students of color and dreamer students. By practicing "critical historiography," one is able to call into question established histories of Composition and provide new models for developing alternative pedagogical approaches to the teaching of Composition today. Thus, my ultimate purpose in writing this book is to elaborate on the theory, history, and practice of critical historiography as a pedagogical approach for Composition students who live in an increasingly multicultural, multilingual society.

By examining a traditional history of Composition Studies, I looked at histories of Composition written by John Brereton, James Berlin, Albert Kitzhaber, and Richard Ohmann. I argue, in part, that these histories do not adequately address minority populations like Chicanxs/Latinxs or African Americans. While Sharon Crowley, Lynn Z. Bloom, and Susan Miller provide a critical analysis of histories of

© The Editor(s) (if applicable) and The Author(s) 2016   195
I.D. Ruiz, *Reclaiming Composition for Chicano/as and Other Ethnic Minorities*, DOI 10.1057/978-1-137-53673-0_10

Composition, these histories also overlook these populations. Specifically, I am concerned with the lack of scholarship about the normal schools in the Midwest and the South and the history of the Southwest in the late nineteenth century.

Furthermore, through a historical comparative analysis, I found that many of the pedagogical changes that took place in the 1960s had already taken place in the early history of Composition. Such pedagogical changes are student-centered learning, collaborative approaches, as well as approaches that considered the backgrounds of students. These kinds of approaches were especially prevalent in black normal schools. I argue that these approaches were long in place within schools that catered specifically to students of color and disadvantaged students and challenged the dominant curriculum representative of the field's genesis, found at Harvard, Yale, and Ann Arbor in the late nineteenth century. As such, I call into question the most common historiographies of Composition, even from those identified as revisionist historians.

The pedagogical implications that resulted from this study are based on the notion that critical knowledge can be learned through literacy—more specifically, a critical literacy that concentrates on questioning commonly accepted notions of history. Furthermore, these pedagogical suggestions are grounded in critical race theory, critical historiography, and critical education theory, which are used to challenge traditional notions of multicultural curricula.

Traditional multicultural curricula, as defined by Paula Moya, can be based on exclusionist premises in that they solely concentrate on identity politics. Instead, Moya advocates for an inclusive multicultural curriculum which challenges the victimhood status often applied to minority students. *Similar to Moya, I argue that an inclusive multicultural writing pedagogy is one that leans on alternative accounts of history for the purpose of looking at subordinated experiences to benefit all students, not just minority students.* This approach goes beyond the use of culturally relevant material by focusing on developing students' rhetorical skills through a critical reading of histories of particular periods or groups.

If this curriculum is adopted in your first-year composition course, the pedagogical implications will vary from context to context. Generally, however, I argue that a historiographic method can provide students with the critical analytical tools needed to analyze current social problems of inequality as well as combat feelings of inadequacy or alienation from mainstream academic culture (see L. Esthela Banuelos' "Here They Go

Again with the Race Stuff"). Just as the 1870s and the 1960s provided students with critical perspectives on history and current social inequalities, the inclusion of these critical practices also necessarily implies making previously excluded histories of minorities and subordinated experiences available to students today. Through a continual commitment to critical pedagogy, one that relies on a Critical Historiographic method, educators, I suggest, will be able to continue the tradition of educational reform. This reform is characterized by attempts to include cultural minorities in institutions of higher education.

In conclusion, given the inseparable connection between education and culture, I view the Composition classroom as one location where educational theory, also known as writing pedagogy in the field, is directly involved in cultural practices. I am an avid practitioner of multicultural Composition pedagogy in my own classroom. I believe in teaching a multicultural curriculum that considers not only mainstream notions of "American" culture but also the "American" culture of ethnic and racial minorities. There is an America that many of us do not remember. This is the America José Martí spoke of—Nuestra America. It is for this reason that I propose concentrating on a multicultural curriculum that will serve a universalist purpose, the education of all of our students, while enfranchising the largest minority population in the U.S.A.—Latinxs.

APPENDIX A

CRITICAL HISTORICAL PEDAGOGY: HOW TO DESIGN A CRITICAL HISTORIOGRAPHIC COURSE

In order to design a critical historiographic course, one should start off with the same premise regardless of what historical event the class will look at in the second half of the course. While there are potentially countless historical events to look at in this type of writing class, first, the students need to become familiar with the various common functions of history. Please consider the following chart in designing your own critical historiography writing course:

Step 1:

A. Reading history:

1. Common conceptions of history
2. History as a study of space and time, issues, and problems
3. Defining history critically: provide some critical reading and rhetorical analytical tools (such as a rhetorical précis)

Here I drew on the following sources: *William and Mary Quarterly*, *American Quarterly*, and *Modern Philology*; Eric Foner's revisionist historical work; and Michel-Rolph Trouillot's *Silencing the Past*.

© The Editor(s) (if applicable) and The Author(s) 2016   199
I.D. Ruiz, *Reclaiming Composition for Chicano/as and Other Ethnic Minorities*, DOI 10.1057/978-1-137-53673-0

B. Writing exercise:

1. Summarize notions of history presented in one of the sources provided that discusses the purpose of history (in this case, Calcott's and Starnes' articles).
2. Discuss at least one critical reading/analytical tool that you plan to use to study a particular historical event.
3. Select one historical event that you would like to study.

Step 2:

A. Choose a historical event:

1. Select at least two sources for learning about this event. Sources may include essays or books.
2. Write a short synopsis of the perspective presented by the two essays or books.
3. Select a primary source, a text written by someone involved in the historical event. It may be an autobiography, an interview, a memoir, a letter, and/or a first-person chronicle.

    Use internet sources or materials located at Special Collections and library archives.
4. Write a short synopsis of primary source material that you have read.
5. Compare the perspective that you have seen in the primary source with those in your secondary sources and note how they differ and what elements are the same.

B. Write a paper in which you use your sources to:

1. Describe the historical event
2. Provide some idea of what is at issue in historicizing this event (i.e., why are there different perspectives on what in fact occurred?). What were the problems or contradictions during that time period?
3. Compare and contrast the different sources as to point out the written perspective inherent in historical writing.
4. Come to some conclusion as to what leads different authors to see the same historical event from different perspectives. Are there differences in class, race, ethnicity, gender, age, generation, and/or century behind the differences or were the texts written at different moments when different issues were prevalent? Are there different or competing/complementary ideologies at work here?

ENGLISH 101

REVISITING THE AMERICAN PAST: THE SPANISH CONQUEST
Instructor: Iris D. Ruiz

Required Text:
Revisiting the American Past, Spring 2007 10A Course Reader

Class Websites:
Warren College Writing Program: http://provost.ucsd.edu/warren/
academiclife/warren_writing/warren_writing.php
   Grammar, punctuation, spelling, and ESL: http://owl.english.purdue.
edu/handouts/grammar/index.html
   MLA documentation style: http://owl.english.purdue.edu/handouts
/research/r_mla.html
   Nonsexist language: http://owl.english.purdue.edu/handouts/gen-
eral/gl_nonsex.html

Course Description: Revisiting the "American" Past
Problematizing History (The First Half of the Course):

The objective of this writing course is to draw upon the argumentation
concepts learned in 10A, specifically, the Toulmin model of argumentation, which utilizes the claims, grounds, and warrants structure in order
to interrogate and produce academic texts. In furthering our knowledge
of how such concepts operate in the sphere of academic inquiry, we will
draw upon an academic debate which has as its major question: What is
the purpose of history? While the discipline of history has been heralded
as one of the leading social sciences serving various humanistic purposes
such as promoting a sense of patriotism and rationalism, instilling morality, providing lessons from the past, and representing us with role models
in the form of heroes so that we might be drawn to be like them, often
times, these purposes are conveyed with no critical stance as to who gets
to decide what historical events get written and disseminated and for what
humanistic purpose. (Lipsitz' work is an example of critical history.) As a
result, one of the defining characteristics of history as a social science is
largely glossed over, namely the social processes at work in the production
of "Official History." So with the investigative purpose of interrogating
the social aspects involved in the process of historical production, I would
like us to consider and interrogate responses to such questions as:

1. What exactly is history?
2. Why is history taught?
3. Who does history benefit?
4. What processes go into the creation of historical texts?
5. How does history account for various indigenous accounts in the realm of American and World History?
6. What does power have to do with historical production? How is it hidden? How is it revealed?
7. What are the issues with current dominant models of historical production such as empiricism and relativism? (Anthony Michel-Rolph Trouillot)
8. How much of history is based on fact? Fiction? Point of view?

CASE STUDY: THE SPANISH CONQUEST (THE SECOND HALF OF THE COURSE):

The purpose of the second half of the course is to put knowledge gained about specific problems with historical production into practice. We'll look at some primary sources that deal with the Spanish Conquest, written by Hernán Cortés in the form of letters to King Charles about his first-person accounts of his meeting with Montezuma and the Aztec empire found in Tenochititlan as well as first-person accounts recorded by the Aztecs themselves and translated into English. Then, we will look at a secondary source (or two) that has drawn upon these sources for the purpose of creating a seamless historical account of the Spanish Conquest (or "The Fall of Tenochititlan") and see how the process of historical production works with a critical eye hopefully gained from the first half of the quarter, where we have been introduced to the various purposes of history and the problems associated with them. This story is ancient—an ancient historical story; however, its importance in terms of understanding the first "Americans" and the first incidents in "American Encounters" is tantamount to understanding what the "Discovery of America" has been predicated upon. The Spanish Conquest took place in 1519, just 27 years after Columbus sailed the ocean blue and "discovered" America. Here, in this historical account, we have one of the first recorded incidents of sixteenth-century imperialism/colonialism of a native culture close to home (San Diego).

Grading Policy
- Assignments 2d, and 3e will receive a letter grade. These grades will be used to determine your final course grade.
- To be eligible to receive a grade on each of the above assignments, you must complete (on time) all of the preceding assignments. For example, to receive a grade on Assignment, you must do Assignments 1a–1d.

Evaluation of Papers
The following questions will be considered when papers are evaluated and graded. All questions may not be relevant to each assignment:

- Does the paper respond to the various parts of the prompt?
- Does the paper make an argument?
- Is the claim clear and plausible? Is it stated and contextualized effectively?
- Is there sufficient and relevant evidence to ground the claim?
- Does the paper effectively select and use material from the course readings to support and validate the analysis? Does it summarize, paraphrase, and quote effectively?
- Does the paper use all relevant details from the readings both to support the claim and to provide a context for the case being made? Does it ignore material that should be taken into account?
- Does the paper demonstrate an awareness of how the argument being proposed fits into the larger set of claims made about the topic in our course readings?
- Does the paper work through the complexities of the material (as opposed to oversimplifying or overgeneralizing)?
- Is the paper well organized?
- Does it cite material from the sources using MLA documentation style?
- Are there sentence structure problems or grammatical errors that interfere with the meaning?

Evaluation Standards at Warren Writing
- An **"A"** essay demonstrates **excellent** work. It has something to say and says it well. It develops its argument clearly and consistently,

demonstrating a complex understanding of the assignment, and does so using varied sentence structures. It often rises above other essays with particular instances of creative or analytical sophistication. There may be only minor and/or occasional grammatical errors.

- A **"B"** essay demonstrates **good** work. It establishes a clear claim and pursues it consistently, demonstrating a good understanding of the assignment. There may be some mechanical difficulties, but not so many as to impair the clear development of the main argument. While a "B" essay is in many ways successful, it lacks the originality and/or sophistication of an "A" essay.
- A **"C"** essay demonstrates **adequate** work. It establishes an adequate grasp of the assignment and argues a central claim. In addition, the argument may rely on unsupported generalizations or insufficiently developed ideas. It may also contain grammatical errors.
- Work that earns a grade of **"E"** or **"F"** is often characterized by the following problems: it fails to demonstrate an adequate understanding of the assignment; it fails to articulate an adequate argument; and/or it contains significant grammatical problems.

Assignment Sequence:

Prompt 1: Synthesis and Definition: Calcott, Starnes, and John L. O'Sullivan:

- According to Calcott and Starnes, what is history's purpose?
- Summarize Calcott and Starnes in relationship to one another, paying particular attention to the various purposes of history presented in both articles. What claims are they making? How does Starnes specifically elaborate on the various purposes of history presented by Calcott? Is there a critical stance present in either of the two articles?
- Using O'Sullivan's "Manifest Destiny" excerpt, apply one or more of the purposes of history to the position made herein:

(1a)	Identify Starnes' main claim and provide specific grounds from the article he uses as evidence for his main claim. (1 pg.)
(1b)	Relational summary: Compare and contrast Starnes and Calcott. (2 pg.)
(1c)	Write Prompt 1. (3 pg.)
(1d)	Revision/Final draft

Prompt 2: Interrogation: Problematizing Historical Production
- Drawing upon four of the readings in the first half of the reader, provide an argument about historical production. This argument should be stated clearly in the form of a main claim and characterized in relation to the purposes that were outlined in the previous essay and one that either Trouillot or Tompkins presents about historical production.
- Pay special attention to summarize each chosen author's main claim/ argument and show how each is complementing, complicating, or qualifying one another. (We will discuss each of these argumentative techniques in class.) You may want to identify the warrants/assumptions that each author is operating from when deciding how each author contributes to the argument about historical production.
- Take care to use specific grounds from the authors when necessary to support your claims.
- Assume your reader has never read any of the articles mentioned so that you may provide relevant context for your claims.

(2a)	Definition: What is historiography? (1 paragraph)
(2b)	What is the relationship between historiography and history? How might this relationship pose a problem for historical education? (1 pg.)
(2c)	Relational summary: Drawing off of Trouillot's and Tompkins' arguments, what are three problems with historical production? (2 pg.)
(2d)	Write Prompt 2.
(2e)	Revision/Final draft

Prompt 3: Putting Knowledge into Practice: Case Study: The Spanish Conquest
- This last assignment seeks to put knowledge gained in the first half of the course into practice by looking at a particular historical event— the Spanish Conquest, also referred to as the Mexican Conquest.
- Choose at least two authors from the first half of the course and argue how the readings on the Spanish Conquest demonstrate and/or challenge their argument/s (Cortés, Portillo, Meyer, and Sherman). For example, do the portrayals of the Spanish Conquest demonstrate the greatness of a hero or of heroes? Do they demonstrate how the stories were meant to instill a sense of morality in their readers? Are

the portrayals meant to justify cruel acts of imperialism or to show the divine providence behind such progress? Are they written from a defensive stance or from an objective stance?

- Jane Tompkin's essay "Problem of History" presents an example of one such argument. She presents an account of her childhood understanding of Indians, the account of her research into scholarly and first-person accounts of the relations between the Indians and the settlers in New England, and a final conclusion. In trying to figure out which historical accounts are true and which are false, she states, "What has really happened in such a case (where contradiction among historical stories is hard to escape) is that the subject of debate has changed from the question of what happened in a particular instance to the question of how knowledge is arrived at" (Tompkins 733). Not only does she show how historical knowledge is created, but she also shows how her own historical knowledge comes into being. In short, questioning the process of how historical knowledge is produced and for what purpose is the driving thread through her essay.

(3a)   Identify J.H. Elliot's main claim. What specific grounds is he relying upon for his translation of Cortés' purpose for writing to the King (Charles IV)? (1–2 pg.)

(3b)   Relational summary: Explain why you think two different introductions were given to the letters of Hernán Cortés? How might these two introductions complicate an unbiased account of the Spanish Conquest given by Cortés? (2 pg.)

(3c)   Point out three incidents in "The Second Letter" that might demonstrate a purpose of history as discussed by Calcott and Starnes. (2 pg.)

(3d)   Identify three points of contradiction between Hernán Cortés letters and the account of the Spaniards arrival in Tenochititlan by the Aztecs in *The Broken Spears*. (2 pg.)

(3e)   In *The Course of Mexican History*, an objective account of the Spanish Conquest is assumed by the inclusion in a textbook of Mexican history. Argue why this particular historical account may or may not be objective and why.

(3f)   Write Prompt 3.

(3g)   Revision/Final draft

BIBLIOGRAPHY FOR "REVISITING THE AMERICAN PAST"

Amin, Samir. *Eurocentrism.* New York: Monthly Review Press, c1989. Print.

Calcott, George H. "History Enters the Schools" *American Quarterly,* Vol. 11, No. 4 (Winter, 1959), 470–483. Print.

Cortes, Hernan. *The Letters of Hernan Cortes* New York, G.P. Putnam, 1908. Print.

Leon-Portilla, Miguel Ed. *The Broken Spears: The Aztec Account of the Conquest of Mexico.* Boston, Beacon Press, 1962. Print.

Meyer, Michael C. and William L. Sherman *The Course of Mexican History* New York: Oxford UP, 1979. Print.

Paterson, Thomas G. Ed. "Manifest Destiny and the War with Mexico" *Major Problems in American Foreign Policy* Lexington, Mass.: D.C. Heath, c1984–c1989. Print

Starnes, D.T. "Purpose in the Writing of History" *Modern Philology,* Vol. 20, No. 3 (Feb., 1923), 281–300. Print.

Tompkins, Jane. "'Indians': Textualism, Morality, and the Problem of History." Web.

Trouillot, Michel-Rolph. *Silencing the Past: power and the production of history.* Boston, Mass.: Beacon Press, 1995. Print.

APPENDIX B

FURTHER SUGGESTIONS/OBSERVATIONS FOR THIS COURSE

- In order to successfully teach a course that focuses on a historical event or issue, it is necessary to familiarize oneself with historical scholarship dealing with the theory of writing history. This familiarity needs to be gained before designing a Critical Historical syllabus. This scholarship will serve as the basis for the course. I have addressed some of this scholarship in Chap. 2, referring specifically to the work of Eric Foner and Michel-Rolph Trouillot.
- The following section includes the reflections on the writing prompts for this course. You will notice that each writing prompt above is followed by a series of tasks. These tasks are steps toward writing the final essay assignment.

For example the "1a" assignment above asks for a simple summary of one of the readings. However, this reading will be a crucial contribution to the complexity of the first essay assignment, which is called "Synthesis and definition." This title refers to the tasks that are involved in this assignment. These tasks are to define and synthesize two or more authors' views on the purpose and function of history. In order to perform these tasks, I ask the students to read texts that discuss the various purposes of history presented in both articles. What claims are they making? How does Starnes specifically elaborate on the various purposes of history presented by Calcott? Is there a critical stance present in either of the two articles?

© The Editor(s) (if applicable) and The Author(s) 2016
I.D. Ruiz, *Reclaiming Composition for Chicano/as and Other Ethnic Minorities*, DOI 10.1057/978-1-137-53673-0

- There are two short writing assignments that are associated with these questions. I first ask them to identify Starnes' main claim and provide specific evidence from the article he uses as evidence for his main claim. This assignment is only one page long. Then, I ask them to write a relational summary where they identify the main claims of each author and compare and contrast them. This assignment is two pages long.
- Writing the above two assignments prepares the students to look at a primary historical document with a critical eye. The students begin to critically engage a historical text by closely examining it in order to identify its historical purpose. Then, they write a draft of what is to be the first graded assignment. Its purpose is more complex than the first two assignments. Specifically, I ask the students to read an excerpt from O'Sullivan's "Manifest Destiny" and apply one or more of the purposes of history to the perspective evident in this text. Last, the students revise the draft for a grade.
- As is evident in the above assignment sequence for essay number one, there are four steps to completing this writing assignment in its entirety, which includes a rewrite of the first draft. The next essay assignment follows a similar pattern, yet it increases in the level of complexity and analysis that is asked of the students.
- There are five steps to completing assignment number two, which asks the students to make an argument about historical production based on readings presented by Samir Amin, Jane Tompkins, and Michel-Rolph Trouillot. These authors present various theories of writing history such as post-structural writing theory, Eurocentrism, empiricism, and social construction. While these readings are theoretical and vary in difficulty, the most challenging reading, for my class, was Samir Amin's. I was aware of the level of difficulty that this text presented and, therefore, I designed one of the shorter writing assignments as an opportunity for the students to give me their version of "Eurocentrism."
- The second graded assignment asks students to draw upon four of the readings in the first half of the reader and provide an argument about historical production. The students are told that their argument should be stated clearly in the form of a main claim and characterized in relation to the purposes that were outlined in the

previous essay[1] and one that either Trouillot or Tompkins presents about historical production.[2]

- This essay assignment follows a similar pattern to the previous assignment in that it asks students to pay special attention to summarize each chosen author's main claim/argument and to show how each is complementing, complicating, or qualifying one another. We discussed each of these argumentative techniques in class.

- As mentioned above, this assignment contains five steps in total, all of which all are writing assignments leading up to the second graded assignment. For the first step, I ask students to write a one-paragraph definition which addresses the question, what is historiography? For the second step, I ask them to consider what the relationship between historiography and history is and how public education's approach to teaching history might be problematic given the distinction between the two terms. This assignment is one to two pages long. The third step is a "relational summary" and asks students to draw from Trouillot's and Tompkins' arguments when they answer this specific question: What are three problems with historical production? This assignment is two pages long. The fourth step is to write a draft of their argument about historical production. While it may sound repetitive, the steps in writing this first draft, which I just went over above, prepare the students to write a well-organized, comprehensive essay which includes a working definition of historiography, a consideration of the difference between history and historiography, and how public education's approach to teaching history functions as either a problem or a solution to historical production.

- I began this course by leading students to gain an understanding of the various theoretical debates surrounding the writing of history and to question traditional notions of history. At this point, they are ready to look at larger textual representations of an historical event with a critical eye. To briefly digress, I think it is important to notice that this pedagogy clearly differentiates from those

[1] These purposes are to contribute to the moral character of a nation, to appeal to a deity, to follow a nation's or person's destiny, or to provide examples of heroism and lessons from the past.

[2] These purposes are more critical in that Tompkins exposes that history is not truth and Trouillot gives a social constructivist theory which critiques history as being one sided. The side that is more often presented in historical narratives, according to Trouillot, is the side of the winners.

addressed earlier on in this book. So far, we have not really talked about the students' individual identities, cultural backgrounds, or language habits. Instead, the subject of culture comes up when we begin to closely examine a historical event that is directly tied to the making of the Mexican culture, namely the Spanish Conquest.

- The second half of this course focused on a "historical case study." The historical event can vary but it should be one textually represented and students should have access to both primary and secondary source material in order to become familiar with the event and analyze the official representations or nonrepresentations of that event. For this particular class, I chose to focus on the Spanish Conquest. I have also taught a critical historical course on the work of Malcolm X. Any other historical event or period can be placed in the case study section of this course. Since not all critical readings may be appropriate for some of the events, teachers have the opportunity to select a critical essay.

- The selection of critical readings depends on the focus that the instructor chooses. Will the focus be the East or the West? Will there be a center? What is interesting about this course is that students also learn that points of view in historical production often benefit those from whose point of view the story is being told. However, if the story is looked at from an alternative vantage point, or center, then that privilege seems to disappear and the moment of inquiry and analysis of the historical event can begin. I have also touched on another possible critical historical case study to be included in the second half of the course in this book. Therefore, it seems that the instructor has some room to influence the direction and focus of the class's critical historical inquiry. As a matter of fact, Damián Baca, author of *Mestiza Scripts, Digital Migrations, and the Territories of Writing* (2008), suggests looking at cross-border relations in order to elaborate Eurocentric ideas of the history of rhetoric and colonial subjugation. He states:

With a greater awareness of Eurocentrism as Dussel articulates it, teachers could also develop a more detached stance toward postmodern theory as it applied to Composition classrooms. A primary pedagogical lesson, that the discipline's long-held periodizations are related to the geopolitics of Western expansion, would assist teachers and students as they together sort out the parallel histories of the field and colonial subjugation. (Baca 143)

Above, Baca refers to "parallel histories" of the field of Composition and Rhetoric. I have demonstrated earlier, in Chaps. 3 and 4, some parallel considerations of the fields of history within the USA. However, what is important to note is that learning that dominant historical accounts of a field or of a region's conquest are often situated from a certain geopolitical center is a worthy pedagogical practice in the first-year composition classroom. Now, I will turn to reflections on the second half of my critical historiographic course, which examined the Spanish Conquest.[3]

CASE STUDY: THE SPANISH CONQUEST (THE SECOND HALF OF THE COURSE)

As stated above, the purpose of the second half of the course is to put knowledge gained about specific problems from historical production into practice. We first look at primary sources that deal with the Spanish Conquest, written by Hernán Cortés in the form of letters to King Charles about his first-person accounts of his meeting with Montezuma and the Aztec empire found in Tenochititlan as well as first-person accounts recorded by the Aztecs themselves and translated into English. Then, we look at secondary sources that have drawn upon these sources for the purpose of creating a seamless historical account of the Spanish Conquest (or "The Fall of Tenochititlan") and see how the process of historical production works with a critical eye gained from the first half of the quarter, where we have been introduced to the various purposes of history and the problems associated with them.

Thus, the writing assignment associated with the reading of Hernán Cortés' letters and Miguel León Portillo's *The Broken Spears* allows students to see first-person accounts of the Conquest and the events leading up to the Conquest. The rhetorical purpose of each primary source is evident *as The Letters* are written to King Charles in an attempt to convince the monarchy of the time that the Conquest was a just, worthy, and beneficial endeavor. On the other hand, when students read *The Broken Spears*, they were able to challenge the Eurocentric perspective evident in *The Letters*. The shift in perspective from Spain to the Aztec perception of events that led up to their (Aztecs) downfall is striking. Interestingly, the text in this book is both in letter and picture form. This type of rhetorical instruction is interesting to analyze and calls upon different types of

[3] Insert information here about the governmental upheaval related to the Mexican History course in Mexico that did not include the Spanish Conquest and stops right at 1500.

reading skills from the students. Baca also calls for a rhetoric that utilizes textual representations in twenty-first-century Composition classrooms as a way to also challenge Eurocentric notions of rhetoric and textual representations. Thus, this exercise, while concentrated on the disruption of the seamless notion of historical production, also calls upon students to encounter various notions of rhetorical production and textual representations in the writing of history.

- The last writing prompt is written in seven parts. It is a more involved and complex writing prompt; thus, the explanation of the prompt at the beginning, which refers to Jane Tompkins article, serves to provide them with guidelines and a model to refer to when thinking about this last critical historical writing task in the first-year writing classroom.
- Here, I would like to take a closer look at steps 3c and 3d[4] that ask students to point out three incidents in Hernán Cortés "The Second Letter" that might demonstrate a purpose of history as discussed by Calcott and Starnes. It is a fairly short assignment; I ask that it be at least two full pages, double-spaced. The length of this assignment is meant to complement and contribute to the final essay assignment and asks students to start identifying various rhetorical purposes behind the historical narrative written by Hernán Cortés. The students were able to identify these rhetorical purposes of the historical narrative because earlier on in the class, they were exposed to various debates about the purpose and function of history. So, at the start, this narrative is read with a critical eye toward identifying the purpose of the text in terms of the justification used for the Conquest as this narrative is written to the King as a means of securing further authority and financial support in pursuing the conquest of Mexico.

The exercise involved in 3c is a necessary step to completing assignment 3d, which asks students to identify three points of contradiction between Hernán Cortés letters and the account of the Spaniards arrival in Tenochititlan by the Aztecs in *The Broken Spears*. I ask that this assignment also be two pages long so as to contribute to the final assignment. In this assignment, students look at primary source material in order to analyze the differences in perspective of the events leading up to the Conquest and the Conquest itself. Since the previous assignment asks students to identify

---

[4] See Appendix A.

a purpose for writing in *The Letters*, students are better able to see why the accounts of the events differ. Students figure out that the purpose behind the writing has much to do with the differing perspectives in these primary texts. What I want to stress here is that the sequence of assignments and the outcomes of the assignments were quite successful in achieving the pedagogical outcomes of a critical historical Composition writing class. There is, in this particular historical event, the European versus indigenous perspective. Including both perspectives and an official historical account of this event allows students to cross-analyze the rhetoric of both groups and the purpose of function of the rhetoric behind each account. This is a complex task that clearly departs from a traditional multicultural curriculum that asks students to concentrate on their own experiences and language using habits, without paying much attention to how such pedagogy might benefit all students and be more universal in a manner that Paula Moya advocates.

BIBLIOGRAPHY

Acuña R. Occupied America. 2nd ed. New York: Harper and Row; 1981.

Aldama FL. Rhet-Comp Borderlands as Cure All? Necessary questions and clarifications (Review). Pedagogy. 2006;6(2):261–87.

Annas PJ. Silences: feminist language research and the teaching of writing. In: Caywood CL, Overing GR, editors. Teaching writing: pedagogy, gender, and equity. Albany: SUNY Press; 1987. p. 3–17.

Apple M. On analyzing hegemony. In: Giroux HA, Penna AN, Pinar WF, editors. Curriculum and instruction. Berkeley: McCutchan; 1981. p. 109–23.

Aronowitz S, Giroux HA. Postmodern education: politics, culture, and social criticism. Minneapolis: Oxford University Press; 1991.

Axelrod A. Minority rights in America. Washington: CQ Press; 2002.

Baca D, Villanueva V (eds.) Rhetorics of the Americas: 3114 BCE to 2012 CE. New York: Palgrave; 2010.

Balester VM, Kells MH, Villanueva V. Latino/a discourses: on language, identity & literacy education. Portsmouth: Boynton/Cook/Heinemann; 2004.

Bañuelos EL. 'Here They Go Again with the Race Stuff': Chicana negotiations of the graduate experience. In: Bernal DD, Elenes CA, Godinez FG, Villenas S, editors. Chicana/Latina education in everyday life. Albany: State of New York University Press; 2006. p. 95–112.

Bartholomae D. Inventing the university. Writing on the margins: essays on composition and teaching. Boston: Bedford, St. Martins; 2004.

Bartholomae D, Elbow P. Writing with teachers: a conversation with Peter Elbow and David Bartholomae. Coll Compos Commun. 1995;46(1):62–71.

Bell D. And we are not saved. New York: Basic Books; 1987.

Bell D. Faces at the bottom of the well. New York: Basic Books; 1992.

© The Editor(s) (if applicable) and The Author(s) 2016   217
I.D. Ruiz, *Reclaiming Composition for Chicano/as and Other Ethnic Minorities*, DOI 10.1057/978-1-137-53673-0

Bell D. Racial realism. In: Creshaw K, Gotanda N, Peller G, Thomas K, editors. Critical race theory. New York: The New Press; 1995.

Bell D. Race, racism, and American law. New York: Aspen Law and Business; 2000.

Benítez M, DeAro J. Realizing student success at Hispanic-Serving institutions. New Dir Community Coll. 2004;127:35–48.

Berlin JA. Writing instruction in Nineteenth-Century American Colleges. Carbondale: Southern Illinois University Press; 1984.

Berlin JA. Rhetoric and reality: writing instruction in American Colleges, 1900–1985. Carbondale: Southern Illinois University Press; 1987.

Berlin J. Contemporary composition: the major pedagogical theories. In: Victor Jr V, editor. Cross-talk in comp theory: a reader. 3rd ed. Illinois: NCTE; 1997. p. 523–54.

Berlin JA. Rhetorics, poetics, and cultures: refiguring College English Studies. West Lafayette: Parlor Press; 2003.

Bernstein R. Dictatorship of Virtue: multiculturalism and the Battle for America's Future. New York: Alfred A. Knopf; 1994.

Bizzell P. Beyond anti-foudationalism to rhetorical authority: problems defining 'Cultural Literacy'. Coll English. 1990;52(6):661–75.

Bloom LZ. Freshman composition as a middle-class enterprise. College English. 1996;58:654–75.

Bourdieu P. The forms of capital. In: Granovetter MS, Swedberg R, editors. The sociology of economic life. Boulder: Westview; 2001. p. 96–101.

Brandt D, Cushman E, Gere AR, Herrington A, Miller RE, Villanueva V, Lu M-Z, Kirsch G. The politics of the personal: storying our lives against the grain. Symposium College English. 2001;64(1):41–62.

Brereton JC (ed.) The origins of composition studies in the American College, 1875–1925: a documentary history. Pittsburgh: University Pittsburgh Press; 1995.

Brodkey L. Writing permitted in designated areas only. Minneapolis: University of Minnesota Press; 1996.

Brodkey L, Robinson L. Not just a matter of course: Lillian S. Robinson talks with Linda Brodkey. The Women's Review of Books. 1992;9(1):23–4.

Cárdenas D, Kirklighter C, Murphy SW. Teaching writing with Latino/a students: lessons learned at Hispanic-Serving Institutions. New York: SUNY; 2007.

Casey J. Proposition 209 Spurs Roundabout approaches to State's issues of diversity. The Guardian; 2007.

Castro T. Hispanics now majority in Texas Public Schools, Districts Assess if they are ready for change. Huffington Post: Latino Voices.

Colombo G. In: Lisle B, Mano S, editors. Framework: culture, storytelling, and college writing. Boston: Bedford; 1997. p. 372–428.

Connal LR. Hybridity A lens for understanding Mestizo/a writers. In: Lunsford AA, Ouzgane L, editors. Crossing borderlands: composition and postcolonial studies. Pittsburgh: University of Pittsburgh Press; 2004.

Crenshaw K, Gotanda N, Peller G, Thomas K (eds.) Critical race theory: the key writings that formed the movement. The New Press: New York; 1995.

Crowley S. Composition in the university: historical and polemical essays. Pittsburgh: University of Pittsburgh Press; 1998.

del Castillo, Griswold R, de León A. North to Aztlán: a history of Mexican Americans in the United States. Illiniois: Harlan Davidson; 2006.

Delgado R. The Imperial Scholar: reflections on a review of civil rights literature. University of Pennsylvania Law Review. 1984;132(3):561–78.

Delgado R. The Imperial Scholar revisited: how to marginalize outsider writing, ten years later. University of Pennsylvania Law Review. 1992;140(4):1349–72.

Delpit LD. The silenced dialogue: power and pedagogy in educating other people's children. In: Villanueva V, editor. Cross-talk in comp theory: a reader. Urbana: NCTE; 1997. p. 565–88.

Douglas W. Rhetoric for the meritocracy. In: Ohmann R, editor. English in America: a radical view of the profession. New York: Oxford University Press; 1976. p. 97–132.

DuBois WEB. The Souls of Black Folk. New York: Bantam; 1989.

Elbow P. Writing without teachers. New York: Oxford University Press; 1995.

Faigley L. Fragments of rationality. Pittsburgh: University of Pittsburgh Press; 1992.

Fischer EF (ed.) Indigenous peoples, civil society, and the Neo-liberal State in Latin America. New York: Berghahn Books; 2009.

Fitzgerald K. A rediscovered tradition: European pedagogy and composition in nineteenth-century midwestern normal schools. Coll Compos Commun. 2001;53:224–250.

Flower L, Hayes JR. A cognitive process theory of writing. Coll Compos Commun. 1981;32(4):365–87.

Foner E. The New American history. Pennsylvania: Temple University Press; 1997.

Foner E. Who owns history?: Rethinking the past in a changing world. New York: Macmillan; 2003.

Foster M, Etter-Lewis G (eds.) Unrelated Kin: race and gender in women's personal narratives. New York: Routledge; 1996.

Foucault M. The order of things: an archaeology of the human sciences. New York: Vintage; 1970.

Foucault M. The archaeology of knowledge. New York: Pantheon; 1972.

Fraser JW. Preparing America's teachers: a history. New York: Teachers College Press; 2006.

Freedman DP, Martha SH. The teacher's body: embodiment, authority, and identity in the academy. New York: New York State University Press; 2003.

Friere P. Pedagogy of the opressed. 30th anniversary ed. Trans. Myrna Bergman Ramos. New York: Bloomsbury; 2000.

Gage JT. Introduction. In: Kitzhaber AR, editor. Rhetoric in American Colleges, 1850–1900. Dallas: Southern Methodist University Press; 1990. p. vii–xxii.

Garro E. It's the fault of the Tlaxcaltecas. In: Manguel A, editor. Other fires. Toronto: Lester and Orpen Dennys; 1986.

Gibson S, Greenburg R, Phillips DB. Chronicling a discipline's genesis: college composition and communication. Coll Compos Commun. 1993;44(4):443–65.

Gilyard K. Voices of the self: a study of language competence. Detroit: Wayne State University Press; 1991.

Gilyard K. African American contributions to composition studies. Coll Compos Commun. 1999;50(4):626–44.

Giroux SS. On the state of race theory: a conversation with David Theo Goldberg. J Adv Compos. 2006;26:13–66.

Grim V. 'Tryin' to make ends meet: African American women's work in Brooks farm, 1920–1970. In: Etter-Lewis G, Foster M. (Eds.) Unrelated Kin: race and gender in women's personal narratives. New York: Routledge, p. 124–140.

Gunner J. Doomed to repeat it: a needed space for critique in historical recovery. In: L'Eplattenier B, Mastrangelo L, editors. Historical studies of writing program administration: individuals, communities, and the formation of a discipline. West Lafayette: Parlor Press; 2004. p. 316.

Gutierrez v. Mun. Ct. of S.E. Judicial Dist. 861 F.2d 1187 (9th Cir. 1988).

Gutierrez, D. The reagan legacy and the racial divide. In: Bobo LD, Dawson MC, editors. DuBois review social science research on race; 2004.

Haefner J. Democracy, pedagogy, and the personal essay. College English. 1992;54(2):127–37.

Hairston M. Diversity, ideology, and teaching writing. Coll Compos Commun. 1992;43:179–93.

Haney-López IF. Is the post in post-racial the blind in colorblind 32. Cardozo L. Rev. 807, 2010. http://scholarship.law.berkeley.edu/facpubs/1816.

Herbert B. A radical treasure. The New York Times. Accessed 29 Jan 2010.

Hillocks G. Teaching writing as reflective practice. New York: Teachers College Press; 1995.

Holquist M. In: Bakhtin MM, editor. The dialogic imagination: four essays. Austin: University of Texas Press; 1981.

Hook JN. Project English: the first year. PMLA. 1963;78(4):33–5.

Hooks B. Ain't I a Woman: black women and feminism. Boston: South End Press; 1981.

Jonas S. Guatemala. In: Prevost G, Vanden HE, editors. Politics of Latin America the power game. New York: Oxford University Press; 2006.

Kanellos N, Martell H (eds.) Hispanic periodicals in the United States, origins to 1960: a brief history and comprehensive bibliography. Houston: Arte Público Press; 2000.

Kantor H, Lowe R. Terms of inclusion: unity and diversity in public education. Educ Theory. 2007;57(3):369–88.

Kelly EB. Murder of the American Dream. Coll Compos Commun. 1968;19 (2):106–8.

Kitzhaber AR. Rhetoric in American Colleges, 1850–1900. Dallas: Southern Methodist University Press; 1990.

Laden BV. Hispanic-serving institutions: what are they? Where are they? Community Coll J Res Pract. 2002;28:181–98.

Lizcano FF. Composición Étnica De Las Tres Áreas Culturales Del Continente Americano Al Comienzo Del Siglo XXI (in Spanish) (PDF). Convergencia (Mexico: Universidad Autónoma Del Estado De México, Centro De Investigación En Ciencias Sociales Y Humanidades). 2005;38:185–232; Table on P. 218. ISSN 1405–1435.

Mariscal G. Brown-eyed children of the Sun: lessons from the Chicano movement, 1965–1975. Albuquerque: University of New Mexico Press; 2005.

Mariscal J. Trouble in paradise. In: Cockburn A, St. Clair J (eds.) CounterPunch. Weekend Edition, March 12–14; 2010.

Martí J. Nuestra America. 3rd ed. Venezuela: Fundación Biblioteca Ayacucho; 2005.

Mejía JA. Arts of the US-Mexico Contact Zone. In: Lunsford AA, Ouzgane L, editors. Crossing borderlands: composition and postcolonial studies. Pittsburgh: University of Pittsburgh; 2004.

Mejía JA. English's 'Other': the rhetorical uses of Spanish in Chicano/a English classes. College Conference on Composition and Communication; 2006.

Miller S. Textual carnivals: the politics of composition. Carbondale: Southern Illinois University Press; 1991.

Miller RE. Fault lines in the Contact Zone. College English. 1994;62(4):389–408.

Moya PML. Learning from experience: minority identities, multicultural struggles. Berkeley: University of California Press; 2002.

Muñoz C. Youth, identity, power: the Chicano movement. London: Verso; 2007.

Murray DM. Finding your own voice: teaching composition in an age of dissent. Coll Compos Commun. 1969;20(2):118–23.

Nef JR. The University of Chicago and the World, 1929–1951. Rev Politics. 1951;13(4):399–429.

North SM. The making of knowledge in composition: portrait of an emerging field. Upper Montclair: Boynton/Cook; 1987.

Octalog. The politics of historiography. Rhetor Rev. 1988;7:5–49.

Octolog II. The (Continuing) politics of historiography. Rhetor Rev. 1997; 16(1):2244.

Ogren C. The American State Normal School: an instrument of great good. New York: Palgrave; 2005.

Ohmann R. English in America: a radical view of the profession. New York: Oxford University Press; 1976.

Ohmann R. Politics of letters. Middletown: Wesleyan University Press; 1987.

Omi M, Winant H. Racial formation in the United States: from the 1960s to the 1990s. New York: Routledge; 1994.

CCC Online, CCCC: Position Statements—Student's Right to Their Own Language for CCC 25; 1974. http://www.ncte.org/ccc/12/sub/statel.html.

Pew Hispanic Center. US-born Hispanics increasingly drive population developments, Pew Hispanic Center Fact Sheet. Washington, DC: Author-Center; 2002.

Pew Hispanic Center Fact Sheet. Hispanics of Guatemalan origin in the United States, 2008. April 22; 2010.

PewResearch Hispanic Trends Project. Between Two Worlds: How Young Latinos Come of Age in America. Pew Research Center. Accessed 1 July 2013.

PewResearch Hispanic Trends Project. Hispanic High School Graduates Pass Whites in Rate of College Enrollment. Pew Research Center. Accessed 9 May 2013.

Pita B, Sanchez R (eds.) Conflicts of interest: the letters of Maria Amparo Ruiz de Burton. Arte Publico Press; 2001.

Pratt ML. Arts of the Contact Zone. Profession 91; 1991.

Prendergast C. Race: the absent presence in composition studies. Coll Compos Commun. 1998;50(1):36–53.

Prendergast C. Literacy and racial justice: the politics of learning after Brown v. Board of Education. Carbondale: Southern Illinois University Press; 2003.

Rajchman J. Michel Foucault: the freedom of philosophy. New York: Columbia University Press; 1985.

Robinson L. Not just a matter of course (interview with Linda Brodkey). Women's review of books; 1992, p. 23.

Roediger D. Towards the abolition of whiteness. New York: Verso; 1994.

Rolph TM. Silencing the past: power and production in the writing of history. Boston: Beacon Press; 1997.

Royster JJ. Traces of a stream: literacy and social change among African American women. Pittsburgh: Univeristy of Pittsburg Press; 1994.

Royster JJ, Williams JC. History in the spaces left: African American presence and narratives of composition studies. Coll Compos Commun. 1999;50(4):563–85.

Ruiz I. Generation 1.5: a border culture in ethnography. Master's Thesis. CSU, Fresno; 2003.

Ruiz I. When does a writing class become something else? 2005.

Salvatori MR. Pedagogy: disturbing history 1819–1929. Pittsburgh: University of Pittsburgh Press; 1996.

San Miguel G. The Fight for Bilingual Education in Houston: an insider's perspective. Houston Hist. 2012;9(1):48–51.

Sánchez R. Mapping the Spanish Language along a multiethnic and multilingual border. In: Noriega CA, Avila ER, Davalos KM, Sandoval C, Pérez-Torres R, editors. The Chicano studies reader: an anthology of Aztlan. Los Angeles: UCLA Chicano Studies Research Center; 2001.

Sánchez R. The function of theory in composition studies. New York: SUNY Press; 2012.

Santoro WA. Conventional politics takes center stage: the Latino Struggle against English-Only Laws. Soc Forces. 1999;77(3):887–909.

Schallart A. Faculty Executive Committee approves diversity requirement proposal. UCLA Daily Bruin. Accessed 30 May 2014.

Shaughnessy MP. Errors and expectations: a guide for the teacher of basic writing. New York: Oxford University Press; 1977.

Simon S. 'The Culture Wars' New Front: U.S. History Classes in Texas. Wallstreet J. Accessed 14 July 2009.

Skinnel R. Institutionalizing normal: rethinking composition's precedence in normal schools. Compos Stud. 2013;41(1):10–26.

Smitherman G. 'Students' Right to Their Own Language': a retrospective. English J. 1995;84(1):21–7.

Smitherman, G, Villanueva V (eds.) Language diversity in the classroom: from intention to practice. Carbondale: Southern Illinois University Press; 2003.

Spear K. Students' right to their own language. Coll Compos Commun. 1974;XXV:1–32.

Spear K. Controversy and consensus in freshman writing: an overview of the field. Rev High Educ. 1997;20(3):319–44.

Stewart D. Some history lessons for composition teachers. In: Roen D, editor. Views from the center: The CCCC Chairs' Addresses 1977–2005. New York: Bedford/St. Martins; 2006.

Strain MM. Defense of a Nation: The National Defense Education Act, Project English, and the origins of empirical research in composition. J Adv Comp. 2005;25(3):513–42.

Three Sonorans. CA school district makes ethnic studies a grad requirement. Three Sonorans News & Analysis. Accessed 27 June 2014.

UCSD Chicano/Latino Concilio. Report card on the University of California, vol. 11. San Diego: A Legacy of Institutional Neglect; 2003. p. 1–6.

UCSD Warren College Writing Website. http://provost.ucsd.edu/warren/academiclife/warren_writing/courses.

Vanden HE, Prevost G. Politics of Latin America the power game. New York: Oxford University Press; 2006.

Villanueva V. On the rhetoric and precedents of racism. Coll Compos Commun. 1999;50(4):645–61.

Villanueva V. *Memoría* is a friend of ours: on the discourse of color. College English. 2004;67(1):9–19.

Villanueva V. Brodkey's Student E-mail to Iris D. Ruiz. Accessed 15 Oct 2006.

Villanueva V. Rhetoric, racism, and the remaking of knowledge making in composition. In: Massey L, Gebhart R, editors. The changing of knowledge in composition: contemporary perspectives; 2011.

Zinn H. A people's history of the U.S. New York: Harper Colophon; 1980.

Zinn H. Making history. The New York Times. Accessed 1 July 2007.

INDEX

© The Editor(s) (if applicable) and The Author(s) 2016   225
I.D. Ruiz, *Reclaiming Composition for Chicano/as and Other Ethnic Minorities*, DOI 10.1057/978-1-137-53673-0

9 781137 536723